THE EARNICORNS

Prof. Dhruv Nath is an angel investor, a mentor to start-ups, an author and a director with Lead Angels Network. Earlier, he was a professor at MDI, Gurugram, and a senior vice president at NIIT Ltd.

As an angel investor, he has invested in over twenty start-ups and mentored a few hundred of them.

Prof. Nath has been a consultant to the top management at Glaxo, Gillette, Nestlé, Indian Oil Corporation, Thermax, Bajaj Auto and Air India, among others, as well as to the prime minister of Namibia and the chief minister of Delhi.

He has a BTech in electrical engineering and a PhD in computer science, both from IIT Delhi.

He has written seven books so far, including *Funding Your Start-up: And Other Nightmares* and *The DREAM Founder*. He has also dabbled in humour with *Welcome to Aaraampur*, a book of humorous short stories about life in the hills of India.

He can be contacted on LinkedIn: www.linkedin.com/in/dhruvnathprof

And yes, he *will* respond ☺

T0290122

THE EARNICORNS

STORIES OF RARE PROFITABLE UNICORNS

DHRUV NATH

PENGUIN
BUSINESS

An imprint of Penguin Random House

PENGUIN BUSINESS

Penguin Business is an imprint of the Penguin Random House group of companies
whose addresses can be found at global.penguinrandomhouse.com

Published by Penguin Random House India Pvt. Ltd
4th Floor, Capital Tower 1, MG Road,
Gurugram 122 002, Haryana, India

Penguin
Random House
India

First published in Penguin Business by Penguin Random House India 2024

Copyright © Dhruv Nath 2024

ISBN 9780143468103

Typeset in Adobe Garamond Pro by MAP Systems, Bengaluru, India
Printed at Replika Press Pvt. Ltd, India

www.penguin.co.in

MIX
Paper | Supporting
responsible forestry
FSC
www.fsc.org
FSC® C016779

Contents

Section VI
Let's Compare These Earnicorns

Section I

The Earnicorns

1

Should You Read This Book?

Hi!

Since you have picked up this book, I assume you are trying to figure out whether you should read it or spend those few precious hours watching your favourite TV show. Over the mandatory beer, of course.

Fortunately, I've anticipated your problem. So let me share with you what it contains, why I wrote it and, most importantly, why you should read it. After that of course, you can decide whether to continue reading it or consign it to your bookshelf in the exalted company of the hundreds of other books already gathering dust over there.

Agreed?

So here goes . . .

First, a bit of background information about myself. No, I don't mean where I did my early schooling, my best friend when I was in kindergarten, my first football match, where I scored a self-goal and was thrown out at half-time, etc., etc. While these facts are extremely important for me, they are completely irrelevant for you. What is relevant is that I have spent several years—well over a decade actually—as an angel investor. In other words, I have been investing in start-ups. I think it's twenty start-ups, but there could be a couple of others that have slipped my mind.

More importantly, I have mentored perhaps a few hundred young founders. It has been a terrific experience and I've had lots of fun. And a huge amount of learning as well. Based on this learning, I've written two books on the subject of start-ups so far, both published by Penguin Random House India. The first one is *Funding Your Start-up: And Other Nightmares*, which I have co-authored with my close friend Sushanto Mitra, the founder and CEO of Lead Angels Network. As you might expect, the book is on the subject of funding ☺. And the second one is *The DREAM Founder*, which I have written alone. This second book covers everything a founder needs to know apart from funding, such as team building, marketing, execution, etc.

Now, the next bit is important, so please focus on what I'm saying. These two books talk about early-stage companies. You know the kind, don't you? Companies that are run by young founders with pink cheeks (sometimes they are also brown—as an author, I don't distinguish between people based on caste, colour or creed), fresh out of college or perhaps a few years into their first job. Armed with that one brilliant idea which they—and their mothers—fondly believe would shake the foundations of planet Earth. I have written about such start-ups, and in case you've read them, I do hope you have learnt something from them.

Now, you would agree that there are some start-ups that have done really well in life. Yes, they may have been started by pink-cheeked founders as before (sorry for the repeat, but I really like the term), but over the years, they have become market leaders in their respective fields. These are companies that have faced problems and challenges at multiple stages and have overcome them to become the giants that they are now. At the same time, their valuations have soared. And the world has created an interesting term for them: They are called **unicorns**—or businesses that have crossed a valuation of a billion dollars.

Unfortunately, there's a catch. Most unicorns have a cute habit: they make losses. And since they are happy making losses—and investors are equally happy to fund them—they keep making losses year after year.

But here's the thing: A few of these unicorns are different. They stand out from the crowd. Because they have had the audacity to make a profit. While the world has been insisting on growth at any cost—and to hell with profits—these companies have actually been making money. Not only that, they have been doing it year after year.

Now, here's a question for you: Wouldn't you like to learn from these companies as well? That rare breed of start-ups that have become unicorns and are profitable at the same time?

Yes, I thought you would.

And that, my friend, is why I decided to write one more book. The third in the series. The one you are holding right now. A book about unicorns that are profitable. Those who faced all kinds of crises over the years, such as the dot-com bust, the global financial crisis of 2008, the Covid-19 pandemic and demonetization, along with several others that I might have missed. Yet, they were able to overcome all these huge setbacks and become the dominant market leaders that they are today. And make money as well. These are companies whose founders are spoken about in hushed whispers in bars—or even boring coffee shops.

By the way, I have coined an interesting term for such companies. I call them **earnicorns**: unicorns that are making profits!

Having made this momentous decision, I had to figure out which companies to write about. And that wasn't too difficult. Because there were four of them that stood out.

Which ones?

Here they are:

Naukri.com (along with its parent, Info Edge)
Zerodha
Dream11
Zoho

These are earnicorns that are highly respected—no, revered—and clear market leaders in their respective fields. And that's where I made my decision. These were the four businesses I would write about. And if you are a founder yourself, you *simply must learn* from them.

But what if you are not a founder? What if you do not have your own start-up? What if you are someone who is simply interested in the fascinating story of these earnicorns? Does it still make sense for you to read the book?

Of course it does, my friend. These are stories about phenomenal companies and their equally phenomenal founders. So there is the story of how Zoho transformed rural Tamil Nadu by recruiting young boys and girls who could not afford to go to a decent college, and nurturing them into becoming star programmers. Or you can read about Nithin Kamath, the outstandingly humble founder of Zerodha, who shocked the nation by charging absolutely no brokerage from investors. Or Sanjeev Bikhchandani, who started Naukri.com from the servants' quarters above his father's garage, using second-hand computers and furniture. And subsequently, grew the business to a point where they have an unbelievable 70 per cent share of the market for white-collar jobs. And of course, Harsh Jain of Dream11, who built a roaring fantasy sports platform when everyone advised him not to!

Yes, sir (or madam), I found these companies truly fascinating when I was researching this book. And I'm sure you'll find them equally fascinating—whether you are a banker, a corporate executive, a priest, a lawyer, a carpenter, a doctor, a programmer, a shopkeeper, a homemaker or just about anyone else.

So do read on—no matter what your background. And I hope you learn as much from these earnicorns as I did . . .

2

Here Come the Earnicorns

Okay guys, let's repeat something that I have mentioned in the previous chapter: Most Internet businesses—including unicorns—are loss-making. At least at the time of writing this book. You see, when they started out, their founders had prayed to God. And this is what God had told them: 'You must not sin. Do not, under any circumstances, make a profit. You must keep making losses. That is the only way your soul will attain salvation!'

Now, how could these founders *not* follow what God had told them? That would have been sacrilege, wouldn't it? And therefore, all these founders happily grew their companies, but kept growing their losses as well.

Interestingly, at the same time, investors also went to God (the same God) to ask for his blessings. And God told them that they must fund growth and not look for profits. Happily, that's exactly what the investors did. They funded start-ups that were growing, even if they were making bigger and bigger losses. And of course, their valuations went up and up and up.

'Big deal,' you might say. 'Everyone knows that!'

Sure, they do. But do you really know why all these companies have been making losses? And why investors continue pumping money into them? Does everyone know that?

Do you?

Well, no.

I thought so, my friend. So let me start by explaining why this has happened . . .

The Coming of the Internet: How Geography Became History

To understand this peculiar phenomenon, I need to take you back in time to the 1990s. Yes, I realize that for many of you, those were prehistoric times. You were not born, and perhaps not even work-in-progress. Or maybe, just maybe, you were in your nappies and couldn't care less. So I must share with you what happened. You see, that was the time when the Internet started becoming popular. And businesses began waking up to the fact that it could dramatically change the way they functioned.

How?

Well, let's look at the pre-Internet era. Suppose you wanted to buy a pair of ready-made trousers. (By the way, it could also be a suit, a shirt, a dress, a skirt, a bikini or anything else that covers or partially covers your body. It'll make no difference at all to my argument.) Now, if you happened to live in Greater Kailash (a colony in South Delhi) you would probably have gone to a shop in Greater Kailash itself, or maybe South Extension or Lajpat Nagar. All colonies in South Delhi. You would definitely not go to Kanpur or Hyderabad or even Bhubaneswar to buy your trousers. Similarly, if you had been living in Jayanagar in Bengaluru, you would probably have gone to a shop in Jayanagar. Or if you were living in Dibrugarh (a town in Assam), you'd go to a shop there and not to one in faraway Chennai.

You don't need to be an Einstein to understand the reason behind this. You would always choose a shop that was close to where you lived. Because you'd need to go there physically, and you would obviously want to cut down on your travel time. And then, of course, the trousers would perhaps have been designed for a person who was six feet tall, whereas you happened to be a proud four feet eight inches in your elevator shoes, so there would be some alteration required.

Which meant another visit to collect them. And you would certainly not want to go back and forth in our traffic-ridden cities and towns, would you? So that's the key: Customers would usually shop only in locations that were close to where they lived.

However, the Internet changed all that. Now, the shop could be based in Mizoram and you could be in Ahmedabad or Coimbatore or Udhampur or anywhere else for that matter. And you could buy your clothes online. In case you needed to get the length altered, no problem. Just share your specs on the Internet and the trousers would be delivered to you in Ahmedabad.

Just take a minute to let this sink in (and to help you think, I've left the rest of the page blank).

Now that you're back from your 'thinking break', here's a question for you: Doesn't this apply to most businesses?

Of course it does. If you wanted to book a holiday in the pre-Internet era, you would meet a travel agent. Both of you would sit across the table, poring over travel guides and maps, with multiple cups of tea. Then you would go home, think about it and perhaps meet the agent once more to close the deal. But in the Internet era, you would do all this online. Earlier, if you wanted to buy lights for your drawing room, you would have gone to a nearby market in your city or town, had a heated argument over parking your car or two-wheeler, and finally bought your lights in a huff. But with the arrival of the Internet, all you'd need to do is go online—along with the mandatory cup of coffee, of course.

I could go on and on and on, but I'm sure you get the picture. Before the Internet came in, businesses could only get customers who lived nearby. In other words, geography was a major constraint. But in the post-Internet era, there was no such constraint. Businesses could be a thousand miles away from their customers and still transact happily. And that leads me to one of my favourite statements:

With the advent of the Internet, geography has become history.

The Focus on Dominance

And now we need to understand what this has done to businesses. You see, when companies realized the opportunities that the Internet had thrown up, they went berserk. They realized that their target market was not limited to just their own neighbourhoods or towns. Their market was the entire country—in some cases, the entire world. Therefore, they started focusing on rapid growth to capture more and more of this HUGE market.

Now, you are aware that large companies have a couple of major advantages over smaller ones. First of all, they have a well-known brand (unless they have done something really stupid, such as fooling their customers). Secondly, they have the advantage of economies of scale. Let's take an example: MakeMyTrip is a giant in the online travel portal space. The brand is extremely well known. They are trusted. So if you wanted to book a hotel, you would definitely prefer them over the tiny, unknown FakeMyTrip.com (assuming, of course, that there is such a company). Besides, given their size and the number of customers they serve, hotels would be happy to give them a fat discount—a part of which MakeMyTrip would pass on to the customer. But poor FakeMyTrip would not get such a discount, and therefore the rates at which they offered hotels to their customers would be higher than those from MakeMyTrip. And that brings me to the key issue: The big, dominant MakeMyTrip would constantly grow even bigger and bigger, at the cost of the smaller FakeMyTrip and all the other smaller travel portals. Finally, a day might come when FakeMyTrip would not be able to survive and perhaps close down!

Please note this very, very, *very* important point: In the Internet world, bigger companies grow bigger and bigger, while the smaller ones struggle to survive and ultimately die. Unless, of course, they have a unique product or service that the bigger guys do not (by the way, this also applies to a lot of non-Internet businesses, but it's much more pronounced in the Internet world). In other words, dominant players—or market leaders—become more and more dominant, whereas the also-rans simply stop running.

Just look around you and you'll see this principle in action everywhere. For instance, there was a time when we had several start-ups in the food delivery space, but ultimately only the two giants, Zomato and Swiggy, survived. In eCommerce, you have the mammoth Amazon, Flipkart and, now JioMart. At best, you could add the Tatas to this list. That's it. All other start-ups in this space have fallen by the wayside—or in some cases they have been bought out by these giants. In cab booking, you have Uber and Ola, and the rest are way, way behind.

I could go on and on and on, but I'm sure you get the picture. If you don't, please read the earlier section again and again. My editor Radhika has categorically told me not to repeat myself.

So let me summarize this in one line:

In the Internet world, dominant players become more and more dominant, whereas the small fry fall by the wayside.

Clear?

Okay, now let me bring in investors. I'm referring to angel investors and venture capitalists (VCs)—those who invest in start-ups. And let me ask you a question: Of these two kinds of companies—the dominant ones and the small ones—which category would investors want to invest in?

The answer should be obvious, isn't it? It's the dominant guys. Because these are the guys who will become market leaders over the years. These are the guys who will ultimately control the market. And these are the guys who will (hopefully) give returns to their investors. That's why investors have been falling over each other to invest in companies that are moving towards dominance. The result? It only gave these companies a further boost. Armed with this investment, the dominant guys simply increased the gap between themselves and the smaller companies and therefore became more dominant!

And were the investors happy? You bet they were. They were delighted and began to dream of the luxury yachts or villas that they would buy with the money they made.

But now for the big question. Founders were looking for rapid growth. And so were investors. But how would they measure growth? At that stage, most companies did not really understand how to make money on the Internet. So they started focusing on visitors coming to their website. The more the visitors, the greater the dominance. Were these visitors generating revenues? Not necessarily. As long as they came to the website, it was assumed that revenues would follow some day.

Therefore, the magic word became *eyeballs*. Get visitors to your site. The more, the merrier. Are they getting you revenues? No?

Anyway, it doesn't matter. Just get the eyeballs. Revenues will come later. So the furious battle for eyeballs began. 'Are your eyeballs growing dramatically month on month? Great. Are you generating revenues? No? No problem—we'll fund you.' As a consequence, valuations kept going up and up like crazy, and the money simply kept flowing in.

Alas, this frenzy could not last. Come March 2000, and with it came the dot-com bust. Or dot gone. Or whatever you want to call it. Investors and founders alike realized that getting eyeballs was simply not enough for a business. It was a bit like customers going to a mall, having a great time window shopping, but then leaving without having bought anything. No sir, any business worth its salt needed customers. Paying customers. They needed revenues.

The fact that many of these companies were set up by tech guys did not help either. Yes, they were very bright tech guys, but tech guys all the same. Many of them had no clue about running a business. They had created great websites, but making money was a completely different ball game. Therefore, their companies floundered. As you can imagine, this caused a huge shake-up in the nascent start-up ecosystem. (Sorry, I don't like jargon, but the word 'ecosystem' seemed very appropriate here. I promise not to use it again.) Eyeballs became a dirty word, and the focus shifted to revenues.

And now, I have a very important question for you. Did the frenzied search for growth slow down?

Come on, my friend. Investors had been looking for rapid growth and dominance, and founders were happy to play ball. There was absolutely no reason for this to stop. The only change was in the way this growth was measured. From the earlier *eyeballs*, it shifted to *revenues*. And the mad rush for growth continued . . .

Now, I'm sure you thought this story had a fairy tale ending, with both founders and investors living happily ever after.

Right?

Dead wrong!

Why?

Very simple. Yes, we had moved away from eyeballs to a far more realistic measure of growth, namely revenues. Unfortunately, that wasn't enough. Because we had actually moved to *revenues at any cost—even at a loss*. And investors were delighted to fund this once again. You see, investors were clear that they (the start-ups) were in a great space and that they (the start-ups) should focus on revenues even if they (the start-ups) were loss-making. And they (the investors) would keep pumping funds into them (the start-ups), because they (the investors) were confident that they (the start-ups) would become dominant players in the market, and at that stage they (the start-ups) would become profitable, giving them (the investors) a wonderful exit.

Aha! So that was the problem. If you were growing by 100 per cent year on year, you were the darling of investors. Too bad if your losses were growing by 150 per cent. And this is how things continued. As long as there was growth, valuations kept going up and up. And mind you, these were valuations of loss-making companies. The word *unicorn* was coined with a lot of fanfare. Then, of course, there were the *decacorns*—or those with a valuation of over ten billion dollars. Not to be left behind were the *soonicorns*—those who were close to the billion-dollar mark. And, of course, the *babycorns*—a term I have coined. All getting measured in the billions of dollars that they were valued at!

However, most of these guys had one thing in common: They were loss-making. And they were proud of it. After all, they were following God's diktat, weren't they?'

But hang on. Here's the twist in the tale: In this ocean of loss-making unicorns, there were a few brave souls who refused to toe the line. They refused to listen to God, at least on this subject. They did not make a loss (except, of course, when they were infants and had to invest). Yes, you heard right, my friend: *They actually made a profit*. And they made it year after year after year. These were the companies that stood out from the crowd of loss-making unicorns. The ones who refused to accept the fact that the only way to survive was to get more and more rounds of funding. The obstinate ones that insisted on creating genuine, profitable businesses.

And this is where I got hooked. As you are aware, I'm an author. I'm always looking for interesting stories to share with you readers. And that's where it hit me. What could be more interesting than the stories of these profitable unicorns?

So that was that. I decided to share these stories with you. As I've already mentioned, I picked four such unicorns—all from different domains. So, I have Zerodha in stock market trading, Dream11 in fantasy sports and Zoho in the B2B SaaS space. And of course, my favourite company, Info Edge, better known for its most successful business, Naukri.com. All Internet businesses, all of them giants and all of them market leaders in their chosen spaces. (Some people believe that Info Edge is not a unicorn, although its valuation is way, way above a billion dollars. Because the formal definition of a unicorn is a company that has reached that magic figure *before* it's listed on the stock exchange. As you are aware, Info Edge got that valuation *after* it was listed. However, it is perhaps the most respected company in the Indian Internet space, therefore I decided to include it in this book. And I'm sure you wouldn't mind!)

Now for my favourite bit. I've already mentioned in the previous chapter that I've coined a term for such unicorns. I call them **earnicorns.** That's right, earnicorns. Unicorns that are actually earning money and not just making heftier and heftier losses year after year. Once this book is out, I hope 'earnicorn' will become a household term, just as the term 'unicorn' has. And of course, as the creator of the term, I'll become famous ☺. But don't worry—I'll still happily sign this book for you.

Before I forget, there is something absolutely critical that I must tell you. None of these founders was chasing valuations. None of them said, 'Ah, all I want is to become a unicorn. That's the sole purpose of my existence. After that, I'll retire and spend the rest of my life on the beaches of Hawaii.' No, they were not chasing valuations—they were chasing their businesses. And because of this, their businesses did well and valuations went up to unicorn levels.

One important caveat: Three of the companies that I have discussed in the book are private limited companies. Therefore, detailed financial data about these companies is not available publicly. Yes, I've been able to get some data from these companies, which I've shared with you. But in any case, my idea is not to give you a detailed financial report. I'll leave that for other authors. My idea is to talk about what's gone behind the numbers—and therefore, what you can learn from it.

We'll See More Earnicorns over Time

And now for something really interesting, so please stop looking at your stupid mobile phone and listen carefully. I've already told you that investors were happy to fund start-ups that were chasing revenues at any cost—even if they were making a loss. In other words, you could keep making bigger and bigger losses and still get funded, as long as your revenues were growing. But there is a limit to this funding, isn't there? Businesses that continue to make losses are not sustainable. They are dependent on the next round of funding. In simple terms, they are not viable businesses. So what if they are called unicorns? And over the years, investors have begun to realize this. Many of them have burnt their fingers. They have got tired of waiting for profits as the losses kept ballooning.

Of course, the Covid-19 pandemic did not help. And neither did the Russia–Ukraine war of 2022. Because inflation went up worldwide, central banks started raising interest rates and recession became a distinct possibility—at least in the developed world. The result? Money became scarce and investors were even more reluctant to invest in loss-making companies. They started looking for sustainable businesses into which they could put their hard-earned money. Importantly, they did not necessarily look for profitable companies. What they looked for was a 'path to profitability'. 'You might be loss-making today, but are you moving towards profitability? Are your losses coming down year-on-year? If yes, we are willing to fund you.'

Businesses realized this. They realized that funding was not a 'God-given gift' that they could pick up whenever they wanted. They had to show a path to profitability. Funding would not be available for survival. You needed to survive on your own. But it would be available for growth.

That's when businesses—including most unicorns—buckled down to the tough task of making money. And it's showing. Yes sir, Internet companies are actually focusing on cutting down expenses and thereby moving towards profitability. So, a few years down the line, you'll see more and more earnicorns.

In the long run, this is great for our country—and the rest of the world. Because we've gone from a thoroughly unsustainable 'eyeballs' to a more sustainable 'revenues at any cost', to today's 'path to profitability'. Yes, my friend, we will see a lot more earnicorns in the years to come. But the ones I have written about in this book will always remain the pioneers. Those whose founders showed the way.

Wouldn't you like to learn from these founders? The likes of Sanjeev Bikhchandani and Hitesh Oberoi of Naukri, Nithin Kamath of Zerodha, Sridhar Vembu of Zoho and Harsh Jain and Bhavit Sheth of Dream11?

You would?

Well, in that case, just turn the page . . .

3

Analysing These Wonderful Earnicorns

So, in this book, you'll hear stories about these four wonderful companies. But over time, I'm sure you'll forget these stories—because your focus would have shifted to the latest *saas-bahu* serial on TV or the next IPL season or even the spicy affairs of our Bollywood actors. Yes, my friend, memory is short, and I can guarantee that a time will come when you'll ask, 'Naukri.com? Zerodha? Did they become earnicorns? How?'

Now, obviously, I don't want that to happen. After all, when *you* create an earnicorn and the country showers awards on you, I would like you to remember me and give me at least a tiny bit of credit, wouldn't I 😊? And this is the problem I kept grappling with as I wrote this book: 'How do I help you remember what I'm telling you about these companies?'

So I thought and thought. And then I thought some more. And more. And suddenly, while taking a shower, it hit me. Yes, I'll tell you these fascinating stories. But I will also analyse these businesses and leave you with two simple phrases—actually acronyms—'PERSISTENT business' and 'PERFECT attitude'. And if you can remember these two acronyms, you will remember the essence of how these four businesses have become successful.

Let's start with the first one, namely the PERSISTENT business:

The PERSISTENT Business

I've already mentioned that I have co-authored a book called *Funding Your Start-up and Other Nightmares* with my friend Sushanto Mitra. This book is based on the many, many businesses that we have been involved in. And this is the key: While writing this book, we realized that *successful businesses had several traits in common*. And businesses that failed were *missing out on the same parameters*.

That's how we created our favourite PERSISTENT framework for successful businesses. Where PERSISTENT stands for:

- P: Problem
- E: Earnings Model
- R: Risks and how you will mitigate them
- S: Size of the market
- I: Innovation
- S: Scalability
- T: Team, starting with the founders
- E: Entry Barriers
- N: Niche
- T: Traction

Now, if you've read that book (more importantly, if you still remember what you've read), you can safely skip the rest of this section. However, my past experience as a professor tells me that people forget what they have read within a few days, if not hours. So I would strongly suggest that you *do* read this section. After that, if you think it was a waste of time because you remembered everything, well, just send me an angry email!

Let's first look at the 'P' in PERSISTENT. Your business needs to solve a problem for the customer—otherwise you don't have a business! That much should be obvious. However, there also needs to be an EARNINGS MODEL—the 'E' in PERSISTENT. Otherwise, my friend, you are not running a business. You are running a charity.

The next letter in the framework is 'S', which stands for SIZE of the MARKET. Critical, isn't it? Because if it's a small market, the business will soon stagnate. Yes, size is critical.

However, sometimes you have large markets, but they are hugely crowded. With several competitors battling for the same customer. In such a situation, it's a good idea to identify a NICHE (the 'N' in PERSISTENT) within the space. And the niche should satisfy two criteria: First of all, it should not be crowded. Secondly, it needs to be large enough. Otherwise you'll stagnate once again.

Then, of course, we have the next 'S' in our PERSISTENT model, which stands for SCALABILITY. In very simple terms, the ability to grow fast. Obviously, this is critical to your business. Because if you don't grow rapidly, your competitors will. They will eat into your market share, take away your customers and potentially kill you. Which is why scalability is so critical.

What are the factors that impact scalability? Patience, my friend—read through this book, don't skip any chapters, and hopefully, you'll get the answer.

Then we have the 'R' in PERSISTENT, which stands for RISKS. I'm sure you would agree that no business is risk-free. And one of the biggest risks to any business is the possibility of competition coming in and taking away your customers. For which you'll need an ENTRY BARRIER—the 'E' in PERSISTENT. Sometimes called *competitive advantage* or *moat*. In other words, something that acts as a barrier and prevents your competitors from entering. Incidentally, if you have an INNOVATIVE solution (the 'I' in PERSISTENT), possibly with a patent or two, that's a wonderful entry barrier. Because, legally, the other guy cannot copy you (assuming, of course, that he is willing to follow the law).

And now for the last two pieces in the PERSISTENT framework. The first 'T' stands for TEAM, which obviously starts with the founders. Finally, you may have a great business model—one that is highly scalable, with a terrific entry barrier and a solid earnings model. In short, you might satisfy all nine components of the PERSISTENT model that we've seen so far. But what's the final proof? The final proof, my friend, is the TRACTION in the business! Are you getting customers? Are they increasing month on month? Are the existing customers staying on or are they quitting? Are your revenues increasing month on month? You see? Traction: customers growing, and revenues growing as well.

So that, my friend, is the PERSISTENT framework. And in our experience, successful businesses tend to be PERSISTENT businesses.

And the PERFECT Attitude

But that's not where the story ends. When I studied these companies, I realized that it wasn't just businesses that had key things in common. Successful *founders* also had certain traits in common. And that's where I created another framework—this time focused on the attitude of founders rather than on the business. I called it the 'PERFECT Attitude'. And that formed one of the cornerstones of my next book, *The DREAM Founder*.

Here's the PERFECT Attitude, as applied to founders:

P: PERSEVERING
E: ETHICAL
R: RESPONSIBLE
F: FLEXIBLE
E: Willing to do EVERYTHING
C: CUSTOMER ORIENTED
T: Builds TRUST

Once again, an acronym which captures the attitude of all successful founders!

Now you know what I'm going to say. That's right. In this book, I have analysed all four businesses using the PERSISTENT framework. And I have also analysed how these founders function, using the PERFECT attitude. And I'm delighted to inform you that all businesses, as well as all founders, fit just perfectly into these frameworks. So if you're planning to create an earnicorn, do remember my words:

> *To be successful, a business needs to be PERSISTENT, and the founder needs to have the PERFECT Attitude.*

Of course, there will be other issues as well—I can't guarantee success, can I? But at least you would have a great starting point.

And on that happy note, I'm taking a break and going out for a cup of coffee and a chocolate pastry.

I'll meet you in the next chapter. Where we'll look at the first of these giants: Naukri.com. And its parent company, Info Edge.

Section II

Naukri.com and Info Edge

4

Naukri.com: The Early Struggles

Dear reader, I'm sure you have heard of Naukri.com, the phenomenally successful giant in the online recruitment space. And its brilliant, charismatic and highly respected founder, Sanjeev Bikhchandani, who was awarded the prestigious Padma Shri by the Government of India in 2021. If you haven't, you're probably living on another planet.

But do you know Sanjeev's story? And how he founded Naukri? And the struggles he had to go through in the early years? And what you can learn from him?

No?

Well, I thought you wouldn't. Now, I must tell you that every time I've met my good friend Sanjeev, I've learnt so, so much from him. And I'm keen to share all that learning with you. So just pick up a cup of coffee, fasten your seat belt, sit back and relax. I'm going to tell you the story of the inimitable Sanjeev and his baby, Naukri.com, along with its parent company, Info Edge.

How It All Began

For a start, I must share with you Sanjeev's family background. No, he was not born with a silver spoon in his mouth. He did not come from a rich business family. His father was a doctor in government service in Delhi and his mother was a homemaker. A typical simple, frugal, middle-class family. Importantly, there was nobody in his family with a business background—no one who could teach him the ropes of starting and building a business. That's right, whatever he did in life, he learnt on his own. And that should be a pointer to you, dear reader. You do not need to have the surname Tata or Mahindra or Ambani to be a successful businessman. Not even Kochhar of Kochhar industries, or Wagle of Wagle, Wagle, Wagle and Associates. You need not come from a family where business is in your blood. You can still create and run a highly successful business!

Fortunately, Sanjeev was a bright young man (he still is 😊) and was able to get admission to St Columba's School in Delhi, and later to St Stephens College for a BA (Honours) in Economics. Both top-notch educational institutions. After which he got a job with Lintas, one of the leading advertising agencies in India. Three years later, he was back to studies—this time at IIM Ahmedabad, the bluest of blue chips in the world of management. While at IIM, he got a plush job with HMM Ltd, the makers of Horlicks, in Mumbai. And with that, I'm sure you thought his life was all set.

But no. It wasn't. There was something lurking at the back of Sanjeev's mind and it simply refused to go away. You see, ever since his school days, he had wanted to do something on his own. And not just something. Something BIG! Yes, there was no one with a business background in his family to guide him, and therefore he realized he would be on his own. And he had absolutely no idea what it took to start and run a business. But like all passionate founders, that did not stop him. No sir, he was clear: 'I will do something big on my own.'

And one fine day, in 1990, a year and a half into his cushy job at HMM, Sanjeev chucked it all up and started his own company. And that, dear reader, was the beginning of his struggles.

Yes, you heard that right. I'm sure you thought setting up the company was an easy journey for Sanjeev. That the moment he started it, customers came in droves, and he needed sacks to collect all the cash that was flowing in. No way, my friend. He wasn't walking into a business that his father had built. Remember, his father was a doctor in government service—as far removed from business as you can imagine. Sanjeev was setting up a company from scratch. And that, believe me, is no joke.

The Early Struggles

Let me take you through those early times. After quitting his job at HMM Ltd, Sanjeev teamed up with a friend. And together they worked on two independent projects: one in the recruitment space and the other one in the area of trademarks. However, a few years later, the two of them parted ways, with the partner working on trademarks and Sanjeev on recruitment. And since this is the story of Sanjeev and Naukri, I will not discuss the trademark business any further. Perhaps in a future book . . .

Sanjeev's company was called **Info Edge**. Now, as you are undoubtedly aware, every business needs a 'corporate office'. And where was the 'corporate office' of Info Edge? You won't believe this: in the servants' quarters above the garage in his father's house. For which the company paid his father a rent of Rs 800 a month. And this plush corporate office was fitted out with—you've guessed it—second-hand computers and furniture. And yes, whenever he had to move around Delhi for meetings, he would do so on an old scooter which he had borrowed from his father!

Dear reader, I hope you've noticed something very important. Sanjeev has always believed in running a frugal business and spending money very, very carefully. According to him, that is the only way to make a profit and build a sustainable business. Let's hear him out:

> To create a viable, sustainable company, your expenses must be lower than your revenues. And to do that, you must run a frugal business. Don't spend on unnecessary things such as plush offices, fancy cars, or business class travel. These will hurt you. Equally important, build these habits early—right from the time you start your company.

And this is most important: How do you ensure that your team follows similar frugal practices? There is only one way. You must set an example for them. You are a role model for them. If you are travelling business class and splurging on a fancy car, can you expect your team to do anything different? So being personally frugal is critical, and you must do this right from the beginning. If you expect your colleagues to travel economy class, and share rooms in a three-star hotel, be prepared to do the same yourself.

And now, for the icing on the cake. Please pick up your cup of coffee and concentrate on what I'm saying. Because I need to talk about the salary Sanjeev took home in those early days.

None.

What? None?

That's right. None.

Why?

Very simple—the company couldn't afford it. Hopefully, at some stage in the future, things would change, but for the moment, there was no salary for the founder. Remember the magic words, 'frugal business'?

Fortunately, his wife was working at that time, so they managed to eke out three square meals a day. By the way, I suspect this is one reason why Sanjeev has maintained a trim figure to this day (sorry, Sanjeev, I couldn't resist this comment 😊).

Anyhow, we now need to take a closer look at the actual business. Please remember, this was 1990 and there was no Internet in India. At least, there was no publicly available Internet. Therefore, searching for a job at the click of a button while sitting comfortably in your living room and guzzling beer, had not even been dreamt of.

But hang on. Yes, there was no Internet. But there were computers. After all, these were not prehistoric times. This was 1990. And using these computers, Sanjeev and his team started off by doing entry-level salary surveys. You see, companies were competing with each other to get bright youngsters from college to join them. And they were desperate to know what the other guy was offering so they could raise their own offer by a few miserable rupees. Until then, these companies would conduct salary surveys on their own. But this is where Sanjeev chipped in. He and his team would get this data by speaking to students from a few top engineering colleges as well as management institutes. And this data would be used to create their salary surveys. Suddenly, employers did not need to conduct their own surveys, which was obviously both time consuming and expensive. They would simply buy the survey from Info Edge. The survey was sold at Rs 5000, and as you can imagine, it was lapped up. Obvious, isn't it—highly valuable information for a few thousand rupees? Over time of course, Sanjeev realized that the value to his customers was far higher, and he was able to price these surveys much higher, typically at Rs 10,000. And so the salary surveys continued.

And yes, I have some good news for you. Sanjeev was finally able to take a small salary from the company.

The Birth of Naukri.com

So that's what Sanjeev started off with: salary surveys. But while this was going on, he was thinking. You see, during the time that he was employed at HMM Ltd, he had noticed something interesting. In those days, the company used to get regular issues of *Business India*, one of India's leading business magazines. And people in the office would read it. But guess what? They didn't read it from the beginning. They would read it back to front!

Yes, you heard right. *Back to front.*

Why?

Actually, if you've ever picked up a copy of *Business India*, you wouldn't ask me this question. Because *Business India* used to carry all its appointment ads for managers at the back of each issue. There were some thirty pages of these ads, and that's what everyone wanted to read.

Some, of course, were keen on applying for jobs. Others were simply figuring out where they stood compared to the rest of the industry, and exploring any potential opportunity that life might throw up. But no matter what the reason, everyone would read these pages. And then of course, they would discuss these jobs, the salaries and the opportunities that they might be losing (over coffee provided by their current employer, of course, but that's beside the point). The key issue was that even people who were not interested in shifting, were looking at these ads.

Then of course, there were the headhunters (more formally called placement consultants, especially in certain parts of Africa, where the term takes on a completely different meaning). Interestingly, many of the jobs that these headhunters had in their kitty, were not even advertised in *Business India*.

Sanjeev realized two things. First of all, there was phenomenal interest in looking around at jobs in the market, and even people not actively looking for a change, were potentially interested. Secondly, the number of jobs that were advertised in magazines such as *Business India* and the like, or in newspapers, was only the tip of the iceberg. A huge number of open positions were not advertised at all and were perhaps tucked away in the bag of goodies that placement consultants carried. And that set Sanjeev thinking. If someone could aggregate all those jobs and put them together in a single database, wouldn't that create an extremely powerful offering?

Unfortunately, as I've already mentioned, there was no Internet in those days. The number of people interested in switching jobs was huge and the number just flipping through—a category that could be converted into jobseekers—was even bigger. But reaching them was the problem.

Somewhere along the line, in 1991, there was a glimmer of hope. Because the government was planning to set up terminals in public places, from which the general public could access specific databases. Sanjeev and his team were excited about this, as it could be the answer to reaching a large number of jobseekers. Sadly, however, the project never took off.

Dear reader, if you've ever met Sanjeev, you would be aware that he never gives up. He keeps trying various options until he finds one that works (if you haven't met him, grab the next opportunity that comes your way). It was just a question of finding a way to make their database of jobs accessible to the huge pool of jobseekers out there. He tried out a franchising model, where franchisees would make the database available to people in their neighbourhood. Unfortunately, this didn't work out. He tried couriering floppy disks to individuals for a fee.* But that didn't work either. Too cumbersome in both cases. Designing the database, getting data about job openings and entering this data into the database—these were easy. The big, big problem was reaching the end user.

By the way, I hope you continue to learn something from Sanjeev's experience. Starting a business is no joke, and I'm sure you've already realized this by now. You'll get hundreds of ideas—each better than the other. Some of these would be discarded quickly. A few would be realistic and you could take these forward. Whatever you do decide on, please remember, you'll have all kinds of problems along the way, and you'll need to try out multiple ways of solving these problems. You might even need to change your business model completely—something that we call pivoting. But you cannot, cannot give up. Keep on at it. Persevere. Keep trying various solutions. Remember, even Sanjeev, one of the most successful founders in the world of the Internet, faced all kinds of problems in his early years. The key is that he didn't give up. And look where he's reached today.

Anyhow, to get back to my story, one fine day the Internet came along. Sanjeev got his solution. And the rest, as they say, is history!

It was 1996, and Sanjeev was attending the IT Asia exhibition in New Delhi. Walking through the pavilion, he came across a particular

---

* For those young people who have no clue what a floppy disk was, it was a small, lightweight, removable disk that you needed to insert into your computer's disk drive. A precursor to today's pen drive. People from my generation have grown up on floppy disks (and cursing them when they didn't function). Perhaps you'll spot them if you watch old movies.

stall with a sign that had 'www' printed on it. Now, you young guys, having been brought up on a diet of the Internet, along with mobile phones and apps, know exactly what 'www' stands for. Yes, it's the World Wide Web—or, in simple terms, the Internet. But back in 1996, it was new. And it was certainly new to Sanjeev (sorry, Sanjeev, it was new to me as well 😊).

Curious Sanjeev walked up to the stall and asked for a demo. And that demo, ladies and gentlemen, was to change his life and the life of every jobseeker in India. Because on that day, Sanjeev figured out the solution to his problem. On that day, he discovered the power of the Internet. And on that day, the seeds for **Naukri.com**—an online job search portal—were sown!

The next few months were both hectic and fun. Obviously, the first step was building the website. For which he caught hold of two friends who were skilled programmers. They built a somewhat rudimentary site, but it served its purpose. Improvements could come later. Then, of course, the website needed daily updates with job data. For this, guess what the team did? They would buy twenty-nine different newspapers every day (and some magazines) and pick up all the job vacancy ads. They also hired data entry operators to compile and enter these into the website.

And then of course, the site needed to be hosted somewhere. For which they needed a server. At that time, almost all such servers were in the USA. They were expensive—the cost of hosting the site was around $25 a month. And the company did not have the money. But, by now, I'm sure you've guessed that little things like lack of money do not deter guys like Sanjeev. He explained the problem to his elder brother Sushil, a professor at the business school at UCLA (University of California, Los Angeles). He also told Sushil that he couldn't pay for the server at the moment. Fortunately, like most elder brothers, Sushil's immediate response was, 'No problem. I'll hire a local shared server so you can host your site. You can pay me later.'

And that was that. Site ready and hosted, data entered, and Naukri.com was all set to launch. The actual launch took place on

2 April 1997. (Yes, Sanjeev avoided 1 April. I'm not sure why ☺. You could ask him when you meet him.)

They started with around 1000 job postings. The early days were not great since the number of users on the Internet was not too large—around 14,000 or so. And bandwidth, which you guys are so used to in today's world, was just about picking up. But it was one of the first attempts in India to use the Internet for business.

It Was Tough to Make Money

And now, I'm sure you have a question. I can guess what it is and I'm coming to it, so please be patient and give me a chance. You see, this was a business and not a charity. So these guys had to make money. Which meant two things. First of all, they needed revenues. In other words, someone had to pay them for the services they provided. And secondly, they needed to keep their costs low—ideally lower than their revenues—in order to make a profit.

Let's start with revenues. I've already told you that these people used to publish salary surveys which were happily bought by various companies. Fortunately, this line of business continued and gave them some revenue, although it wasn't a huge amount. They needed much higher revenues because the new business they had launched, namely Naukri.com, needed a lot of money for it to stand on its own feet and become viable: money for developing the site, money for marketing, and of course, overheads such as salaries and rents. And the salary surveys they used to conduct provided only a fraction of this money. So the big revenues had to come from Naukri itself. That simply *had to be* the mainstay.

Sanjeev was very clear that they would not charge jobseekers. As I've already mentioned, at that time there were only around 14,000 Internet users out there, and it was important to get as many of these users as possible to land up on their website. Not only that, it was vital to make sure these users kept returning. And this would only be possible if access was free. So that much was clear—they could not charge users. But since they had to make money from somewhere, they needed to charge companies. For posting their ads on the site.

Unfortunately, as you can imagine, companies were not really interested in shelling out money till they saw an adequate number of jobseekers coming to the website. And to get a large number of jobseekers, Naukri needed to spend on marketing. So it was a typical chicken-and-egg situation. Companies wanted lots of jobseekers before paying and to get jobseekers, Naukri needed money.

Fortunately, these guys started getting press coverage. You see, the Internet was an exciting new phenomenon and was growing rapidly in the country. And the media always latches onto such things. Yes, you already had Yahoo!, Hotmail and all the other popular Internet-based applications in the USA. But Naukri.com was home-grown. It was Indian. Not only that, this one actually targeted Indians living in India, unlike other Indian websites such as Khoj, Samachar and Rediff.com, which were targeting NRIs in the USA, because that's where most Internet users lived. And so, the Indian media happily latched onto it and started writing about it. In fact, over time, Naukri.com gained massive media coverage. As a consequence, the number of users kept going up. The fact that it was free to use was another huge factor in getting users onboarded. And of course, word of mouth helped.

And guess what happened next? That's right. As the number of users went up, employers began to get interested and were willing to pay for their ads to be posted on the site. At that stage, Naukri was charging Rs 350 for a job posting, and they also offered their clients a larger package—Rs 6000 per year for unlimited postings. During the first financial year, namely 1997–98, 80 per cent of the job ads were free. In this year, the company earned a revenue of Rs 2.35 lakh. Not a huge amount, but it was a start. In the second year, 1998–99, more businesses started paying and revenues jumped to Rs 18 lakh. And that is when Sanjeev realized that this was no longer an experiment but a serious business. Which is when he decided to focus on the Naukri.com business and stop the salary surveys.

(Potential founders, please note: When you've figured out that one business is working out well and has significant potential to grow, that's the time to focus on it.)

The following year, 1999–2000, was even better. Revenues ballooned to Rs 36 lakh. And—hold your breath—they actually made a profit of Rs 1.80 lakh. Yes, my friend, this is where Info Edge actually made their first profit. A start-up in the Internet space, which was notorious for all those (happily) loss-making businesses, actually made a profit!

Aha! Now that we are talking about profits, we need to talk about costs. And I'm sure you've guessed the rest. To control costs, Sanjeev was once again forced to not take a salary. For the second time since he quit his cushy job at a multinational company. But by this time his wife had given up her job, so the money had to come in from elsewhere. That's when he took up a job with *The Pioneer* newspaper as the consulting editor of their career supplement, titled *Avenues*. In addition, he also conducted CAT classes to help potential MBA aspirants get into one of the IIMs. By the way, this is an approach often used by successful founders when their main business is in the process of being built, and is not yet generating enough money on its own. Doing something in parallel which brings in the cash. For instance, tech founders take on programming assignments. Some do consulting. Others conduct classes. All temporary of course, but they do bring in valuable cash. After all, not only the business, but even the founders' digestive systems need cash to survive, don't they?

Those were real tough times for Sanjeev. He once told me that he would wake up at 6 a.m., reach the Info Edge office by 7 a.m., work until 12 noon and then go across to the office of the *Pioneer*. After office hours, he would return to Info Edge, work until midnight, and then crash. But come 6 a.m. the next day, he would be up again for the same punishing schedule. Day after day, month after month, for three years.

Let's hear what Sanjeev has to say on surviving through those tough times:

It was tough going in the first few years of the business. And
during this phase, I learnt two extremely important lessons, which
I would like to share with the readers of this book. First of all,
you must be frugal. Something that I've already mentioned earlier.
Secondly, please remember, building a great company is a lifetime
commitment. It's not a one or two-year job. Don't create a business
with the objective of selling it in the next few years. Remember the
wonderful dialogue from the famous Hindi movie *Deewaar*: Be a
'lambi race ka ghoda' (In simple terms, as a founder, you must be
in the game for the long run.) If your attitude is, 'Let me try this
for a couple of years; otherwise I'll take up a job,' sorry, my friend,
that won't work. Yes, you'll have all kinds of problems along the
way, but you've got to keep on at it. You need patience, you need
persistence. And most importantly, you need to put in lots and
lots of hard work. Remember, *'Company khoon paseeney se banti
hai. Paison se nahin.'* (A company is built from blood, sweat and
sometimes tears. Not money!)

And perhaps the most important lesson of all: You can only
do all of this if you are passionate about your chosen business.
You must enjoy building your company. That is what will support
you all the way. I had a really tough time in the early years of my
company. But I really liked what I was doing, even though there
was no money. I was in control of my life. My priorities were
being set by me and not by a boss. That's perhaps the biggest
reason why I carried on through those struggles.

And that's a message for all of you readers out there: When things are
not going right for you and you are frustrated, wanting to tear your
hair out (assuming you still have some left to tear out), remember,
even hugely successful people like Sanjeev went through the same
tough times as you. Keep trying, keep experimenting, be frugal and
hopefully something will work out.

And with that last bit of gyan, let's take a break. I'm a bit tired of
writing and I'm sure you are tired of reading. We'll meet again in the
next chapter. Where I'll tell you about the time Hitesh joined Sanjeev.

5

The Sanjeev and Hitesh Show

In the life of any company, there are certain events which have a huge impact on its fortunes. And in February 2000, there was one such hugely positive event at Info Edge. Because this was when Hitesh Oberoi joined Sanjeev. Ever since then there has been no looking back, as the two of them took the company to the phenomenal position it is in today. And today, Hitesh is the MD and CEO of Info Edge.

Now, who is Hitesh Oberoi, you might ask? Well, if you are into the world of business in India, you obviously know him. But just in case you don't, let me tell you a bit about him. And we'll start with college. Hitesh did his BTech in Computer Science from IIT Delhi in 1994. By the way, I also did my BTech from IIT Delhi. However, I passed out a full seventeen years before him, and therefore I never met him. More important, he did not have the privilege of being ragged by me ☺. Fortunately, he quickly got over that disappointment and inevitably did what most bright youngsters do. That's right, he did his MBA from the prestigious IIM Bangalore in 1996.

Having completed his MBA, he joined Hindustan Unilever Ltd (HUL) and was there for the next three years, looking after sales and distribution in the ice cream division.

But this is where the itch began. You know the symptoms, don't you? That's right: 'I need to do something different. Something on my own.'

Hitesh Joins Info Edge

During this time, Hitesh happened to meet our very own Sanjeev Bikhchandani, whom he had known for some time. Sanjeev realized that Hitesh's background in FMCG sales and distribution would be invaluable for Info Edge. Together, the two of them could make the company boom. And then Sanjeev said something that would change the course of history. Well, not quite, but it would definitely change the course of the history of Info Edge. He said, 'If this is what you want to do, let's do it together.'

And that was that. Hitesh joined Info Edge as a co-founder. Interestingly, he didn't join the company for Naukri. He joined to start another Internet-based business within Info Edge. The business was called Bachao.com, and it provided users with deals and discounts on purchases. However, fate had other things in store for him, and if you'll wait patiently for a bit, I'll explain what happened.

By the way, like Sanjeev, Hitesh also came from a typical middle-class family, where the only constant was a fixed salary at the end of each month. No business people, please. So why did he take the plunge and get into an uncertain, highly risky business? Well, the best person to tell us is Hitesh himself, so let's hear him out:

> If you've grown up in a business family, by the time you are an adult, you are ready to start something on your own. Because that's what you've been hearing day in and day out. It's almost in the blood. Now, I came from a service-class family and did not have this kind of upbringing. However, there was something interesting happening in India during the eighties and nineties. Almost a revolution, you might say. Because IT professionals, with no background in business, were building extremely successful IT companies. Companies such as Infosys, HCL and Wipro. And that's when I felt I should also take the plunge. In any case, even if I had to quit the business and take up a job again, I would not

have faced a problem, given that I had degrees from IIT and IIM.
And that was that. I jumped in and joined Sanjeev at Info Edge!

So that was that. However, it wasn't all smooth sailing for Hitesh—
at least on the personal front. You see, when he was working at
HUL, he met his future wife, a young lady named Rimy. Now
I don't want to get into the details of their romance, how they
bunked office to watch movies, or where they went to have
chaat in Delhi, etc., etc. (you know the drill, don't you?). But,
as in all Hindi movies, there was the inevitable catch. Rimy came
from a Keralite Christian family and Hitesh was a blue-blooded
Punjabi Hindu.

Aha! Now it gets interesting, doesn't it? You see, in those days
this sort of thing simply wasn't done. Rimy's parents were hoping
for a nice Keralite Christian boy for their daughter. Definitely not a
Punjabi Hindu boy. No way! Fortunately, however, the story had a
happy ending. You see, Hitesh's job with a leading multinational—
with retirement benefits as well—was the sweetener, and his in-laws
relented. But then came the twist (it gets to be more and more like a
Hindi movie, doesn't it?). When Hitesh dropped the bombshell: He
was quitting HUL to start something on his own.

Can you imagine the earthquake this caused? 'As it is, our son
in-law is a Punjabi Hindu boy. But at least he has a good, stable job.
Now he's gone and chucked it up.' Fortunately, Rimy's parents agreed
once again (perhaps Hitesh's experience in sales had something to
do with it), and the wedding did take place, around the time Hitesh
joined Info Edge. And now they have two lovely daughters: Megha
and Misha.

Incidentally, around the time that he switched from HUL to
Info Edge, Hitesh bought his first car.

And can you guess which car it was?

No, it wasn't a Mercedes. Or a BMW. Not even a miserable
Honda City. It was a simple Daewoo Matiz, one of the smallest and
lowest-cost cars in the Indian market.

Dear reader, please note something that is very, very important to this story: All this while, I've been talking about Sanjeev's frugal personal habits. And here was his co-founder with exactly the same kind of thinking!

Anyhow, before I proceed with the Info Edge story, there is one more thing I must tell you about Hitesh. And it has nothing to do with the company. At least, I don't think it does. When I met him in his office in Noida, near Delhi, I expected to be offered coffee and cookies. That's the done thing during meetings, isn't it? Coffee (or tea, if you prefer) and cookies.

Yes, I did get my coffee. But guess what? No cookies. We were served butter popcorn!

Butter popcorn?

That's right. Butter popcorn. Hitesh is inordinately fond of butter popcorn and all his visitors are treated to this exotic delicacy. And given the amount he consumes, I'm sure it has had a bearing on the phenomenal success of the company he heads!

And so our meeting continued, interrupted by the crunch, crunch, crunch of the yummy butter popcorn . . .

The VCs Get Interested

Anyhow, we must get back to serious business now. You see, Info Edge had been growing at a decent pace since the launch of Naukri.com in 1990. It was definitely not a giant, but yes, there was growth. As I have mentioned earlier, in the financial year 1999–2000, the company had clocked revenues of Rs 36 lakh, along with a small profit of Rs 1.80 lakh. Now, when a start-up starts growing, and (incredibly) makes a profit as well, what do you think happens?

That's right, investors start getting excited. Which is exactly what happened to Info Edge. 'An Internet portal for classified job ads? That too in India, where the number of employment opportunities as well as jobseekers is HUGE? And to top it all, a profitable business? Wow,

we are interested. Please take our money. We want to invest in you.'
That's what the investors said.

But look at Sanjeev's reaction, 'Sorry, we are profitable and
growing. We don't need your money!'

Yes, my friend, in this world of start-ups, where every founder
and his grandmother is desperately searching for funding, here was
someone who had the audacity to say no.

But, of course, there was a problem, which Sanjeev realized
over time. You see, this was the time that Internet businesses were
being launched across the world as though there was no tomorrow.
Even within India, the Internet was beginning to boom, and dot-com
companies were being launched right, left and centre. The area
of online job portals was also beginning to heat up and Naukri
already had an aggressive competitor called JobsAhead. Not only
that, JobsAhead had actually raised two rounds of funds totalling
a staggering Rs 33 crore, from Chrysalis Capital, a VC firm.[*] With
this money, they recruited a large team and developed a product
that was better than that of Naukri.com. Something that both
Sanjeev and Hitesh admitted. (Please note their willingness to
accept this. Successful people are more than willing to accept the
fact that competition could be better than them. But then they do
something about it. Which is one reason why they are successful.)
You see, Naukri had a basic website where they put up recruitment
ads. But JobsAhead also maintained a database of applicants, which
employers could search through, figure out which applicants they
were interested in, and then call them over for interviews. As you
can imagine, this helped HR departments cut down the effort in
recruiting manpower.

But there was more. Not only did JobsAhead have a good
product, they also used their funds to advertise on TV, which, as you

---

[*] 'JobsAhead gets Rs 11 crore funds injection', agencyfaqs!, 3 May 2001, https://
www.afaqs.com/news/advertising/2497_jobsahead-gets-rs-11-crore-funds-
injection.

are probably aware, is among the most expensive modes of marketing your product. They had the money. So they used it.

And what was the effect on our very own Naukri? Well, I've already told you that in the world of the Internet, it is critical to scale up rapidly. If you don't, the other guy scales up faster than you, eats into your customers and your market share, and ultimately kills you. Sanjeev and Hitesh realized this. The game was changing from a small, uncertain, wobbly market to something potentially huge. With an aggressive competitor and perhaps bigger ones lurking around, just waiting to get in. In this environment, Info Edge could not remain a small, cute company. No way. They had to grow big to survive.

So, what do you think they did? Simple. They went back to the investors who had earlier contacted them, namely ICICI Venture (the VC arm of ICICI Bank which invests in start-ups). But this is when something really interesting happened. And I don't want to steal Hitesh's thunder, so let's hear it from him:

> Before investing in any company, a VC needs a detailed business plan. And obviously, ICICI Venture asked us for one. But Sanjeev and I looked at each other. We didn't have one! We *did* have some projections, but everything was extremely fluid. You see, in those days, no one really knew how to make money from an Internet business. We were experimenting and didn't know how things would pan out. Things were changing virtually every month. And in such an environment, how could we have a firm, credible plan?
>
> Anyhow, ICICI Venture needed one, so we had to create one. However, it was a very conservative plan. And ICICI Venture said, 'Sorry, your plan is too conservative. We need much more growth!' That was it.
>
> Fortunately, ICICI Venture realized the potential of our business. Maybe they had an inkling of the explosive growth that was likely to take place in the Internet, and therefore, in Internet-related businesses. In any case, what we were charging

employers per ad in Naukri was around Rs 350, whereas newspapers would charge far, far more. Therefore, with more and more users getting access to the net, they expected a larger and larger number of employers to switch from newspapers to the cheaper Naukri.com. My guess is that they realized we were being conservative. Therefore, they did decide to fund us.

Dear reader, please stop here for a moment, and notice the humility of the man. He didn't say, 'We knew everything.' He simply said, 'We didn't know how to make money!'

Back to my story. On 8 April 2000, ICICI Venture signed a shareholder agreement with the company and made a commitment to invest Rs 7.29 crore, for a 15 per cent equity stake. The investment would come in tranches (which is fairly common in such cases) with the first tranche being approximately Rs 3 crore. So Sanjeev and Hitesh got the money. (Sorry, Info Edge got the money. It didn't go into their pockets, if that's what you were thinking.) And guess what? They promptly put half of it into a fixed deposit in a bank!

Now hang on. Isn't that crazy? You work so hard to get money from investors, and then you put it into a fixed deposit. What a silly thing to do!

No, my friend. It wasn't silly at all. It was one of the wisest decisions our two founders made.

Why?

Well, let's listen to Sanjeev on the subject:

Once you've got money from investors, treat it as sacred. The fact that you've got the money doesn't mean the commitment to your investors ends. It has just begun. Will you now splurge on first-class travel and five-star hotels? No way! That's the last thing investors want. What they want is for you to build a great, sustainable company. And great companies are capital-efficient. They use their money frugally.

And this is the key. If you have too much money available, you will get into bad habits. You will start spending on unnecessary luxuries. Companies that have too much money sloshing around tend to use it sub-optimally. And then you will not be able to build a profitable, sustainable business. Use money frugally. And a good way to be frugal is to be slightly scarce with regard to cash.

Aha! I'm sure you get it now. Sanjeev and Hitesh were clear that they were not chasing growth at any cost. Their philosophy was certainly not, 'Keep making a loss, and keep raising money'. And that's why they put half the money into a fixed deposit, so that they would continue to run a frugal business.

My friend, can you now see how Info Edge has always been a viable, profitable company? And it was growing—although not at the hectic pace that several Internet companies were. Just compare this with the gamut of loss-making Internet companies that have been proudly raising money year after year after year . . .

And this is the key: *Because Info Edge was profitable, they did not need funding for survival. They needed funding for growth.* Which is why they approached ICICI Venture and took money from them.

Finally, since you've been waiting patiently, I must tell you what happened to Bachao.com. You see, ICICI Venture wanted Info Edge to focus on the Naukri business and shut down (or sell off) everything else. Sanjeev and Hitesh listened carefully to them, found merit in this suggestion and accepted it. That's when they shut down Bachao.com.

And that's when Hitesh moved into the Naukri business full-time. To focus on setting up the product, marketing, and sales functions.

The Dot-Com Boom and Crash

Having received their funding, Sanjeev and Hitesh thought their troubles were over. But of course, you and I know better, don't we? Because this was 2000. This is when the dot-com bubble burst. Now, I've already spoken about this in Chapter 2, but I need to tell you a bit more. As I've mentioned earlier, when the Internet came along, the world—especially the USA—was super excited. This was a new technology that could potentially transform the way people shopped or did business. And of course, consumers were delighted. Everyone simply *had to buy a PC*. What was a *luxury* earlier had become a *necessity*.

And that further spurred the revolution in Internet businesses. Founders fell over each other to launch the next big thing. eBay.com, Pets.com, Boo.com, Webvan.com and hundreds of similar businesses were launched. All with a '.com' in their name. And all focused on grabbing the Internet market.

And what was the effect on investors? Well, they started licking their lips and opened up their wallets (sorry, cheque books). Here was a once-in-a-lifetime opportunity to invest in Internet companies that were going to take over the world. Those were days when interest rates were low, so these guys could easily borrow money from banks and invest it in these Internet companies. And it wasn't just angel investors and VCs. Many of these companies got listed on the stock market, and therefore, even the common man (*aam aadmi* in Indian parlance) could invest in this glorious opportunity.

Now, you might be aware that in the US stock market, there is a specific index for tech stocks called the Nasdaq. Rather like our Sensex or Nifty, except that it is only composed of tech stocks. Obviously, many of these newly minted Internet companies (the bigger ones) were part of the Nasdaq. And would you believe it— during the period from 1995, when the Internet craze took off, to March 2000, the Nasdaq actually grew by over 400 per cent.[*]

Yes, my friend, founders created Internet companies and investors poured money into these companies like there was no tomorrow.

---

[*] Adam Hayes, 'Dotcom Bubble Definition', Investopedia, 13 June 2023, https://www.investopedia.com/terms/d/dotcom-bubble.asp.

Unfortunately for them, that's exactly what happened. There *was* no tomorrow. At least, not for most of these companies. Because in March 2000, the world went through the infamous dot-com bust. And that's when investors pulled the plug. Businesses that were only getting eyeballs and could not get funding died a sudden, violent death. Those which were heavily loss-making and therefore dependent on funding collapsed as well. Giants such as Pets.com, Boo.com, Webvan and many, many more, simply disappeared from the face of the earth—sorry, Internet.

Of course, during this time, we also had the terrible tragedy of 9/11 and the world was shaken out of its slumber. Suddenly, people wanted to run to safety and not invest in risky, loss-making Internet companies.

I'm sure you know the rest. From a peak of 5048.62 on 10 March 2000, the Nasdaq collapsed to 1139.90 on 4 October 2002—a gigantic fall of 76.81 per cent.[*]

Yes my friend, this was the time the dot-com bubble burst.

And What Happened to Info Edge?

Nothing much!

Nothing much? You mean an Internet company that was not impacted by the dot-com crash?

Yes, sir. That's exactly what I mean. Because Info Edge was a genuine company. It was generating revenues and these revenues were increasing year on year. And most of all, it was profitable. It was not focusing on growth at any cost. And here's the key: *Info Edge did not need external funding to survive. It did not even need funding to grow—it was growing anyway. It only needed funding to grow faster.*

Of course, with the mayhem around them, the founders were scared. After all, who wouldn't be? But they survived because they

---

[*] Adam Hayes, 'Dotcom Bubble Definition', Investopedia, 13 June 2023, https://www.investopedia.com/terms/d/dotcom-bubble.asp.

were running a real, profitable business, and not one that was chasing eyeballs.

Finally, let me summarize the philosophy of Info Edge with one of my favourite quotes from Sanjeev:

The customer's money is far more important than the investor's money.

What does this mean? Simple. Focus on your business. If you do that, you'll get customers. These customers will give you revenues. And then investors will come to you. On the other hand, if you focus on getting funding rather than building your business, you might not get customers—or, at least, you will get less of them. And if that happens, why would investors come to you? They are looking for a business that earns growing revenues, aren't they?

And with that bit of wisdom from Sanjeev, let's end this chapter.

6

Growing the Business

And now, let's understand how Info Edge used the funds they had raised. Or more specifically, the Rs 1.5 crore they were left with after the fixed deposit. Obviously, they began spending on marketing—meaning expensive ads and direct mailers. In fact, within the first couple of months, they had spent around Rs 70 lakh, or around a fourth of the first tranche of funds they had received.

And what was the result?

Nothing significant. No major growth in business. There was a large market out there for employment ads, but they were not able to tap it. It was so frustrating.

But that's when Hitesh, the master of sales and distribution at Hindustan Unilever, had an idea. He realized that this was a new concept. And when you have a new concept to sell, what do you do? Simple. You sit across the table with your customer, and patiently explain your offering. Assuming of course, that the customer is willing to patiently listen to you. Then you answer his questions, clear up his doubts, and hopefully get him to agree to spend a measly Rs 350 for posting an advertisement on your portal. Interestingly, this wasn't the approach being followed by new-fangled Internet businesses across the world. They simply splurged and splurged and then splurged some more, on ads and email campaigns. But Hitesh believed that closing deals in a completely new space, such as the

Internet, required face-to-face meetings. And that's why the company needed to get into sales mode.

Sales, Sales, Sales

So on an experimental basis, the company took on four salespeople. Wonder of wonders: Within just four months, each of these guys was generating an average of Rs 50,000 per month in sales. And there is more. The total expenditure that the company incurred on each salesperson was Rs 22,000 per month, including his salary, conveyance, shared desks and all other overheads. In other words, for each salesperson they were making a margin of Rs 28,000 per month.

And with that, ladies and gentlemen, Info Edge had found what they called their 'repeatable profitable unit' or RPU: *the salesperson*. They had figured out how to grow profitably. And that's when Hitesh went all guns blazing and added salespeople. Not from the IIMs or IITs. He recruited simple graduates from lesser-known colleges. Why? Well, they wouldn't be selling space satellites. They would be selling a Rs 350 ad for jobs on their portal. That did not need an IIT or IIM degree. It needed smart, presentable youngsters, with good communication skills. And here's the key: These young graduates were delighted to get the job at a fraction of what Naukri would have had to pay MBAs. In fact, within two years, they had added 240 salespeople across eleven cities.

But there is something else I must tell you. It wasn't just the sales guys who were selling. No sir, both Sanjeev and Hitesh were very much part of the gang. No sitting in an air-conditioned ivory tower and giving instructions. No way. In fact, both of them spent a lot of their time on the field, making sales calls. Here is what Hitesh says:

> We had to get clients. And to do that, as founders we had to show the way. Unlike HUL, Info Edge was not a huge multinational with lots of highly experienced salespeople. So, Sanjeev and I led the way in making sales calls. I would spend around twelve days a

month travelling around the country, making sales calls. And then I'd come back to Delhi and continue making calls here. It didn't matter whether I was making a call to a small company or a large one. It didn't matter whether I was meeting a senior person or a junior one. The order might simply be worth Rs 350. But the call had to be made—and I made it. Often, even junior people kept me waiting at the reception for an hour. But as a founder, you don't have a choice. You make sales calls. Period.

And Sanjeev was the same. No hang-ups about making sales calls. That's how we were able to survive without spending too much. And that's how we trained our sales guys—by taking them along with us on these calls.

By the way, as you can imagine, the tragic 9/11 event was the lowest point in the business. At that time, Sanjeev and Hitesh thought they were dead. Because they now had no hope of getting further funding, and the business had not yet picked up sufficiently. But that's where they personally took on the responsibility of wading through the crisis. 'We'll get the business, and we'll personally make sales calls,' is what they famously said. And during the month of October, following 9/11, guess what? Hitesh made eighty-five sales calls, and Sanjeev made sixty-five. That, my friend, is leading by example. That's taking responsibility!

We'll Do Whatever the Customer Wants

Now, at this stage, Hitesh realized something very important. You see, in this business, they were trying to wean employers away from advertising in newspapers—something these employers had been doing for ages and were comfortable with. Therefore, two things became important. First of all, Naukri had to provide whatever services employers were getting from the print media. You couldn't tell the customer, 'Please switch to advertising on the Internet. We realize it's a new, untested medium. And we realize that you have been successfully using the print medium so far. But please advertise with us. Oh, we almost forgot. You will need to put in a lot of extra effort to advertise with us!'

Makes sense?

So let's first take a look at the extra effort. You see, advertising in newspapers was typically done through a local advertising agency. Importantly, these agencies would do the formatting and layout of the ad, including writing some of the text. But with Naukri, the employer had to do this himself before submitting the ad. So what did Naukri do? Simple: They just asked their customers to send them an email. Naukri would do the layout and formatting.

And there was more. Naukri would receive all the resumes in response to each ad, collate them, print them out, and then send them to the customer. An additional service, as you can see. That's how customer-focused our founders were.

As you can imagine, this created a wonderful 'network effect'. As the number of Internet users grew, the number of jobseekers on the Naukri website grew as well. And that made it more attractive for employers to post their ads there. Which, in turn, made it more attractive for jobseekers, and therefore more and more such people started coming to the site. You see? The chicken-and-egg problem had effectively been solved. Because more users led to more ads, which in turn led to more users . . .

Dear reader, you've seen that both these founders have always been customer-focused. No, that's too mild a statement. They were actually obsessed with their customers. And that led to a major addition to the Naukri business. You would recall from the previous chapter that their competitor, JobsAhead, maintained a database of applicants that employers could search through, figure out which applicants were suitable, and then call them over for interviews. Now, since Hitesh and Sanjeev were constantly in touch with their customers, they received feedback that this feature was extremely useful. In fact, this was a major reason for the success of JobsAhead.

And that's when, in 2003, they decided to launch their own version of this database, which they called Resdex (Incidentally, both Sanjeev and Hitesh admitted that they had made a mistake by not launching this earlier. Yes, my friend, they squarely took responsibility for it.) So employers could now search through Resdex and thereby identify potential candidates. And this had another benefit. During the meetings that each salesperson had with a potential client, the client could actually search through the database and see that there were enough good, usable resumes. In other words, the client was able to gain confidence that it was worth going ahead with Naukri as a recruitment partner. Yes, it did take time to build up. After all, they *were* playing catch-up with JobsAhead. But over time, it added significant value to their offering.

But there's more to this story. Over time, our founders realized that they could actually charge for Resdex. In other words, instead of putting out ads, employers could simply access the Resdex database for a fee. And that really turbo-charged the business, as Naukri's revenues shot up from Rs 8 crore in 2002–03 to Rs 240 crore in 2007–08. Today, Resdex contributes over 70 per cent of Naukri's revenues, and most of their profits. Fascinating, isn't it? The biggest contributor to the Info Edge business—and something that Sanjeev and Hitesh launched simply because they were so, so customer-oriented!

Of course, as more and more services such as Resdex were offered, and as the number of users grew, guess what? Naukri increased their prices. And yet, employers kept coming back for more. In fact, by 2005, their most expensive product was priced at a staggering Rs 3 lakh per year. Yes, you heard it right—Rs 3 lakh! And it was still cheaper than what newspapers were offering. As you can imagine, the productivity of the sales team also shot up over time. Remember, they were initially selling only ad postings worth Rs 350 each. And each salesperson would sell perhaps three of four such postings per day. But now, they could sell far more expensive products, and were therefore getting sales worth several times their salaries!

The 'Monster' Competitor

So Naukri had successfully warded off the challenge from other Indian competitors, including JobsAhead. And you thought that was when our crack team of Sanjeev and Hitesh could sit back and relax. Perhaps, lying in hammock on a beach, with a can of beer in their hand. Without a care in the world.

Right? Isn't that what you thought?

Well, think again. Founders cannot afford to relax. Yes, they *can* have beer. And as far as I'm aware, they can also lie down in a hammock. But they must remain aware of what's going on around them. Because the world doesn't stop. The world keeps moving on and throwing fresh challenges at you. And in the case of Naukri, it was a truly 'monster' challenge. In the form of the global leader in online job search, Monster.com. A company that was present in thirty countries when it entered India sometime in 2001.

And just to add to the fun, the popular newspaper, the *Times of India*, also launched its own portal, Timesjobs.com in 2004. Obviously, the newspaper was happy to promote the site extensively. Something that Naukri could not afford to do. And then something further happened. In an attempt to capture a large chunk of the Indian market, in May 2004, Monster.com bought out JobsAhead, paying a total of Rs 40 crore for the acquisition.[*]

As you can imagine, these competitors posed a challenge for Naukri. But then, Naukri was used to challenges. You know that by now, don't you? Yes, they emerged unscathed from this challenge as well.

How? Well, three main reasons. First of all, these were very early days in the history of online jobs. It was by no means a saturated market, and there was huge scope for everyone to grow.

---

[*] 'Monster Acquires JobsAhead,' Updated 6 Feb 2013, https://www.business-standard.com/article/companies/monster-acquires-jobsahead-104052601101_1.html.

Secondly, Naukri had always been a market leader in the space. They already had a huge number of employers posting jobs on their site. And this became an entry barrier. Because jobseekers would obviously go to sites that had a large number of job opportunities. And the network effect I've just spoken about, ensured that both job opportunities as well as jobseekers kept growing on Naukri. Now, it is not easy for a newcomer to beat the network effect. Because the big get bigger. Monster might have been the world leader in jobs but it had a small presence in India. Even after buying out JobsAhead, it remained smaller than Naukri in India. And the network effect did the rest.

And now, for the third reason: Hitesh believes that a major reason for their success in warding off competition, was their 'feet-on-the-street' model. Where individual sales guys would sit across the table and convince their clients to buy their products, including the low-value products. Monster did not use this model.

The result? Naukri maintained its lead, although Monster was a close second. In fact, by 2004–05, Naukri had raced to revenues of Rs 47 crore. Largely because of a sales team of 400 people.

But then something happened which effectively stopped the race, leaving only one winner. In 2008, we had the global financial crisis with Lehmann brothers and several other giants collapsing (Don't tell me you aren't aware of this. If you aren't, well, read about it. I cannot tell you everything.) With huge corporations simply dying, Monster's global business plummeted. And with that, it dropped out of the two-horse race in India. Well, it was still there, but it was no longer a serious competitor to Naukri. Fortunately, the financial crisis had a lower impact in India and Naukri's business continued. The result? Naukri was the clear, undisputed market leader once again.

Now, there is something else you need to know. As long as Naukri was small, technology was not really an issue. Response times were decent and there were no significant outages. But as they began scaling up, the volume of transactions began to take its toll. Therefore, according to Sanjeev, Naukri has been investing heavily in technology and product upgradation. And they continue to do so till today. Because that's the only way they can support the burgeoning volume of transactions.

The IPO

Somewhere during the pitched battle with Monster (which now included JobsAhead), Info Edge decided to go ahead with an IPO, or Initial Public Offer, where they would get listed on the stock exchange. This was in October 2006, and Info Edge became India's first Internet company to be listed on both the Bombay Stock Exchange (BSE) and the National Stock Exchange (NSE).

It's interesting to see the reason for the IPO. No, it wasn't because ICICI Venture wanted an exit; in fact, they had already got a partial exit well before the IPO. Actually, there were multiple reasons. First of all, they had JobsAhead and later, the giant Monster.com breathing down their neck. And to compete, they needed money. Plus, Sanjeev and Hitesh believed that an IPO would help them gain more credibility and therefore build their brand. Of course, it was also good for their individual shareholders, such as employees with ESOPs who wanted to cash out.

So Naukri got their money and grew and grew and grew. At the time of writing this book (2023), they command a phenomenal 70 per cent share of the white-collar jobs market in India. A spectacular success story, if ever there was any.

But wait. That's only part of the story.

Because Naukri has three siblings as well. You see, Info Edge has been building three more businesses—namely Jeevansathi, 99acres and Shiksha.com.

Wouldn't you like to read about them?

Okay. Just turn the page . . .

7

We Are in the Business of Online Classified Ads

Jeevansathi.com

Dear reader, let me take you back to 1999 for a bit. Having launched Naukri.com, Sanjeev tried out another experiment, this time in the area of matrimonial matchmaking. You know how it works, don't you? Most marriages in India are 'arranged marriages'. 'Love marriage' is a bit of a dirty word. (By the way, in case you have had a love marriage or are planning one, please forgive me. In any case, this is definitely not my personal view, although I *did* have an arranged marriage 😊.) You see, the concept of arranged marriages is a tradition that has been handed down from generation to generation in perhaps 90 per cent of Indian families. Why? Because you need to marry someone within your caste. And sub-caste. And of course, you must marry into a family that has roughly the same social status as yours. Horoscopes must match. And God help you if you want to marry someone from another religion. You would most probably be ostracized by the entire family and knocked out of every family will. No, that would simply not do. And so, arranged marriages are the norm.

How does it work? Well, there are certain 'aunties' whose goal in life is to arrange matches. You should see the gleam in their eyes when they are stalking their prey, and the supremely smug look on their face when the match actually takes place. Job done, off they go in search of the next marriageable boy or girl.

The problem, of course, is that the database of eligible boys and girls that each of these aunties possesses, is severely limited. And unless the boy in question is willing to marry the first thing in a sari that the aunty puts up (or conversely, the girl is willing to marry the first thing in pants), sometimes these matchmaking efforts do not take off. Which leads us to the next big thing, namely family pundits. Or even marriage brokers, who make tons of money from matchmaking. You've seen their ads, of course, while travelling by train and looking out at the walls of the village houses as you pass them by. (If you haven't, my friend, you haven't really been on a train journey in India.) But once again, the database of eligible young people that each broker possesses, is not too large. So, if you are finicky, you are unlikely to get a match.

Then, of course, you have classified ads in the newspapers—where every boy is highly qualified and handsome with a six-figure income, and every girl is slim, fair and beautiful (what a wonderful country)! Here, the database becomes larger. You have a lot of such newspapers floating around, with several pages full of classified ads in each of them. The problem is, how many newspapers—and how many pages of ads—can you go through? You would perhaps need to be retired to go through all those ads every day. And of course, after a point you are confused because all girls are beautiful and all boys are handsome, so you simply give up and open the inevitable can of beer to recover!

Fortunately, there is a solution. What if all these classified ads were put into a computerized database? And made accessible through a website. Where you could feed in your specifications, such as religion, caste, location, preferred background, etc., etc. And voila—the website responds with those potential brides or grooms who meet your criteria. Suddenly, you have access to lots and lots of potential matches. And you do not need to go through pages and pages of classified ads in multiple newspapers, to decide which of those matches you were interested in. Wouldn't that be just wonderful?

And that, my friend, is exactly what Sanjeev figured out. Which is why, on an experimental basis, he launched **Jeevansathi** in 1999. A matchmaking site for marriages. They say that marriages are made in heaven, but Sanjeev and his team were hoping to make them on Jeevansathi!

However, there is more to this story. Remember, when Info Edge had raised funding, the investors, ICICI Venture, had wanted them to shut down everything else and focus on the Naukri business. That's when they shut down the Bachao business. And that's also when they sold off the Jeevansathi business. In retrospect, this turned out to be a great decision, because in the subsequent mayhem caused by the dot-com crash, focusing on one single business definitely helped the company to stay alive.

Jeevansathi: The Second Innings

But that was not the end of the Jeevansathi story. By 2004, Info Edge was making a decent amount of money, and had cash available. And that's when Sanjeev and Hitesh had a brainwave: 'Why not buy Jeevansathi back?'

Now, I know you are dying to ask me a question: 'Why buy a completely unrelated business?'

Good question. Actually, it wasn't a completely unrelated business. You see, Naukri was essentially into matchmaking. Between employers and jobseekers. And so was Jeevansathi, but this time between potential brides and grooms. So Jeevansathi was a portal, where brides and grooms could put up their resumes as well as requirements and hope for a match (actually, it was usually their desperate parents, egged on by their nosey neighbours and family members, who would put up these resumes, but that's beside the point).

Aha! I can now see the gleam in your eyes. That's right, both Naukri.com and Jeevansathi.com were doing something similar: They were letting people or companies put up classified ads, and helping in matchmaking. Yes, there was a difference in the way the customers were charged. In the case of Naukri, the employers paid to list their ad, whereas listings were free on Jeevansathi. Instead, they charged for the phone number of the family that had put up the ad. That apart, the two businesses seemed very, very similar.

Effectively, Sanjeev and Hitesh had broadened their business to one more category of classified ads. And that was smart, wasn't it? Had they got into the business of manufacturing biscuits or supplying babies' diapers online, it would have been a huge mistake, because these businesses were very, very, VERY different from their original business. Too defocused. Instead, they got into a somewhat similar business, where the learnings from Naukri could be used.

And now for the killer: With this acquisition, the focus of the company had changed. It wasn't a job portal any more.

It was a company running classified ads on the Internet. A company that was into online matchmaking!

But Were the Two Businesses Really Similar?

So Sanjeev and Hitesh had got into classified ads in a different area. And since they understood the business of recruitment, they assumed matrimonials would be similar.

Right?

Wrong.

Yes, Jeevansathi was based on classified ads. And yes, it focused on matchmaking. But the similarity ended there. Naukri was connecting employers with jobseekers. In other words, it was providing matchmaking services between businesses and individuals. But Jeevansathi was connecting individuals with individuals, or at best, individual families. So where the company was selling ads to a few thousand companies in Naukri, they actually had to sell to lakhs and lakhs of individual families in Jeevansathi. The result? Well, Hitesh's brilliant strategy of 'feet on the street' would not work. You see, it was relatively easy for the Naukri salespeople to meet someone in the HR department of a company. After all, there was a limited number of companies to deal with. But how would this work with matrimonials? You couldn't have salespeople knocking on every door, and politely asking, 'Sir (or Madam), do you have a marriageable son or daughter in your family?' Ridiculous, isn't it? This was an out-and-out consumer service, and it needed hefty marketing spend. And a lot more time than Naukri. Yes, word of mouth would help, but there was no choice—marketing spend was a given.

There were other differences as well. In the case of Naukri, once they had a client, there was a decent chance that the client would stay with them for years, giving them recurring business. After all, they would keep recruiting people, wouldn't they? But what about Jeevansathi? Unless India became the divorce capital of the world, once a customer was married, hopefully he or she would stay married. These were definitely not repeat customers—thank God. Plus, the average cost of a matrimonial ad, which Jeevansathi was attempting to replace, was much lower than the cost of an employment ad. Also, in the case of Jeevansathi, they had to focus on two very diverse sets of people: the individuals who were getting married, and the parents, many of whom were either terrified or extremely suspicious of anything remotely online.

And there is still more. As I've already mentioned, marriages in India almost invariably take place within the same community, caste, or even subcaste. Just check out the matrimonial pages the next time you read your newspaper, and you'll find that most of them ask for an Aggarwal match, or a Kayasth match, or a Punjabi Kshatriya match, or something similar. In other words, it's a very fragmented market. For instance, you couldn't tell a Kashmiri Brahmin family, 'We have the most wonderful Keralite Christian matches for your daughter.' No way. Consequently, word of mouth, which is essential for any business to grow, would be extremely localized. So if Jeevansathi were to successfully initiate a Marwari Maheshwari match in north India, it would have absolutely no impact on any Lingayat matches in Karnataka, or Iyengar matches in Tamil Nadu. Word of mouth, if any, would simply spread amongst Maheshwaris in the north, which meant even more marketing spend.

The net result, of course, was that Jeevansathi required far bigger marketing spend than Naukri did. And that meant they needed to focus on specific geographies where they had a good chance of becoming one of the dominant players, rather than going all out across the country and spending tons and tons of marketing money.

Finally, there was one more major difference between the two businesses. Unlike Naukri, Jeevansathi had large, entrenched competitors—each operating in specific geographies. And that's when Hitesh and Sanjeev sat down over the inevitable coffee (and butter popcorn, in the case of Hitesh) to figure out which geography to build their business in. They realized that south India already had a dominant player in BharatMatrimony, with a large, established network and word of mouth. Therefore, it made sense to look at other parts of India. And that is how they decided to focus on north and west India, which did not have any huge, entrenched competition. As you can imagine, the strategy worked. Jeevansathi is today a strong number 2 in north and west India after Shaadi.com, and number 3 nationally.

Dear reader, there is a key message in all of this. When you get into a business, you really don't know the pitfalls you will face. Sanjeev and Hitesh thought Jeevansathi would be very similar to Naukri, but it actually turned out to be very different, even though it was still a matchmaking business. As you can imagine, building Jeevansathi was tough going. In fact, it has been a loss-making business all along.

However, I've spoken to Hitesh, and he believes that the future holds out hope for this business. Wait until Chapter 10 to read all about his views.

99acres.com

So Sanjeev and Hitesh had re-positioned their company from a job portal to a company in the business of online classified ads.

Essentially matchmaking. Then, of course, they started hunting for other large areas that worked on the principle of matchmaking. And the next obvious one was real estate, so they launched **99acres.com**.

Aha! Real Estate. A yummy business where you have suitcases full of cash. And *benaami* (essentially fraudulent) deals. And everyone falling over each other in order to reduce 'valuations'. All with one sole intent: fooling the taxman.

But hang on. Before you get carried away, let me tell you that the actual business was none of the above. No sir, there were no cash dealings, no undervaluation, and absolutely no attempt to reduce stamp duty or any other taxes for that matter. After all, you wouldn't expect this from supremely ethical, squeaky-clean guys like Sanjeev and Hitesh, would you? This was pure and simple, utterly boring matchmaking. Bringing buyers and sellers (or landlords and tenants) together. Once that was done, 99acres was not involved. They had absolutely no role to play in the actual transaction.

So, what were they doing? Well, as you are aware, real estate deals are often done through a broker. Or by placing classified ads in the newspaper. What 99acres did was provide a portal where these ads could be posted for a fee. Buyers (or tenants) would then be able to see these ads, and get in touch with the appropriate sellers (or landlords). Online matchmaking once again, wasn't it?

However, there was a catch. Once again, Sanjeev and Hitesh had assumed that the business would be similar to the Naukri business, and therefore all their past learning could be applied here. But as in the case of Jeevansathi, there were fundamental differences. You see, real estate has three kinds of clients who put up ads: builders, brokers, and individual property owners. Large, organized builders were the closest to Naukri's corporate clients, so this was a B2B business, and the tried and tested 'feet-on-the-street' sales strategy would work. But for the smaller builders, brokers, and property owners, it was a B2C business and Hitesh's strategy would not work. Which meant that 99acres had to switch back to the advertising model, and that meant higher marketing costs.

And there was more. You see, brokers are usually far less sophisticated than corporates. Consequently, 99acres had a lot of poor-quality listings, which could potentially impact the 99acres brand. Obviously, this had to be avoided at all cost. Therefore, 99acres put together a team of 'property verifiers', who would physically go to properties that had been listed, to verify the address as well as other parameters that had been mentioned in the listing. The obvious consequence was higher costs!

Dear reader, I hope you are getting the message. Once again, what appeared to be a similar business to Naukri was actually significantly different. And Hitesh and Sanjeev discovered this only after they had jumped into it.

By the way, this business also had significant competition, and that too, well-funded competition. So you had MagicBricks.com from the Times Group, as well as Housing.com, which had received significant funding. As in the case of Naukri, Sanjeev and Hitesh realized that they needed money to stay ahead of these competitors. And that's when they raised another round of funds, this time through a QIP. (For those who are not aware of what this strange abbreviation means, it stands for Qualified Institutional Placement. Essentially, a method by which listed companies sell shares to specific investors. By the way, the company had to raise money through a QIP once more, when they were hit by the dreaded Covid-19 pandemic.)

Fortunately, 99acres was able to establish a lead over its rivals, even though it was a slender lead, unlike the almost monopoly-like status of Naukri. Yes, the business remains loss-making at the time of writing this book, but there are reasons for that, which we'll discuss later in Chapter 10. In any case, the losses are marginal. And the indications are that it will soon turn profitable.

Shiksha.com

And then there is **Shiksha.com**. Now, don't get me wrong; this was not a business where they taught *Old MacDonald Had a Farm* to toddlers. Or the slightly more sophisticated periodic table to older kids. This was once again a classified ads and matchmaking service in the area of education. Where colleges and universities could list themselves, and students would then be able to figure out which ones they wanted to shortlist and ultimately evaluate. Shiksha also provided other information, such as user reviews.

Fortunately, even though the market was small, Shiksha became the market leader in classified ads in this space—and remains so till date. And yes, it is profitable.

And on that profitable note, let's end this chapter. Take a break, go for a stroll or perhaps pour yourself a cup of coffee.

We'll meet again in the next chapter.

8

We'll Also Grow Inorganically

So we've taken a look at four different businesses within Info Edge. These are their core businesses and all of them fall broadly in the area of online matchmaking. However, there is something else that these four have in common: They are all home-grown. They have all been built from scratch (strictly speaking, Jeevansathi is partially home-grown, because it was started within Info Edge, but was sold off for a few years and then bought back).

Now, there is a term we use for this kind of growth. We call it 'organic growth'.

However, since you are smart (you bought this book, didn't you?) you would be aware that this is not the only way to grow. A company can also grow by investing in another company or even fully acquiring the other company. That's what we call 'inorganic growth'. And now, I'm sure you can guess what I'm about to say. Info Edge started off by growing their four core businesses organically. But they also invested in—and sometimes bought out—other companies. In other words, they were growing inorganically as well.

Why did they do this? Well, in most cases, it was because the company they were acquiring provided a service that was a useful value-add to what Info Edge was providing. And rather than building this service from scratch—which would take time—Info Edge simply acquired a ready-made business. It's a strategy followed by many large firms when they want to grow rapidly. By the way, such an investment is often called a 'strategic investment'. Where the investor sees the start-up as a good extension to their existing business. Importantly, strategic investors do not look for an exit. Because the company they invest in becomes an extension to their own business.

So now that you are the proud possessor of three brand-new terms, let me share with you some of the acquisitions made by Info Edge.

In November 2004, they bought a small company called **Quadrangle**, which was into executive-level recruitment. In simple terms, a head hunter for managerial positions. You see, in any recruitment transaction, Naukri was only getting a small chunk of the fee that the employer paid—the fee for putting out the ad. Head hunters would get far more—typically the equivalent of one month's salary of the candidate. And for senior-level positions, this amount could go into several lakhs, which is something Naukri was missing out on. And that was the reason for acquiring Quadrangle.

Then, in 2016, they acquired **AmbitionBox**, an online start-up that provided reviews about potential employers, and thereby helped jobseekers identify great companies to work for. In 2019, they acquired **IIMJobs**, which was a specialized version of Naukri for management jobs. And then, in 2021, they acquired Bengaluru-based **Zwayam**, a B2B platform that helped employers recruit and manage manpower. In the same year, they acquired **DoSelect**, a skill-assessment platform for hiring people and helping them develop. All Internet-based businesses, and all in the space of manpower recruitment, training, and management. In other words, all of them adding value to the existing Naukri business.

Info Edge Becomes a VC—Well, Almost

And now for the next step—when Info Edge became a VC.

Well, actually, that's not strictly correct. I saw that you were yawning, and had to say this to wake you up.

But seriously, the company did do something that felt uncannily like a VC.

What?

You see, Info Edge had already made several strategic investments that added value to their core businesses. Even after this, they had cash left over, thanks to their relentless focus on running a profitable and sustainable business. The question was: What should they do with this spare cash? An obvious answer was to perhaps diversify into other businesses. The problem was that the four businesses they were currently running were taking up huge chunks of management time. And they didn't have any more management time. After all, every human being needs to sleep for at least a few hours a day, doesn't he?

And that's when an idea began to take shape. 'We have the cash to launch new businesses, but not the time. Why don't we look for great tech businesses with great founders? We'll invest in them, and let the founders run the businesses. So rather than becoming strategic investors where we run those businesses, we become financial investors in them.'

And isn't that exactly what VCs do?

However, there was one fundamental difference. The founders were clear that they would only invest in businesses that they understood reasonably well. They understood the Internet, they understood consumers and they understood the FMCG sales process. And so they invested in businesses which were into these areas.

And that had a significant impact on their investee companies. *Because people at Info Edge could advise them.* You see, VCs are usually staffed with analysts, often with no background in running a business (sorry, VCs). But Info Edge was staffed with people who were actually running successful businesses. Therefore, their advice to their investee companies was based on real-life experience, which was obviously more valuable.

Incidentally, this is a common practice with several large companies, and such companies are sometimes called 'Corporate VCs'.

Welcome Policybazaar, Zomato and More

So that was that. Info Edge used their excess cash to make financial
investments in attractive start-ups. Starting with **Policybazaar**,
the well-known giant insurance aggregator, in 2008. Interestingly,
Policybazaar was also into matchmaking—this time between
insurance providers and individuals who wanted insurance. And
there was one more huge plus point. Yashish Dahiya, the founder of
Policybazaar, and Hitesh Oberoi had studied together at IIT Delhi.
(And yes, I have anticipated your question. I haven't ragged Yashish
either 😊.) So there was a certain comfort in working with him.
After all, if you've spent four years together in a college hostel, you
know each other inside out, don't you?

As you are aware, Policybazaar became a phenomenal success
story. A clear market leader in its chosen space. Sanjeev and Hitesh
realized that they had backed a winning horse, and they continued
to invest in it. Today, Info Edge holds a 13 per cent stake in the
company. And they're in no hurry to sell, because they see the value
going up and up . . .

And then there was their second major financial investment—in
an interesting company called Foodiebay.

Foodiebay?

Dear reader, I'm willing to bet that you haven't heard of this
company. At the same time, I'm also willing to bet that you *have* heard
of **Zomato**. But here's the interesting part: Foodiebay and Zomato
are one and the same company. Yes, what you know as Zomato today
was launched as Foodiebay. And that was another fascinating start-up
where Info Edge made a significant financial investment.

Why?

Well, they were once again in the ad listing space. Where Naukri
listed jobs, Foodiebay listed restaurants, along with the food menus
of those restaurants. So people could browse through the Foodiebay
website and then decide which restaurant to go to. It seemed to be
a large market and it became much bigger with the boom in smart

phones, and of course, the ubiquitous Internet. Therefore, it appeared to be a good area to invest in, although the company had almost no revenues at that time. Plus, Hitesh and Sanjeev had met Deepinder Goyal, the founder of Zomato, and were comfortable with him. (Incidentally, Deepinder was also from IIT Delhi. My junior—and from the same Aravali hostel as me. Sadly however, I never ragged him either ☺.) So in August 2010, Info Edge decided to invest Rs 4.7 crore in Zomato—sorry, Foodiebay.

By the way, in those days, Zomato was a restaurant listing company, which is how it caught the eye of the Info Edge founders. There was no food delivery. In fact, the company went on to become the leader in the restaurant listing service in India, and even expanded its presence to South-East Asia, West Asia, Europe and even the USA. Later on, as you are aware, Zomato moved into food delivery and is one of the two leaders in this space today—the other one being Swiggy. And since the company was consistently doing well and growing, Info Edge continued to invest in it, just as they had done in the case of Policybazaar.

And here's the icing on the cake. As you are aware, Zomato went ahead with its IPO in July 2021. Info Edge sold part of their stake for Rs 357 crore and made a phenomenal return of sixty-five times on their investment. And that's not the end of the story, because they still hold a 14 per cent stake in Zomato.

Of course, there were a lot more financial investments, such as **ShopKirana** and **Shiprocket**, but if I go into all of them, this book will probably be twice its current size, so I decided against it. You are welcome to read about these investments on the Internet!

And Then: the Funds

Now for something really interesting. After Info Edge made their early investments in Policybazaar and Zomato, the founders realized that financial investing was a full-time activity, with huge potential. It perhaps needed a different division. That's when they created Info

Edge Ventures, the 'VC arm' of Info Edge, and put Rs 750 crore into it. And guess what? In 2010, Sanjeev handed over day-to-day operations to Hitesh and decided to focus on Info Edge Ventures. Hitesh would focus on the four core business areas: recruitment, real estate, matrimonials and education. Interestingly, all acquisitions within these four areas were also part of Hitesh's domain.

But there was more drama in store. Because then there was the Covid-19 pandemic. And during the lockdown quarter, the star division of Info Edge, namely Naukri, actually de-grew by 44 per cent year on year. Naturally, there was panic. And no one had any clue how Covid-19 would pan out. There was no way Info Edge could afford to put more money into Info Edge Ventures. In fact, they had reached a situation where they might need to take money back and focus on their core businesses.

But that's when Temasek, the well-known Singapore based investor—backed by the Singapore government—stepped in. They were happy to partner with Info Edge, and provide money as well as expertise in the tech domain. In return of course, they expected to benefit from the India growth story. A win-win for both, as you can imagine.

In this context, let's hear out Kitty Agarwal, a partner at Info Edge Ventures:

> We have four funds as of now, and there are two different focus areas. Some of them focus on the kinds of investments Info Edge has been making in the past, such as market places and other consumer-focused businesses, for instance, ShopKirana and Shiprocket.
>
> The other funds are much more long-term, typically focusing on technologies that might bring returns over several years. They invest in businesses that involve a lot of R&D and create intellectual property. For example in deep tech, and the entire electric vehicle space.

So that's it. Info Edge acquired some businesses. And they made financial investments in others. And finally, they launched funds which would make these financial investments.

And that concludes the inorganic growth story of Info Edge. At least, it concludes what I wanted to share with you.

But now for something that every successful organization prides itself on:

Its culture.

In the next chapter . . .

9

Culture and Corporate Governance

Dear reader, I'm sure you would agree that most successful organizations have one thing in common—their culture. How they treat their people, and how they build and nurture their teams. And how these people, in turn, treat the outside world, such as customers and partners. A great culture would mean that people take ownership. They look forward to coming to work in the morning, and take pride in the work they do. They learn, they grow and at the same time they have fun. They are fair and ethical in their dealings with customers. And, of course, they stay on. On the other hand, a terrible culture is one where employees are constantly cribbing, perhaps scared to disagree with the boss, and are just waiting to get home to their chilled bottle of beer so they can vent all their frustrations. And of course, they could just get onto Naukri.com—as customers this time—looking for the next opportunity 😊.

Right? So, let's understand the culture at Info Edge. In fact, I'll share just one incident, and then leave you to figure it out for yourself. You remember the global financial crisis of 2008, don't you? That's when the world went into a tizzy, and large companies such as Lehmann Brothers collapsed. And of course, it impacted companies in India as well. Obviously, recruitment hit a new low and Naukri's business went into a trough.

Now what do Internet companies do when hit by a crisis? Obvious, isn't it? Pink becomes their favourite colour, and lay-offs their favourite term, as pink slips are handed out ad nauseum.

So what did Info Edge do?

No one was laid off!

That's right, *no one was laid off*. But that's not all. The senior people in the company took a voluntary cut in salary *so that the junior people could get an increment*. Yes, my friend, in that crisis, when the world was melting down, Sanjeev realized that senior people could afford a cut. But for those earning low salaries, their families were heavily dependent on their monthly paychecks. And, therefore, not only were they given their monthly salaries, but their increments as well, when they were due!

Of course, the salary cuts at the top were voluntary, but as you can imagine, Sanjeev and Hitesh were the first to take this 'voluntary' cut. Culture flows from the top, you see!

It's things like this that have led to such trust in the company and its management. That's what has created strong ownership in the minds of the team: 'My company looks after me through thick and thin. And therefore, I will also look after my company.' That's why people join Info Edge. They don't leave.

As I spent more and more time with people at Info Edge, I began to get a sense of the culture they had built. You see, the company believed in taking on good people—irrespective of their qualifications—and then giving them the space to work independently. Hitesh puts it very well when he says:

> Great ideas need not come from the top. They could come from anywhere. And we encourage that. It's not a hierarchical organization where the manager is always right. Whether it's junior or senior guys, we believe in empowering them and giving them opportunities to prove themselves.
>
> As an example, in the early days, the user would access the Naukri portal from his laptop or desktop over the web. But once

the mobile phone boom began, we needed to give access through an app. The problem was that the app user interface had to be completely different from the web user interface—and none of us had any idea how to design it (by the way, please notice the humility of the man once again). Fortunately, we found a great designer. But guess what? He was just a year out of design school. Anyhow, we gave him the task and he did a great job. Without any interference from us!

And here's something more. While doing my research for this book, I met Sumeet Singh, the smiling, affable chief marketing officer at Info Edge. And she showed me an award that she had received. It was a plaque with the words 'We value you' engraved on it. According to Sumeet, anyone who stays on in the organization for five years—and subsequently multiples of five years—gets that award. It isn't based on performance. Team members are recognized for simply being part of the organization. Wonderful way to show that the company cares, isn't it?

And now a word about profitability. After all, this is a book about earnicorns, isn't it? It's not that the company was against highly qualified people. It was just that qualifications didn't really matter to them. They wanted good people. Whether qualified or not. Whether they came from top institutes or average ones. Whether they were experienced or raw. They just wanted good people. You can see an immediate side benefit—this lowered their manpower costs. And since people stayed on and didn't leave, well, that cut down on recruitment and training costs as well. Can you now see one more major reason why Info Edge has remained profitable all along?

It All Starts from the Top

That's obvious, isn't it? You cannot have the founders following unethical and unfair practices, being completely non-transparent in their dealings, not caring about their teams and yet expect the team to be different. Simply wouldn't work, would it? It's the founders who lead the way. And in this context, I must share with you some more incidents:

The first incident relates to Sanjeev. A few years ago, he was asked to join the board of directors of MakeMyTrip, the leader in the online travel space. As you are aware, directors need to spend time in board meetings, for which they are usually paid. In this case, Sanjeev was offered shares (ESOPs) in MakeMyTrip.

But guess what he did? He didn't take the shares in his name. He said that he would be spending time with MakeMyTrip, but this was not his personal time. The time belonged to Info Edge. Therefore, he took the ESOPs in the name of Info Edge.

Can you imagine anyone making such a wonderful gesture? Incidentally, MakeMyTrip listed on the stock exchange later on, and Info Edge was able to sell these shares at a profit.

And that, my friend, is Sanjeev for you.

Now for the second incident. As you can guess, to gather material for this story, I spent a lot of time going through the annual reports of the company. One of the reports pertained to the financial year 2021–22, the year of the dreaded Covid-19 pandemic. Now, as you are aware, the first item in any annual report is a statement from the chairman or managing director summarizing the past year. Where he talks about issues such as growth, new launches, strategies, directions, etc. Unfortunately, in this particular financial year, Info Edge had lost four of its team members to Covid-19. And guess what? The annual report did not start with growth, or any of the other issues that the MD was supposed to talk about. It started with an obituary for the four unfortunate team members who lost their lives to Covid-19.

That's Hitesh for you.

And finally, one more incident which I was personally involved in. And this related to the famous 'butter popcorn' meeting with Hitesh. Immediately after this meeting, I had to meet Sumeet. Now Sumeet's office was in the same building as Hitesh's office, but on a different floor. Naturally, I expected to be given directions on how to reach her office. Or at best, Hitesh's executive assistant would have accompanied me there.

But no. Guess who accompanied me to Sumeet's office? That's right—the busy, busy managing director and CEO of Info Edge—Hitesh Oberoi. It took him perhaps ten minutes, but he took that time out to walk me there.

That's Hitesh once again.

And that, my friend, is how Sanjeev and Hitesh have built a wonderful culture at Info Edge. Not just by talking about it. But by setting an example!

Corporate Governance

Before I end this chapter, I must tell you a bit about corporate governance at Info Edge. Now, if you follow business, you would at least have some idea about the term. But if all you watch on TV are *saas bahu* soaps and the only research journals you read are *Filmfare* and *Stardust*, let me explain what that means. Here's the formal definition from Investopedia:*

> Corporate governance is the system of rules, practices, and processes by which a firm is directed and controlled. Corporate governance essentially involves balancing the interests of a company's many stakeholders, such as shareholders, senior management executives, customers, suppliers, financiers, the government, and the community.

Clear?

I bet it's not. I'm sure you're as confused as I was. But then I sat down to figure out what this really meant. And I realized that it's really quite simple:

So here's a simpler definition—this time from me:

---

* https://www.investopedia.com/terms/c/corporategovernance.asp.

Be fair. Be ethical. Be transparent. Don't hide stuff. Don't fool anyone. Don't avoid bad news; if there is a problem, please, please share it with whoever is likely to be affected, whether it is customers, employees, shareholders, or anyone else. Follow rules. Fulfil your commitments on time. And finally, have a system of rules and processes to ensure all this. Starting from the top. In other words, from the board of directors.

Quite simple, isn't it? In fact, if you think about it—and I know you can—it's really a formalization of the culture of the organization!

And now to get back to Info Edge. Given the phenomenally strong belief of the founders in building a wonderful culture, you can imagine how perfect the corporate governance would be. Let me share just one example of this before I end this chapter:

You see, in the third quarter of FY 2022–23, this highly profitable company, Info Edge, actually posted a huge loss. As much as Rs 116 crore.

Why?

Well, as part of their strategy for inorganic growth, they had made a strategic investment in a property-related start-up called **4B Networks**. A company that provided an Internet platform aimed at brokers, helping them connect with both property developers as well as buyers. Something that would have been a great addition to 99acres.com.

So far so good. But then our founders (the founders of Info Edge, not 4B Networks) realized that things were not going too well with their investment. There was too much cash burn, and 4B Networks needed to raise funds, which wasn't happening. Worse, there were some financial transactions which the founders at Info Edge were not comfortable with, especially given their strong standards of corporate governance. And the financial reports that Info Edge was supposed to receive were not forthcoming.

So what did our founders do? I'm sure you can guess by now. When they realized that things were not going well, they wrote off the entire investment of Rs 276 crore in 4B Networks.

Now, this was in the third quarter of FY 2022–23. They could easily have kept quiet about the issue. Or perhaps written off the investment in bits and pieces, so as to keep making a profit in each quarter. But no. They were clear. This was bad news, and it was their duty to inform shareholders as soon as possible. Because of this write-off, Info Edge made a loss in this quarter. And that's what I mean by corporate governance at Info Edge. That's what I mean by being ethical. And that is why everyone and his grandmother trusts Sanjeev and Hitesh.

By the way, I am involved in the stock market and I happen to own shares of Info Edge. And I can say this from personal experience—this is one company where I am never worried about any wrongdoings. In today's world of raids by the ED (enforcement directorate), you would never have heard of raids on Info Edge. No way.

And now you know why.

Finally, let me end this section with a super punch line from Sanjeev:

In the final analysis, your reputation is your only asset.

Giving Back to Society

So you've met Sanjeev and Hitesh. And you've seen how they've built a wonderful organization, one that is a market leader in most of the areas they operate in. And of course, it is profitable, which is a rarity in the Internet world.

But I need to tell you more. They haven't just built their own organization. They believe in giving back to society as well. Sanjeev and Hitesh are among the founders of Ashoka University, where they have put in their personal money. In case you are not aware, Ashoka is a leading university in the areas of humanities and science, based in Sonipat, Haryana, around fifty kilometres from Delhi. The university focuses on both teaching and research in diverse subjects such as environmental studies, entrepreneurship, physics, psychology, history, economics and many more. Hitesh is also one of the founders of Plaksha University based in Mohali, near Chandigarh, which has been set up to focus on technology. Both universities have a very high standing in the world of academics (I should know, since I have been in academics myself.)

By the way, the company is not far behind either. It has established an InfoEdge Centre for Entrepreneurship at Ashoka University from its CSR (corporate social responsibility) funds.

Isn't that a wonderful way to give back to society?

10

Info Edge: Today and Tomorrow

So that's the story of our first **earnicorn**, Info Edge.

And where is the company today? Well, for the financial year 2022–23, they achieved a consolidated revenue of over Rs 2700 crore. They have been growing at a CAGR (compounded annual growth rate) of 21 per cent, which is extremely healthy for a giant company. Interestingly, during this year they made a pre-tax profit of more than Rs 140 crore, in spite of writing off the entire investment in 4B Networks.

And what about the individual businesses? Well, Naukri clocked revenues of over Rs 1700 crore, and has a 70 per cent share in the white collar jobs market—and you cannot possibly do better than that. 99acres did Rs 280 crore, Jeevansathi did Rs 78 crore and Shiksha, Rs 117 crore. Naukri had a huge operational profit of 60 per cent. Shiksha was profitable as well, whereas 99acres and Jeevansathi made a loss. Please note that these are approximate figures. I have not gone into three decimal points because that's not really relevant.

And now for the big, big, BIG question: Why are two of the businesses profitable whereas the other two are not? You see, Naukri has been profitable ever since the 1990s. Shiksha has also been profitable for several years, although it is a small division, and therefore does not have much impact on the company. But 99acres has been loss-making, although it is now close to breaking even and should do so in the near future. Jeevansathi has also been loss-making and it's somewhat further away from breaking even.

Why is this? The management is the same. The company philosophy and the culture are the same. Customers are happy in all divisions. So why do two divisions stand out? That's the question I asked Hitesh. And this is the invaluable gyan I got from him:

Making Profits in the Internet World—Naukri

First of all, I will repeat one of my favourite statements—except that this time it's come from Hitesh:

> *With the coming of the Internet, geography has become history.*

In simple terms, before the Internet era, your competitors were local. But now they can be anywhere in the country—or perhaps anywhere in the world.

And that makes a huge difference. Take, for instance, the friendly neighbourhood kirana store. Since the target segment for this business is highly localized, there is no scope for dramatic growth. Therefore, the owner focuses on his existing customers. Much of the time these customers do not leave him. In any case, a lot of the business is based on personal relationships. And there are no competitors from far away to threaten his business, so there is a reasonably comfortable status quo.

But the moment kirana stores go on to the Internet and become online grocery shops, all that changes dramatically. Now there will be similar online grocery shops across the city, all competing for the same customers. With everyone trying to grab market share. And remember, on the Internet it is easy for the customer to switch loyalties. Because the next guy is just a click away. The result? Lots of marketing spend, perhaps discounts, and a major focus on constantly improving the service and the offerings, just to be able to hang on to your customer.

Of course, all this costs money. A whole lot of it. And that, my friend, is the issue. Just listen to Hitesh:

> In the Internet world, any company that is a clear market leader is able to make money. Because they have built a certain brand and a certain credibility, and can therefore charge for it. They can set their price so as to make a profit. Plus, market leaders have the largest volumes, and therefore economies of scale kick in. This puts them in a great position—their costs are lower than the others and they can demand their price. So in the Internet world, the market leader is the best placed to make money. The number two could make some money, for reasons similar to those of the market leader. But it would be less than the money the leader makes. And as you go down the ladder, the rest of the businesses make less and less money. In fact, many of them are likely to make a loss. And that's the fundamental problem with Internet businesses—you need to be a clear market leader, or at least close to one, to be profitable.
>
> Now, Naukri is in a great position in the market. We are a dominant player, with over 70 per cent market share in our chosen segment of white-collar jobs. So we can set our price. Plus, we run a very frugal operation, so our costs are low. And in any case, since we are a large, dominant player, we get economies of scale. In other words, we have an advantage from both sides: We can set our rates, and at the same time we are a low-cost operation. That's what makes Naukri very interesting, because we charge less than our competitors and yet make a profit.

And there is more. According to Hitesh, because of its sheer size, Naukri takes care of 40 per cent or more of the recruitment needs of their clients. In other words, the monopoly-like status of Naukri makes them almost indispensable to their clients. It actually creates an interesting 'exit barrier' for the client. If the client moves away from Naukri, where else would they fulfil this 40 per cent of their recruitment needs from? And of course, the fact that the company has always been strongly customer-focused and trustworthy, means that the employer has no need to go elsewhere. That is why Naukri has never spent too much on marketing. And that's one reason why it has been profitable all along.

What about Jeevansathi.com?

Jeevansathi, on the other hand, is not a market leader. As I've already mentioned earlier, the Indian market has three large players in this field, namely Bharatmatrimony, Shaadi.com and Jeevansathi. And they're all in more or less the same bracket. Since there is no clear leader, everyone is trying to gain market share, and get into a clear leadership position. Consequently, all these businesses have two problems: On the one hand, revenues go down, because everyone tries to dole out discounts and schemes to grab the customer. On the other hand, the cost of acquiring the customer is high, because everyone is spending on marketing. Which is why no one makes significant profits, although Bharatmatrimony and Shaadi.com do make some money. Jeevansathi is number three in this race and that is one of the reasons why they haven't been able to make money so far.

And Jeevansathi has one more disadvantage compared to Naukri. They have one-time customers (thank God). Therefore, customer acquisition is a repeated cost every time. Which is one more reason why Jeevansathi remains a loss-making proposition.

And What about 99acres.com?

In the real estate space, 99acres is the market leader in the country, but not by much. It has a share of around 40 per cent of the market, unlike Naukri, which has a 70 per cent market share in its chosen segment. There are two other major, well-funded players, namely MagicBricks and Housing.com, which have been around for several years now. And both of them are snapping at the heels of 99acres.

In other words, 99acres is not a clear leader and therefore does not enjoy the kind of benefits that Naukri does.

But there is more. Real estate is a highly cyclical industry, and it has been in the dumps for several years now. It went through a tough transition when the government brought in the RERA (Real Estate Regulatory Authority) Act to ensure a certain level of transparency and control in an otherwise highly opaque sector. This was a blow to the industry which thrives on coloured money and other unethical practices. Then there was GST, which took a while to get assimilated into the system. And finally, the dreaded Covid-19 pandemic. In other words, for one reason or another, real estate has had a tough time for the past many years. In fact, the industry has barely grown and therefore no player has been able to make money.

What of the Future?

Well, Naukri is firmly entrenched as the market leader. They have weathered storms such as JobsAhead, Monster.com and, currently, LinkedIn as well as TimesJobs. They have successfully waded through tsunamis such as the dot-com bust, the global financial crisis of 2008 and of course, Covid-19. So far, they have onboarded over 1,10,000 employers. They continue to surge ahead, and for all the reasons mentioned earlier, they will remain highly profitable.

Shiksha is also a clear market leader, although in a much smaller space, and they continue to be profitable.

Regarding 99acres, the real estate cycle is now picking up. Fortunately. And cycles in this industry are long. The market is large (in fact, globally, real estate portals are bigger business than job portals). Therefore, the expectation is that the next few years would be good for the industry. Secondly, 99acres is a bit like Naukri, in the sense that some of their customers, namely brokers and builders, are long-term customers. For these, customer acquisition is a one-time cost. And of course, 99acres is the market leader, although by a slim margin. At the time of writing this book, they are almost profitable and Hitesh is confident that things will turn around soon.

In other words, three businesses within the Info Edge stable are either going great guns, or are expected to turn the corner. Namely, Naukri, Shiksha and 99acres.

Jeevansathi remains an issue, but given that they are close to the two market leaders, the founders continue to back the business. And anyway, a lot of the development and marketing costs have already been spent. Hopefully word of mouth will now kick in, and the business will eventually become profitable.

Of course, there is always the possibility of consolidation in the industry, where two companies merge and create a clear market leader in the space.

Will that happen?

Who knows?

And with that, I come to the end of the fascinating story of the earnicorn, Info Edge, and its wonderful founders, Sanjeev Bikhchandani and Hitesh Oberoi. In their entrepreneurial journey, they've had ups and downs, but have always come out with flying colours.

And this is a great time to repeat one of Sanjeev's famous quotes:

Company khoon paseeney se banti hai. Paison se nahin. (A company is built from blood, sweat and tears, not money!)

11

Let's Analyse the Earnicorn: Info Edge

So that was the fascinating story of the highly respected, profitable giant in the space of online classified ads, Info Edge. Perhaps the first **earnicorn** in India. And its wonderful founders, Sanjeev Bikhchandani and Hitesh Oberoi.

Now, I've already told you that I would be analysing each company using the frameworks I had discussed in Chapter 2. However, there is one caveat: Each of these companies actually has multiple business lines. I could, of course, analyse all of them. But that would take several pages and make this book a lot thicker (and more expensive for you). Therefore, I decided to focus on the most well-known business within each company. In the case of Info Edge, it's Naukri.com. I leave it to you to analyse the other businesses. And don't worry, I will not charge you any royalty 😊.

Naukri.com: The PERSISTENT Business

Let's start with the PERSISTENT framework. And just to refresh your memory, here it is again:

- P: Problem
- E: Earnings Model
- R: Risks and how you will mitigate them
- S: Size of the market

- I: Innovation
- S: Scalability
- T: Team, starting with the founders
- E: Entry Barriers
- N: Niche
- T: Traction

Obviously, Naukri is solving a PROBLEM for both employers as well as jobseekers. That's the 'P' in PERSISTENT. And yes, they do have an EARNINGS MODEL (the 'E'), because employers have to pay to put up their ads on the site—even though many of them did start by posting ads for free.

Now, SIZE OF THE MARKET (the first 'S') is interesting. When Sanjeev launched Naukri, there were enough companies wanting to recruit manpower, and there were more than enough individuals who were interested in these jobs. So that was not a problem. The issue was the very small number of such individuals who had access to the Internet—just about 14,000 at the time of the launch. In other words, it was a tiny market.

But the potential was huge, assuming that more and more users would get hooked on the Internet over time. Sanjeev banked on this growth in the Internet, and therefore decided to focus on this potential market. The rest, to use a cliché, is history.

By the way, that's an interesting message for all of you readers (and founders) out there:

You might not have a huge market right now, but as long as the potential is large, well, you could be in business!

Then of course, we have the next 'S' in our PERSISTENT model, namely SCALABILITY. You see, the size of the market simply tells you how large the opportunity is. Scalability tells you whether you can grow your business within this large market. And how fast you can grow. Obviously, this is critical to any business. Because if you don't grow—and grow fast—your competitors will, they will eat into your market share and perhaps kill your business.

Clear?

So how scalable is Naukri.com? Well, as you've already seen, they have been able to grow fast, and they have been market leaders ever since they started the business. And they have been able to onboard over 1,10,000 companies. Huge, isn't it?

But what is it about the business that allowed them to scale rapidly? Actually, the answer is simple. It is a technology driven business and not a manpower driven one. For a moment, just imagine what would happen if Naukri were running the same business without the Internet and without technology. They would then need a lot of manpower: to maintain the database of jobs as well as candidates, to match potential candidates with jobs, to send the appropriate resumes to employers and so on. And what if they wanted to double their revenues? Well, they would need to double their manpower as well. Which is not easy. They would then have to train these people. And some of them would leave because they were being offered a higher salary elsewhere. In which case, Naukri would need to replace them and train the new employees.

Then there is the infrastructure. They would need office space for all these guys, which would again take time, cost, as well as effort. After all, these people couldn't sit on the pavement, could they?

You see? It takes time and costs money to add people, especially if you need to add a lot of them. And that is why manpower-intensive businesses find it tough to grow big and that too, fast. Fortunately, Naukri is not a manpower-intensive business. It is technology-driven. To double their revenues every year, they do not need to double their manpower. And that is why they have always been highly scalable. (For a more detailed explanation of scalability and more examples, please check out either of my books, *Funding Your Start-up and Other Nightmares* or *The DREAM Founder*. And I'm not asking you to buy them. I'm sure you could borrow a copy from one of your friends and conveniently forget to give it back!)

And now for the 'E' in our PERSISTENT model, namely ENTRY BARRIER. What's an entry barrier? Very simply, something in your business that prevents your competitor from entering and taking away your customers and your market share. It's a 'barrier' that prevents your competitor from 'entering' your business.

In the case of Naukri, one significant entry barrier is the network effect, which I've spoken about in Chapter 6. Simply put, more jobseekers lead to more employers putting up ads on the site, which in turn, leads to more jobseekers coming to the site. Which once again leads to more employers putting up ads. And so on. As you can imagine, this becomes a great entry barrier *because it takes time to build*.

Related to this is the brand. As more and more employers and more and more jobseekers land upon the site, the Naukri brand builds up. So an employer wishing to advertise would think of brand Naukri. And a jobseeker looking for an opening would look for brand Naukri as well. Of course, the fact that Naukri is a frugal operation is a huge bonus because they can charge the client a lower fee and still be profitable. As you can see, there are several reasons why Naukri has been able to build up a phenomenal entry barrier over the years.

And now for the TEAM. By now, you would agree with me that Sanjeev and Hitesh have been able to build a wonderful culture within the organization. They give people responsibility early on, and help them grow. Of course, rewards and recognition help, too. Both monetary, in the form of ESOPs, as well as the 'We Value You' award at the end of every five years. All these and many more, have ensured that the company has been able to get good people who stayed on with them. And because of the kind of environment they have created, the team is highly productive. A great team, in ways more than one.

Finally, as I keep repeating, Naukri has always been the market leader in its chosen space, with a 70 per cent market share in the white-collar job market and revenues of Rs 1700 crore, the last time I checked. In addition, they have been able to onboard over 1,10,000 companies. Their TRACTION has always been higher than that of their competitors. And knowing Sanjeev and Hitesh, it's likely to continue.

What's the bottom line?

I thought you would get it, my friend—Naukri has always been a PERSISTENT business!

The PERFECT Attitude

Dear reader, I'm sure you would agree with me (at least I hope you do) that everything flows from the top. From the attitude of the founders. Right?

So let's take a look at the attitude of our two friends, Sanjeev and Hitesh.

But first, I must let you into a secret. While researching companies for my earlier book, *The DREAM Founder*, I had met Sanjeev a few times. In these meetings, he had shared with me his thoughts on how important it was for founders to have the right attitude. Of course, I added my own masala to it (I call it value addition), and converted it into the inevitable framework—the PERFECT attitude. So in a way, Sanjeev is responsible for the framework. By the way, I did offer him a share of my miserable royalty, but, thorough gentleman that he is, he politely refused 😊. In any case, I'm sure he earns far, far more from his business.

Why have I told you this? Simple. Because Sanjeev always practises what he preaches. And I can't think of a founder with a more PERFECT attitude. Incidentally, Hitesh is very much in the same category—which is why they've made such a wonderful team for over twenty years.

Just to remind you, here's the PERFECT attitude once again:

P: PERSEVERING
E: ETHICAL
R: RESPONSIBLE

F: FLEXIBLE
E: Willing to do EVERYTHING
C: CUSTOMER ORIENTED
T: Builds TRUST

Let's start by looking at three of these qualities, namely CUSTOMER ORIENTED, FLEXIBLE and PERSEVERING. Remember, when Sanjeev was working at HMM Ltd, he realized that people were keen on scanning through ads for jobs in business magazines. In other words, there were two potential customers he could help: the companies, whose ads he could take to jobseekers, and the jobseekers themselves. But he also realized that jobseekers would need to go through various magazines and newspapers. And that's when he thought about collating ads from various sources, making them available at one single location, and making this data easy to access. Thereby making life easier for these jobseekers while at the same time making a far larger number of jobs available to them. And that's being CUSTOMER ORIENTED, isn't it?

Collating these ads was the easier part. The tougher part was getting them to these jobseekers. And that's where Sanjeev tried all kinds of options. He tried to participate in the government's scheme, where they wanted organizations to provide databases, so that individuals could access them. But, of course, the government shelved that plan. Next, he tried to make their database of jobs available to franchisees, so that jobseekers in the vicinity could access it. That didn't work either. He tried couriering floppy disks to individuals for a fee. Even that didn't work. Finally, what did work was the advent of the Internet, and the creation of the Naukri.com portal, where jobseekers could access the jobs database through their PCs.

Dear reader, I hope you have noticed how FLEXIBLE Sanjeev was. He tried out multiple ways to reach jobseekers. And of course, you know that the entire process started in 1991, but Naukri was launched in 1997. *Six long years.* If that is not being PERSEVERING, frankly, I don't know what is. Remember

Sanjeev's wonderful statement which he picked up from the iconic Hindi movie *Deewaar*?

Be a *'lambi race ke ghoda* (be in the game for the long run)*'.

Then of course, Hitesh joined him. And he realized that the Internet was a new medium. Spending crores and crores of rupees on marketing to attract corporates and get them to put up their ads on Naukri, would just not work. Corporates were likely to be sceptical. Someone needed to sit across the table with them and patiently explain the benefits of putting up their ads on Naukri. Yes my friend, Hitesh was equally CUSTOMER ORIENTED. He realized the concerns of employers and framed his strategy accordingly. Even after the sale, as you've seen, he was more than willing to do the customer's work. Work such as formatting the ads, posting them on the portal (remember, the Internet was a new phenomenon, and many customers did not know how to use it), collating the resumes that had come in, and finally printing them out and submitting them to the customer. Just to make it easier for him.

Finally, how can I forget the launch of Resdex? The biggest contributor to Naukri's revenues, which was launched purely because Hitesh and Sanjeev kept meeting customers and getting feedback from them.

Now for the willingness to do EVERYTHING. I think the best example of this is when Naukri had to make sales calls to customers. Remember who led the team in making these calls? Sanjeev and Hitesh, of course. And who sat in an ivory tower and gave instructions? No one. I recall asking Hitesh about this. And he just laughed. His response was classic:

That's the only way to do it. As founders, we had no choice.

And there is something else that Hitesh had said (I'm sorry I'm repeating this, but it's important):

We had to get clients. And to do that, as founders we had to show the way. We made a huge number of sales calls—to senior people, to junior people. Sometimes, even junior people kept me waiting at the reception for an hour. But as a founder, you don't have a choice. You make calls. Period.

And Sanjeev was the same. No hang-ups about making sales calls. That's how we were able to survive without spending too much. And that's how we trained our sales guys—by taking them along with us on these calls.

Dear reader, if you are planning to start a business, remember what Hitesh said: 'As founders, you have no choice. You must be willing to do everything.'

And now for being RESPONSIBLE. You've already seen what Sanjeev and Hitesh did when the dot-com crash and the subsequent 9/11 event took place. Business was down and both of them took full RESPONSIBILITY for getting it back on track—by making sales calls, more sales calls and still more sales calls.

But that's not all. RESPONSIBILITY goes far beyond this. For instance, if you've made a decision and it goes wrong, what do you do? Blame someone else? No way. Take responsibility for your decision or action. On the other hand, if something goes right, do you take all the credit? Of course not, my friend. Share it. In fact, give your team the lion's share of credit. Only then will they TRUST you. And only then will they function like the highly motivated, charged-up team that that they need to be.

Here are a couple of examples of things that went wrong: For the first several years, Naukri didn't launch a resume database—and that was a blunder, for which Sanjeev and Hitesh took full responsibility. And when they finally did launch Resdex, it was a star. Similarly, after receiving funding for Naukri, they banked on advertisements. The strategy bombed and Sanjeev squarely took the blame. Later, of course, Hitesh put together a sales team, and there was no looking back.

Then of course, the decision to make a strategic investment in 4B Networks, which had to be completely written off. Both Sanjeev and Hitesh made it very, very clear that it was their decision, and they took the blame.

But what about something that had gone right? Did the founders take the credit? No way. You've already seen that when Naukri had to create a phone-based app, the founders readily admitted that they had no idea what the user interface looked like. And the entire credit went to the young designer, who was just a year out of college.

Here, I must share with you something else that Sanjeev told me:

> Given that I am the founder and the public face of the company,
> I get the credit for most things that I haven't done. Yes, when we
> started the company, most of the ideas were mine. But in the past
> ten years or so, almost no idea has been mine. All the credit goes
> to the extremely talented team we have.

Dear reader, can't you just smell the humility of the man? I certainly could when I was speaking to him.

And finally, ETHICS and building TRUST. I've already mentioned one incident involving Sanjeev, where he was asked to join the board of directors of MakeMyTrip. For which he was offered shares in the company. But as I've already mentioned, he didn't take the shares in his name. Instead, he took the shares in the name of Info Edge. Why? Because as a director attending board meetings at MakeMyTrip, he would be spending time that belonged to Info Edge. Brilliant example of ethics, isn't it?

And the fact that Sanjeev and Hitesh—along with the board— wrote off the entire investment in 4B Networks. Because they did not want to hide bad news from their shareholders. That's ethics once again, isn't it?

So you have the founders being strongly customer-oriented, willing to do anything, taking full responsibility when things went wrong and being two hundred per cent ethical.

That's why they were able to build TRUST: in the minds of their customers, the team members at Info Edge, their shareholders and just about anyone else they came in contact with.

And that, my friend, is as close as you can ever get to a PERFECT attitude!

The Profitable Business

Dear reader, you can't imagine how delighted I was to write this chapter. In my earlier books, I had created two frameworks—the PERSISTENT business and the PERFECT attitude of the founders. And I had created them to evaluate start-ups. But here was a giant, Info Edge, that fitted beautifully into both frameworks. In other words, the frameworks were applicable not only to fledgling start-ups, but to mature companies as well. Even giants.

However, there is one major parameter that I missed out on when creating these frameworks. The need to focus on making the business profitable—because that's the only way to make it sustainable. Otherwise, you are constantly at the mercy of investors. And in all humility, I accept my mistake. You see, like Sanjeev and Hitesh, I'm also RESPONSIBLE ☺. In fact, I thought of changing my PERSISTENT model to PPERSISTENT, just to bring in that extra 'P' for PROFITABLE. Or even changing the PERFECT attitude to PPERFECT. But after several mugs of coffee, I decided to let the models remain. Ddidn't sound good, you see!

Anyhow, let's get back to what we were discussing. Namely, how Info Edge has remained profitable right through, despite the inevitable ups and downs. In this context, one of the first things I learnt was the value of being frugal. And that obviously starts with the founders. Because people see what the boss does, rather than what he says! Right from the initial days, when Sanjeev operated from his father's servants' quarters with second-hand furniture and computers, to the time when they got their first investment and put half of it into a fixed deposit. And the fact that both founders would stay in low-cost hotels—definitely not five-star ones—and travel by auto just to cut costs. And thereby set an example for the rest of the team.

Plus, our founders were just not interested in the typical mantra of Internet companies, namely 'growth at any cost, even if you make a loss'. No way. They were very clear that they wanted to run a profitable, sustainable business where they did not need to keep going back to investors with a begging bowl (sorry guys, but I feel strongly about this).

Interestingly, there were several things the company did, where the purpose was not to cut costs but to be more effective. But these had the effect of reducing their costs as well. For instance, you've seen that they were extremely customer-oriented, helping them at every stage and adding on products that they might find useful. The result, of course, was that customers wouldn't leave them—and therefore they did not have to incur huge costs in getting new customers to replace the ones that had left.

And then of course, the fact that they recruited people for what they could bring to the table, rather than their qualifications. Because that meant they were able to bring in lots of people who did not have fancy MBA degrees but were able to contribute significantly. Which, in turn, brought down their manpower costs. Again, the idea was not to shun fancy degrees but to take on people on merit!

Plus, since they were market leaders, they could set their terms. And when you combine that with a low-cost operation, it means that you can charge less than your competitors do and still make a profit. Brilliant, isn't it?

But I think the biggest thing Sanjeev and Hitesh did was to build TRUST in everyone—whether employees, customers, investors, or just about anyone else who was involved in the Info Edge story. To me, the best example of this was the fact that they never resorted to large-scale lay-offs during tough times. Instead, they took a voluntary cut in salary, just so that junior folks would get their increments. That's what created ownership in the minds of their team. 'This is my company. They look after me even when the chips are down. So I'll look after them. And I won't leave.'

And that's true of customers as well.

I think this was among the greatest things I learnt about the company and its founders.

And on this note, let me end this story with one last statement: If you are running a business, please make sure it's a PERSISTENT business. Run it with just the PERFECT attitude. And focus on making it PROFITABLE!

That, my friend, is my learning from Sanjeev and Hitesh, and the wonderful, wonderful **earnicorn** they have created.

Section III

Zerodha

12

Zerodha: Where It All Began

A few years ago, one of my students came up to me, almost falling over himself in his excitement. 'You know, I've discovered a new stockbroker. They're called Zerodha. And true to their name, they don't charge any brokerage at all,' he gushed.

'How can that be?' was my immediate retort. They've got to make money somehow, don't they? This must be a marketing gimmick. They'll make losses and disappear in no time.'

'I know, but it's true. They don't charge any brokerage at all.'

Now, this was too good to be true. A stockbroker who didn't charge brokerage? This simply had to be investigated. So I put on my favourite Sherlock Holmes cap and got into action. And I realized that what my student had told me was absolutely true. These guys did not charge their investors any brokerage at all. At the same time, they were phenomenally profitable.

Intrigued, I dived deeper into the business. And what emerged was a truly fascinating story. The story of one man who had taken his company to the number one position in an extremely crowded space—a space where brokers would bend over backwards to grab clients from each other. A man who was able to disrupt a business that had existed for a hundred years or perhaps more. Not only that, this company was making bigger and bigger profits every year. And that's when I decided that I simply *had* to include the story of this man and his phenomenal company in my book.

Fortunately, Nithin Kamath, thorough gentleman that he is, readily agreed.

Wouldn't you like to hear his story?

Well, just read on . . .

It All Began with Trading

Nithin's story began in 1997, when he was introduced to trading on the stock market. Now here, I must digress for a bit. Some of you might understand trading, but I suspect there are many who don't. So this bit is to explain the concept of trading to you. If you understand it, you are welcome to skip this section and use the time saved for something more productive, such as going out for a smoke!

You see, there are broadly two kinds of people who work the stock market. First of all, there are the 'investors'. These are people who buy shares in, say, Reliance Industries, and then hang on to them for months. Perhaps years. In the hope that the company will do well and the share price will rise. The key here is that investors are people who buy shares for the long term.

Now, I'm sure you are aware that share prices never have a smooth rise or fall. They move up and down every minute. Just take a look at the business channels on TV, and you'll get what I mean. And that's where traders jump in. You see, traders are people who look at short-term movements in share prices. Where short term could mean a day, a week, or even a couple of months—but definitely not years. So a trader might buy 100 shares of Reliance Industries one morning, on the assumption that the share price will go up by the end of the afternoon. And when that happens, he happily sells his shares and makes a neat profit. Of course, the price could also go down, in which case he makes a loss. By the way, we call this 'day trading', or sometimes 'intra-day trading'.

As you might imagine, short-term share price movements are very tough to predict, and even experts often get them wrong. Trading is speculative in nature and is therefore risky. But that doesn't stop traders, who perhaps like the adrenaline rush it gives them.

F&O Trading

Now, let's take this a step further. Assume you believe that the share of Reliance Industries will go up somewhere in the short term. But you can't really figure out when. It could be today, tomorrow or even a couple of weeks later. In any case, price movements within a day are very tough to predict. So rather than trading intra-day, you would prefer to trade over a longer period, say a month.

Makes sense? So what do you do? Well, you buy these shares and hang on to them until the end of the month. Now let's assume the price today is Rs 2000 per share, and by the end of the month it goes up by 10 per cent to Rs 2200. You would then have made a cool profit of Rs 200 per share or 10 per cent. Which, of course, you are welcome to blow up on your favourite brand of alcohol.

However, traders are restless people. They want more. 'Ten per cent profit in one month? And I need to pay the full price of the share upfront? I want more. Give me something better.' And that 'something better', ladies and gentlemen, is what we call 'Futures and Options Trading'. Or simply F&O trading!

Now, at this stage, I must clarify something. F&O is a complicated subject. There are books, books and more books on the subject, and my purpose is not to make you an expert. In any case, I'm no expert. It took me several sessions over beer with friends to even begin to understand it. So this will be a highly simplified explanation—perhaps oversimplified. My purpose here is simply to tell you enough so that you understand the Zerodha story, and don't stop reading in frustration.

Okay? So let's start with 'futures'. And we'll take the example of Reliance Industries once again. As before, you expect the price of this share to rise by the end of the month. So you make a commitment to the stock exchange that you will buy it at the end of the month, *but at today's price.* And this is the key: You are not buying the share. *You are making a commitment to buying it at the end of the month, but at today's price.* In other words, you are entering into a contract. In F&O terminology, *you are buying a futures contract.* If, as expected, the share price does rise, you make a neat profit. But if it falls, you suffer a loss.

Obviously, there needs to be a corresponding seller, who expects the price to fall, and therefore he commits to selling it at the end of the month, but once again at today's price. So if the price falls, as he expects, he makes a profit. Conversely, if it rises, he makes a loss.

I hope that's clear so far?

Now let me complicate things a bit. Since you are not actually buying the share, but only making a commitment to buying it at the end of the month, you do not need to pay the entire price today. Instead, you pay a fraction of the share price. A token amount, essentially, to seal the deal. And this token amount is called 'margin'.

My friend, let me stop here for a bit. I can see you getting confused. The symptoms are clear—eyes glazed, blank look on your face, beer refills getting more and more frequent. Don't worry; it's happened to me several times while I was writing this book and grappling with the subject. So let's take a few numbers, and hopefully things will become clearer.

As before, we assume that Reliance Industries is currently trading at Rs 2000. And you buy a futures contract where you commit to buying 100 shares at the end of the month, but at today's price. In other words, at Rs 2000 (in actual practice, the price would be a bit different from the price of the underlying share, but that doesn't change our argument significantly). The key is that you are not paying the full price for these shares. You are paying a margin, which is a fraction of the price. And let's assume this margin is Rs 400 per share. So for 100 shares, the margin money works out to Rs (100 x 400) or Rs 40,000.

Once again, we assume that the price of the share goes up by 10 per cent to Rs 2200 by the end of the month. So you would have made the same cool profit of Rs 2200–2000, which is Rs 200 per share, or Rs 20,000 for 100 shares.

And, therefore, you have made a profit of 10 per cent. As before. Right?

Wrong! *You have actually made a profit of 50 per cent.*

Why? Because you didn't put in the full Rs 2 lakh. You put in only Rs 40,000, on which you made a profit of Rs 20,000!

Wow. Great, isn't it?

Now, if you've understood this example, you've understood the basic concept of futures trading. The share price goes up by 10 per cent, but you actually make a profit of 50 per cent! Of course, you also need to pay a few other charges, such as brokerage as well as taxes, so your profit comes down a bit. But the fact remains that you've made far, far more than the 10 per cent you would have made otherwise. By the way, we call this 'leveraged trading'. Because you leverage a small amount to do a far bigger trade.

And now for the next scenario: Suppose you had got out from the wrong side of the bed (or perhaps seen the face of the wrong neighbour). Whatever the reason, let's assume the share price goes down by 10 per cent to Rs 1800 at the end of the month. Now, you've already made a commitment to buy 100 shares at Rs 2000 each. Therefore, at the end of the month, you incur a loss of Rs 20,000. But this is the key: You don't lose Rs 20,000 on an investment of Rs 2 lakh, or 10 per cent. You lose Rs 20,000 on the Rs 40,000 you had put in. *In other words, your loss is 50 per cent.*

Terrible, isn't it? And that tells you how risky leveraged trading can be. *You can easily magnify your profits, but you can just as easily magnify your losses.*

So that was futures trading. Then, there is 'Options trading', where you do not commit to buying the share at the end of the month, but only to have the *option* of buying it. Once again, you do not need to pay the full price of the shares upfront but only a margin amount.

My friend, if conventional trading sends the blood gushing through your veins (or arteries—I'm not sure which), you can imagine what F&O trading would do. That is why it is such a popular concept among traders. By the way, most traders accept the fact that they'll make a loss a few times, provided they make profits overall. Yes sir, these are traders. Very different from investors, who have a long-term view.

Finally, I have some great news for you. That's the end of this lesson in complex financial mathematics. If you've understood whatever I've shared, that's wonderful. You are far smarter than me. But if you haven't, don't worry. Just keep in mind the one key statement I've made: *F&O trading can easily magnify your profits, but it can just as easily magnify your losses.*

In any case, with all the terms you've just learnt (even if you haven't understood them), aren't you in a great position to impress all the ladies—or gents—at the next party?

The Kamath Brothers Were Traders

And that brings me back to where I had started. Nithin Kamath was a trader. Yes, he was an engineer as well, but his first love was trading. I would have loved to check his blood pressure, pulse, and other similar parameters when he was into his favourite occupation, but so far I have not been able to. However, that's not relevant to us, so we'll let it pass. The point is that after his engineering degree, he got into stock trading full-time. Incidentally, his younger brother and co-founder, Nikhil, was also into trading. And, according to Nithin, his brother was a far better trader. (I hope you've noticed the humility of the man. That too, in a person who has disrupted the stock market by creating the most respected brokerage firm in the country.)

Anyhow, Nithin continued his foray into the exciting world of trading. And then of course, he borrowed money to trade more. Unfortunately, he lost this money. Now, if you had borrowed money and needed to return it, what would you do? Simple. Figure out some other way of earning it back, isn't it? So you could return the money?

And that's how Nithin took up a job in a call centre—on a 'princely' salary of Rs 8000 a month.

By the way, Nithin was delighted with this job. And to understand why, we need to hear him out:

> Working in a call centre was just perfect for me because I used to work in the night shift. And that left my day free for my first love—trading. But that was not the only thing. Call centres were great places to work in because they had a lot of good-looking girls. So not only was I able to continue to trade, I also had a great time in the call centre.

Incidentally, I hope you can make out Nithin's sense of humour? I've gone through his personal web page as well as several of his interviews, and humour is one thing that stands out.

Anyhow, Nithin worked nights in the call centre. And then, in 2005, he met his future wife, Seema. In the call centre—where else? Purpose served, he quit the call centre (sorry, Nithin, that was a joke 😊). However, he did not quit trading. No way. In fact, one day he happened to meet someone who was hugely impressed with his performance as a trader. This gentleman asked Nithin to trade with his money. And then there was no looking back. More and more clients wanted Nithin to trade with their money, and he ultimately reached ten clients. But that was still not the end. At this stage, Nithin decided to become a sub-broker with Reliance Money, a major broker in those days. And life carried on . . .

But Nithin Was Itching to Do Something Different

Now, at this stage, let me ask you a question: If you've been doing something for ten years, wouldn't you feel a bit tired? Tired of doing the same thing day in and day out? Wouldn't you want to do something else?

That's exactly what happened to Nithin. He wanted to take a break. He wanted to do something different, but something where the brothers could use their experience as traders. As you can imagine, the answer was obvious: 'Why not start a broking business? We have a lot of experience in trading. We understand the problems that traders face with most of the current brokers. So let us create a brokerage which will take care of all these issues.' Interestingly, as in the case of Sanjeev and Hitesh, the Kamath brothers came from a service-class family. There wasn't a drop of business in their blood. But when you really want to do something, can your family background ever be a deterrent?

No way.

And that, dear reader, is how the idea of Zerodha was born.

13

The Launch

So Nithin decided to launch a broking business.

Now, let's understand his thought process. First of all, he realized that 99 per cent of the transactions on the stock exchanges were done by traders and only 1 per cent by investors. In other words, if he wanted to run a large, high-volume business, he would need to cater to traders. Yes, investors were also welcome, but the focus of the business would be traders. And of course, it had to be an online brokerage. After all, he was targeting young people, wasn't he?

And then he surveyed the competitive environment. You see, they were getting into a space which was already very crowded. Brokerage businesses in India had been in existence for decades—perhaps even longer. There were major, established brands. For instance, major banks such as ICICI Bank and HDFC Bank had set up brokerage divisions. Then there were large, stand-alone brokerages, such as Motilal Oswal Financial Services, Anand Rathi Financial Services, India Infoline Finance and the like. There was no way the Kamath brothers could be copycats and still survive and grow. They had to be different.

Fortunately, as I've already mentioned, both brothers had been trading for some years, and were aware of the problems that traders faced with existing brokers. If they could solve these problems, they would stand out from the crowd. And that's exactly what they decided to do.

Essentially, they decided that their brokerage platform would be:

- Low-cost
- Transparent
- Fast and easy to use

We'll Charge a Flat Brokerage Fee of Rs 20

Let's start with 'low-cost'. And here, our young friend Nithin did something that changed the face of the Indian brokerage industry forever. You see, during their trading years, the Kamath brothers had seen a major flaw in the system. A flaw that had to do with the brokerage fee charged by most brokers—which was a percentage of the value of the trade. You see, it's very easy for a broker to say, 'I'll charge you just 1 per cent of the value of each trade.' Sounds tiny, doesn't it? Well, if the value of your trade is Rs 1000, 1 per cent works out to just Rs 10. So it *is* tiny. But just increase the value of the trade to Rs 10 lakh, and you are paying a brokerage of Rs 10,000. That's not tiny, is it?

And that's not all. Remember, traders are not like investors. They don't buy (or sell) and go to sleep. They are active throughout the day. They might do multiple trades during each day. And that's where the amount of brokerage they pay can increase dramatically.

Nithin realized that a lot of people who were keen to trade would perhaps not do so because of the high brokerage charges. Especially young people like him. So there was a large market out there just waiting to be tapped, if only the brokerage fee could be reduced. And the villain of the piece was that so-called tiny percentage. According to Nithin, 'Whether you do a trade for Rs 100 or Rs 1 lakh, the effort and cost for the broker are the same. So why should he charge more?'

That's when he picked up a cup of coffee and began to think. And then he took a refill and thought some more. And more. And at the end of the nth refill, it hit him. (I'm not too sure what the value of 'n' was, but you are welcome to ask him when you meet him. And do let me know, so I can incorporate it in the next edition of this book.) That's when the decision was made. 'I will not charge a percentage from my clients. I'll charge a flat fee of Rs 20 per trade!'

My friend, can you imagine anything more revolutionary? Here were brokerages that were charging Rs 10,000 per trade (under the garb of a miniscule 1 per cent commission, of course). And suddenly, there was this upstart called Zerodha, which charged only Rs 20. That's it! So you could do ten trades in a day and pay only Rs 200 to the broker. Around the cost of a cup of coffee.

And now for the HUGE question. How on earth would the business make money? After all, the other brokers were not fools. If they were charging a percentage of the traded amount as their brokerage fee, there must have been a reason. So how would Zerodha survive *and* make a profit?

Very simple. They had to manage costs. Starting with the cost of the software they used. As you can imagine, a brokerage platform is a fairly complex piece of software, and the cost of this software would be a major component of their total costs. And Nithin had no choice. He just *had to control this cost.*

How?

Well, fortunately, he had an ally. The National Stock Exchange, or NSE, which was—and still is—the premier stock exchange in the country. In an effort to encourage the investing and trading culture in the country, the NSE had created an Internet-based platform for trading, which they called NOW. And the best part? NSE had made it available to brokers without any charge. Nithin and his team studied the platform, found it acceptable and decided to use it—at least for a start. Thereby reducing their costs. And that, as you can imagine, had a direct impact on their profitability.

We'll Be Completely Transparent

And now we come to transparency. You see, in addition to providing a trading platform to users, most brokers also provide them with research reports. Essentially, they recommend to their clients the shares they should buy or sell. However, this has its own set of problems. What if the broker himself has bought shares of a particular company and is keen to ensure that the price of the share goes up? If he were an unscrupulous broker, what would he do? Simple: recommend it to his unsuspecting clients so that they buy it as well. And in the process, the price does goes up. But the poor, unsuspecting client has no idea what is happening behind the scenes.

Now, Nithin was very, very clear. He would stay away from such recommendations. He would be completely transparent. Clients had to make their own decisions and not be swayed by what he said. Yes, he would educate them—something that we'll see in a later chapter—but that was it. No recommendations. By the way, such brokers, who do not offer additional services such as research reports, are often called discount brokers. A concept that already existed in the USA, with well-known Internet-based brokerages such as Charles Schwab and eTrade following this approach. But it was certainly new to India.

There was also a side benefit to not giving recommendations. Since they did not have to compile such reports, their costs came down. And I'm sure you can guess what that did. That's right, it made the Rs 20 brokerage even more viable.

But there is still more to transparency, so please keep reading. You see, when you trade on the stock market, there are several other costs involved, apart from the direct cost of the shares you are buying or selling. There are taxes, there are demat charges (don't bother about this term; I won't mention it again), there are penalties if you don't trade enough and therefore the broker doesn't make enough money . . .

Now, in those days, most brokerage firms were highly opaque. They didn't really tell you exactly how much a particular trade would cost. Well, they probably had these details in the fine print of the agreement the trader had signed, but it was perhaps a forty-page agreement. How many traders would have read each word—and equally important, remembered it? No way. Not possible. Therefore, most traders would happily trade without really knowing what their trades would cost them.

So what did Nithin do? Simple. He made this system transparent. In fact, he was the first to do so. Which meant that the user would know exactly what his costs would be *before executing a trade*. There were no hidden costs. And then he could decide whether or not to go ahead with the trade. And that, my friend, is transparency!

So, you've seen how the brothers built a trading platform which satisfied two of the conditions they had laid out. It was low-cost and it was utterly transparent. But what about the third condition? The fact that it had to be fast and easy to use?

Patience, my friend. I assume you do plan to continue reading this book. And if you do, you'll discover how. For the moment, let me talk about the launch.

The Launch

So that was it. Everything was ready for the launch. Except for the name. Now remember, Nithin wanted to create a brokerage platform that would make things easier for traders. Something that would remove all barriers for them, making it low-cost as well as easy to use. And one day, it hit him. He thought of the Sanskrit word 'rodha', meaning barrier. And since he wanted to remove all barriers or in other words, make it 'zero barrier', well, you can guess what happened. That's right, the company was named **Zerodha**. Completely apt, wasn't it?

So, with a lot of fanfare and blowing of bugles, the low-cost, highly transparent online brokerage service, Zerodha, was launched. In 2010. Here's what Nithin says about those initial days:

> We started out as a small team. We had no pedigree education,
> no background in tech, no experience, but we had a passion for
> capital markets and the intent to help other traders like us.

Can you think of a better example of humility?

It Wasn't All Hunky-Dory: The Credibility Issue

So Zerodha was launched. But there is something interesting that happened during those early years. You see, when a business charges much less than the rest of the market, the first question that comes to the customer's mind is credibility. Remember, in this business, customers are buying and selling shares through the broker. And, in the process, they are trusting the broker with their hard-earned money. Therefore, the credibility of the broker becomes extremely critical. And that was the issue. Here was an unknown upstart that charged only Rs 20 for a trade, whereas all the known, established brokers in the country were charging much more. In this situation, what would traders think? 'Stay away from this guy. He could be a fraud. He might run away with my money.' Or perhaps something a bit less damaging: 'Maybe his service quality will be terrible. Maybe their website will be horrible. No, I'd rather stick to the trusted, more expensive brokers!'

Isn't it? Isn't that what you would think? Of course, you would! And you would be entirely justified. That's why the first few years of the business were tough. It took time for traders to be convinced. They came to Zerodha in drips and dribbles, and growth was slow. In the first year, they managed to get a meagre 3000 customers. And by the second year, they had reached just 10,000. Yes, it was slow going, but the Kamath brothers stuck to their guns and refused to give up.

And that's a message for you, dear founder. When you see a wonderful, highly successful business, it's easy to get carried away and imagine that they've had it easy all along. But that's rarely the case. The first few years are almost always tough. You've seen the case of Naukri and now you've seen Zerodha. And you'll see two more hugely successful businesses as you keep reading this book. They all had a tough time initially. So what's the message for you? Don't give up. Hang in there. Keep trying multiple options. Keep pivoting. And hopefully you'll emerge a stronger business from those tough times.

Anyhow, to get back to our story, that was how Zerodha was launched.

Of course, there is a lot more. But for the moment, let's take a break.

We'll continue with the story in the next chapter . . .

14

We Won't *Take* Money, So We Must *Make* Money

And now, you need to get into 'thinking mode'. Remember the Naukri story, where I had said that every business needs to have an entry barrier? Something in the business that makes it tough for competitors to enter the business and take away their customers? Something unique, that is tough to copy? Remember?

Now, Nithin had offered his customers a flat brokerage of Rs 20. Wasn't that a wonderful entry barrier?

Of course not. How could that possibly be an entry barrier? After all, every large, established broker could easily offer a similar flat fee, and push Zerodha out of business. Please remember, offering a discounted price is never an entry barrier, simply because it is so easy to copy.

No, my friend, the key to an entry barrier is that it has to be tough to copy. Ideally, it should take months, if not years, to copy. And for Nithin, the product was the entry barrier. Because the customer was the key to success, and for the customer, the product was the key. So the entry barrier simply *had to be* the product.

Now clearly, the product had to be significantly better than what competitors had. It had to be easy to use. And fast—even after scaling up. Just imagine a situation where a trader wants to buy a share whose price is rapidly going up. He enters the details and waits nervously, chewing his nails all the while. And since the website is slow, he starts nodding his head . . . and then he nods some more . . . and more . . . until he finally falls asleep. In the meantime, of course, the share price has already shot up! (By the way, this is a bit of an exaggeration. I'm not saying that share prices don't go up. It's just that most traders do not fall asleep when sitting in front of their terminals. However, I'm sure you get the message.) In a nutshell, Zerodha had to ensure fast response times. And yes, they would also need to come up with better and better versions of the product on a regular basis to ensure that they retained their entry barrier.

For the moment, their product was NSE's NOW platform. However, all brokers had access to NOW so that could never become an entry barrier. Therefore, they had to develop their own unique product. Their own platform. And that meant that they needed money.

Fortunately, there was a time-tested method adopted by most Internet-based businesses which Zerodha could also use: Raise funds from investors, use them to develop the product, spend heavily on marketing and grow. Of course, that would have meant hefty losses, but that was not an issue. Investors were happy to fund loss-making businesses, as long as they were growing.

Wouldn't that have been a sensible approach? To keep raising funds and keep growing, while at the same time continuing to make losses?

Right?

Wrong. Dead wrong. Maybe that's what most Internet businesses would have done. But that is certainly not what Nithin did.

So what did he do? Well, just pick up a cup of tea (for a change) and read on . . .

We Won't Take Money

Nithin was clear that he would not take money from investors. And just to ensure that you get the message, I'll repeat it. *Nithin did not take money from investors!*

What? An Internet giant that never raised money? Completely bootstrapped? No series A? No Series B, C . . . ? How is that possible?

Yes, my friend, it *is* possible. It *did* happen. Zerodha never raised funding. And according to Nithin, that is one of the biggest reasons for their success. Let's understand why.

You see, in the beginning, no one really wanted to fund them. No VC and no angel network. Stockbroking was just too crowded a space. But then the company started growing. Wonder of wonders, they were actually making a profit as well. Something that was taboo amongst Internet businesses. And that's when the VCs woke up. 'Profitable growth? We haven't seen such a thing in Internet businesses. These guys must be doing something right. Come, let's invest'. And the VCs came in droves.

But hang on. Those wonderful VCs, with their even more wonderful dollars and yen and rupees, were in for a rude shock. Zerodha didn't want their money. Yes, you heard right. *They didn't want investor money.* Because they were growing anyway. And they were also making a profit—which was ploughed back to fuel further growth. The VCs coaxed and cajoled Nithin. 'Take our money; you'll grow a lot faster,' they said. But Nithin was adamant. Polite, as always, smiling as always, but firm, 'Sorry, we don't need your money!'

Now, if you are familiar with the world of start-ups and Internet businesses, I'm sure you are as foxed as those poor VCs were. How could these guys *not* take funding? When every Tom, Dick and Harry—sorry, Anil, Sunil and Murli—was just desperate to take money from investors. At a time when Series A, B, C . . . going up to the last few letters of the alphabet, were the 'in thing'? Here was a company that said 'NO'.

The best person to explain the logic behind this strange decision, is obviously Nithin himself, so let's hear him out:

> We took a conscious decision not to take money from VCs. And in hindsight, that was perhaps one of the best decisions we have ever taken. You see, once you take money from these guys, they get involved in running the business. Which means that you need to go to them before taking any decisions—especially the major

ones. And that slows you down. To survive in the Internet world, you need to be nimble. You need to take quick decisions and run, and you can't do that if you have to wait for someone else's approval every time.

And there is another thing. External money comes with too many conditions and too many constraints. A founder needs to take decisions that he believes are good for the customer and good for the company. Importantly, these might not be the greatest decisions for the investor. For instance, VCs are always keen to get an exit, but that might not be the best decision for the company. So we didn't take money from investors, and therefore we didn't have to keep anyone happy, except our customers.

In a way, Zerodha is like the great-looking college girl that everyone wants to date, but she is not willing.

By the way, I hope you can see Nithin's trademark humour in action again? Anyhow, there is more, so let's listen to him once again:

Unfortunately, success in Internet businesses has been measured by the amount of money you have been able to raise from VCs. And, of course, the valuation at which you've raised it. 'Take money' has been the mantra. Instead, it should be 'make money'. We did not have spare cash floating around, so we had to figure out ways to make money. And I think that has been one major reason for our success.'

And that, dear reader, gives you Nithin's philosophy in a nutshell:

Since we did not 'take' money, we had to 'make' money.

Brilliant statement, isn't it? And doesn't it sound uncannily like Sanjeev Bikhchandani of Naukri? When you have too much money available, you have a tendency to spend it. Even overspend it. Your focus is growth, growth and more growth. It is not profitability.

You don't need to be profitable because you are getting the money from investors anyway. You are not building a genuine business. So, where Sanjeev and Hitesh took a round of VC money and put half of it into a fixed deposit, Nithin actually went a step further: He didn't take money at all!

Building the Product: The FOSS Advantage

So there was no investor money available to Zerodha. But, as we have seen earlier, they simply *had to build a product that was different*. A product that would become their entry barrier. A product that was flexible enough so they could add features over time, and sustain their entry barrier. But they couldn't spend much on it, because they didn't have the luxury of funding.

So what did they do?

Well, they used FOSS to build their product.

FOSS? What kind of animal is this?

It's not an animal, my friend. FOSS stands for 'Free and Open Source Software'. Now, I realize that this is not a book about software, and I'm sure you didn't expect to read silly things like this when you bought it. But to understand the Zerodha story, you do need to understand the concept of FOSS. Of course, if you already know how FOSS works, you are welcome to skip this section.

So here goes . . .

You see, if you wanted to deploy a piece of software, such as a trading platform in our case, you would most likely to go to a software vendor. This vendor would usually have a pre-packaged software product, which they would customize to your specific needs, and then deploy it for you. The plus point, obviously, is that you would not need to spend months, or perhaps years, developing something. You could start off fast. But the obvious disadvantage is that it would cost you lots of money. In addition, you would be limited to the features that this packaged software provided. And there's a third problem. You would need to pay annual maintenance charges to this vendor to take care of bugs, changes and upgrades to the software. And, of course, if you wanted to enhance this software, well, you would be completely dependent on the time frames the vendor gave you.

Now, the key issue in this entire drama is that the *vendor owns the 'source code' for the software* and no one else has access to it.

What is source code? Well, you see, the computer is a digital animal. It can only understand strings of zeroes and ones. Something that we call 'machine language'. A typical machine language program would look something like this:

```
0110110110011011
1001000100010101
0101000000110010
1001000001110000
0101010101111111 . . .
```

Great. Wonderful. This is what computers understand. But here's the catch: Most human beings would have a decided aversion to writing programs in 0s and 1s. And most programmers are human beings, aren't they ☺? So programmers would need a different kind of programming language. Something that is closer to English.

And that's why programming languages such as Java, C++, and Python were invented. These are called 'high-level languages' as against 'machine language' that the computer understands.

Here's a very, very, VERY simple program in one such language:

```
begin
a := a+1
end
```

This program instructs the computer to increment the value of a number 'a' by 1. So if 'a' had the value '5' before this program was executed, its value becomes '6' after the program is executed.

Therefore, we have high-level languages for humans to program and we have machine language that the computer understands and executes. Obviously, someone needs to translate the high-level program into machine language, so that the computer can understand and run the program. That 'someone' is itself a program called a 'compiler' or 'interpreter'. And now for the last piece of gyan: The program (also called code) written by a programmer in a high-level language is called 'source code', whereas the translated version in machine language is called 'object code'.

Aha! I'm sure you're getting it now. When a vendor sells software to a client, they only give them the object code. Strings of zeroes and ones. *The source code remains under heavy lock and key with the vendor.* Which means that the client, or anyone using the software, cannot make any changes to the software. They can only run it. All control remains with the vendor.

Now, if you are familiar with software guys, you would know that they are a somewhat unique species within the human race (I was a software guy once, so I should know 😊.) They dislike control. They believe that software is something that should be available to everyone to use, modify and enhance. Why should it be the prerogative of some stupid vendor, who can then charge astronomical sums to let his poor clients use it?

No way. Programmers were angry with this whole business of software being owned by the vendor. And angry programmers don't just sit and crib. If they have a problem, they do something about it. And in this case, they did. Several software guys got together and created a movement against this kind of 'proprietary' software. They called it the 'FOSS', or 'Free and Open Source Software' movement.[*] A movement where programmers would develop software and make the source code available to other programmers. To use, modify and do whatever they wanted with it.

Now, this is critical, so I'll repeat it: *The FOSS movement made the source code available to other programmers!* Not just the object code. So the others could use it, modify it, improve upon it, build on it . . .

---

[*] Unesco.org: https://en.unesco.org/freeandopensourcesoftware.

My friend, can you imagine the phenomenal impact of this development? Because now, rather than just the vendor making changes to the software they owned, charging heavily for these changes, and taking their own sweet time over it, the software was now available to anyone to change. So when you *did* have a problem, or wanted to make changes, you were not dependent on the vendor. You could make the changes yourself.

And there is more. Several programmers created small pieces of programs (sometimes called components), which were freely available to others to use. Users would stitch these programs together, add their own programs, and voila—you had a larger program (let's call it a super-component). And so on. In fact, you could build a complete system in this manner. As you can imagine, the community swelled and then swelled some more, with more and more programmers gleefully joining the bandwagon. (By the way, when I use the term 'free', I mean 'freedom to use, modify and enhance'. It does not necessarily mean 'no charge', although in many cases such software is available without any charge. And that's the other key issue: FOSS software tends to be much cheaper to build, deploy and modify.)

Now, this might be the first time you've heard the term FOSS. But you would definitely have heard of some of the famous software products that were developed using FOSS. For instance, most mobile phones except Apple iPhones use the Android operating system—the software that acts as the interface between you and the instrument. And guess what? Android is FOSS-based. I'm sure you've heard of the Linux operating system for computers. That's FOSS-based, too. And so is the web browser, Firefox. For techies, so is the Apache web server . . .

So that was a very brief and highly simplified tutorial on the subject of FOSS. And now, I'm sure you've guessed what I'm going to say. That's right: A large part of the software for Zerodha was developed using FOSS. You see, Nithin and Nikhil were traders. They understood the innards of trading, and they understood the issues with the stockbroking business. But neither of them was a techie. Neither of them could take up his pen (sorry, fingers) and furiously type away to create a computer program. But that's when Nithin met Kailash Nadh, a tech whiz. Kailash had a PhD in AI (artificial intelligence) from Middlesex University in the UK. More importantly, Kailash was a highly active member of the FOSS community. In fact, he went a step further. He was, and still is, an evangelist for the FOSS movement!

Need I say anything more? Kailash was impressed with Nithin's vision for the company. And he explained to Nithin how FOSS could be used in building the Zerodha platform. That was it. Kailash joined the team in 2012 and has been the CTO (Chief Technology Officer) ever since. And he and his team built Zerodha's software using the FOSS concept.

How did that impact costs? Well, first of all, they could use existing components that other programmers had built. Which obviously cut down their costs. And they were not dependent on vendors for changes to the software. They could make these changes and enhancements themselves. Which meant savings in time as well as cost.

So Kailash, along with a small team of programmers, built the next version of the Zerodha platform using FOSS in 2015. The platform itself was called **Kite.** Why Kite? Well, according to Nithin, it's because kites are light, they fly high in the air and they are fast. Need I say more?

By the way, Nithin has famously said that Zerodha has probably saved a few hundred crores of rupees by using FOSS, and has built high-speed, scalable and responsive systems in the process. And that, my friend, is how their product has become one of their major entry barriers.

Marketing on a Shoestring Budget

So that's how Zerodha built its software. But that's not all. You might have a wonderful piece of software, and your clients might be delighted with it. But ultimately, you are running a business, and you need to generate revenues. And to do that, you need to spend heavily on marketing, don't you? How often have you heard something like, 'Such and such company spent over Rs 400 to earn Re 1 of revenue?' Very common, isn't it? That's the done thing in the Internet world. And, of course, these companies make up those phenomenal losses from investors, who are queueing up to invest in them.

However, this was definitely not the approach adopted by Zerodha. Nithin was clear that he was running a sustainable business. And to run such a sustainable business, he could not afford to splurge and splurge on expensive marketing campaigns. No, there simply had to be another way. And that other way was 'word of mouth'. Let's hear him out once again:

> If you have a great product, you should not need to market it. If people are happy with it, they will keep using it. And then they will talk to other people, who will join in as well. Right through our journey at Zerodha, we have focused on building a great product. Something that the customer really loves. Something that sets us apart from the others. This could mean response time, simplicity, ease of use, support—anything that makes the customer's life simpler. Which of course, means that we have been continuously enhancing the product. And that has really been possible because of our CTO, Kailash, and FOSS.

Of course, the press also had a role to play. No one in India had heard of a broker charging a flat fee, so this was splashed all over the business media. Which obviously helped.

So Zerodha did not splash out on marketing. But surely, they had a sales team with the usual hefty targets and fat incentives if they met these targets? People who would respond to even a fleeting interest shown by a potential client? Or, they must have had a hyperactive call centre with agents chasing the hell out of anyone whose number they happened to have? If you had to grow and you didn't spend on marketing, wouldn't you at least need an aggressive sales organization?

Well, my friend, you obviously don't know Nithin. He *did* have salespeople, but they did not have targets. Yes, you heard that right; *his salespeople did not have any targets.* It gets more and more crazy, doesn't it? No hefty marketing and no sales targets. So how did Nithin expect the company to grow?

Nithin has always been very clear about one thing (actually, he's been very clear about many things and this is another one of them). He strongly believes that sales targets lead to a lot of mis-selling. You see, when you have a stiff target to chase, you are under pressure to meet it. And a lot of unwanted practices creep in, such as making wrong commitments or pressurizing the client to close the deal. This has always been taboo for Nithin. He believes that his customers are the best salespeople for the company. This is what he says:

> Do what is good for the customer. If there is a product or service that is good for the customer, we will make it available to him, even if it doesn't make us money. It'll keep him happy and he will not only stay with you, but will also bring in other customers. So if it's good for the customer, it's good for the business. We believe in the dictum, 'Customers first, rather than profits first.' If you put customers first, profits will follow.

Finally, let me take you back to Nithin's famous statement, 'Since we didn't *take* money, we had to *make* money'. From whatever you've read so far, I'm sure you've seen this in action. The use of FOSS cut down their development costs, in addition to making the software highly adaptable and scalable. The focus on the product and keeping the customer happy ensured that customers didn't leave. And these 'happy customers' brought in other customers through word of mouth, which meant that Zerodha did not need to incur marketing costs.

Can you now see the makings of a solidly profitable organization?

And on that profitable note, we need to end this chapter.

Go for a nice, lo-o-o-o-o-o-o-o-ng walk.

And come back fresh for the next chapter . . .

15

We Won't Charge Brokerage at All

And now for the blockbuster decision that changed the face of the Indian stock market. That's right, I'm referring to the one thing everyone talks about—zero brokerage.

How did this happen? How could any sane entrepreneur charge nothing at all for a service? Not just once but repeatedly? How could Zerodha make a profit when several clients were using their platform to buy and sell shares, and paying absolutely no fee as long as they were around? Wouldn't they incur hefty losses? What a ridiculous decision!

My friend, you probably know Nithin by now. You would know that he does not make ridiculous decisions. And he definitely doesn't like to incur a loss. There was a very solid reason for this decision, so let's find out what it was . . .

It all happened one Friday in 2015, when Nithin, Kailash and another colleague were sitting at Bengaluru airport, waiting for a flight to Kochi. As luck would have it, the flight was delayed. And the three young men were hanging around, sharing a beer along with the inevitable peanuts. (I'm not sure if they were fried peanuts, but that's not relevant to the story, so we'll let it pass.) Naturally, the discussion veered around to their business, and the fact that the number of clients they had was still not great.

Now, this was the key: They also realized that 99 per cent of their transactions, and therefore 99 per cent of their revenues, came from

3

traders. Investors contributed just 1 per cent. Obvious, isn't it? If you are an investor, and you do even fifty transactions in a year (which, by the way, is quite a large number) you would still be paying Zerodha only Rs 20 x 50 or a total of Rs 1000 in the year. Peanuts.

Suddenly, while munching peanuts along with his beer, Nithin had a brainwave. The kind of brainwave that came to Archimedes in his bathtub. The kind that comes only once in a lifetime—if at all. 'Hey guys', he said excitedly, 'Why are we hung up on this miniscule revenue from investors? Why not make investing free?'

And with that, Nithin sat back and continued munching peanuts with a grin on his face. While the other two simply stared at him— beer mugs suspended in mid-air.

'Free?' they finally managed to blurt out.

'Yes, free,' said Nithin, as the grin on his face became even broader.

Kailash and his colleague looked at each other. Had Nithin gone crazy? He certainly didn't look it, but you could never tell. However, as the beer flowed and three sets of teeth continued their chomping on the peanuts, the sheer audacity of the suggestion hit them. And in their excitement, they almost missed their flight.

Dear reader, I'm sure even you are wondering what the hell was going on, so let me not keep you in suspense any more. You see, Nithin realized that the bulk of their revenues came from traders. Very little from investors. Bringing the fee down to zero for investors, would have a miniscule effect on their overall revenues. But the optics would be phenomenal. They could imagine the entire country waking up and saying, 'Zero brokerage? My God, what's this? Let's find out!' It could potentially lead to an explosive growth in the number of investors joining them. Not only that, with this message going around the country, they would even be able to add more traders. And the icing on the cake? Many of the investors joining them might later convert to trading. Which was the core business of Zerodha, anyway.

And that was that. The decision was made on that Friday evening and announced the very next morning. Yes, my friend, you heard right. The very next day—Saturday. Because they had no VC, no investor to check with. No convincing, no taking an Excel sheet to their VC. No sitting across the table and poring over projections and the possible implications of the decision. And if you recall, this is exactly the reason why Nithin decided against taking investor money. Speed. Agility. Remember, if you don't have investor money, you can make decisions on the spur of the moment.

As you can imagine, this decision received phenomenal press coverage, which, as you know, is zero-cost marketing. And of course, word of mouth spread like wildfire, 'Who is this broker who is not charging any fee at all?' 'My God, we must check them out.' 'Zero brokerage fees? Never heard of it. We must join them.' Of course, you can guess what this did to the financials of the company. Huge word of mouth, massive press coverage and zero marketing costs. Yes, my friend, both revenues and profit simply went up and up.

Now, in this context, I must share something very important with you. Was this a decision that was made based on some complex analysis? Did these guys have a huge Excel sheet which they pored over for days? Did they project the implications of this momentous decision over and over again?

No, my friend, they did not. There was no Excel sheet and there was no analysis for days on end. This was an instinctive decision. And that's a message for you. Yes, you do have wonderful tools, such as spreadsheets, available to you. And you can go gaga playing around with numbers. But sometimes decisions need to be made based on gut feel. As a CEO or even as a manager, you need to move away from too much analysis and ultimately trust your instinct. Which is what Nithin did. Remember, this decision was made over beer and peanuts. In the lounge at Bengaluru airport, and not in some stuffy conference room. And look where it took the company!

And now for the grand finale. In 2016, the *Economic Times* published a list of the top ten businessmen to watch out for. Number one on the list was Mukesh Ambani, and number two was—yes, you've guessed it right—our young friend, Nithin Kamath. But please note the utter humility of the young man. Nowhere did he brag about the fact that he was placed next to Mukesh Ambani in the list of promising CEOs. Nowhere did he strut around, chest all puffed up, and tell the world that he was the biggest. No sir. Nithin quietly went about his business of building Zerodha. Yes, the world sat up and sang praises about him. But Nithin would not blow his own trumpet.

And that's something truly endearing about the man!

Why Not Mutual Funds as Well?

So that was how Nithin brought in lots of investors, on the assumption that some of them would become traders over time. Now, what was the logical next step? Well, as you are aware, many investors do not invest directly in shares. They invest in mutual funds instead. Over time, some of them move to direct investment in shares and ultimately become traders as well. So why leave out this segment of the market? No way. And that's where Zerodha launched their next product, **Coin**, through which investors could buy and sell mutual funds. Smart, wasn't it?

One question: Did they charge for Coin?

Well, they did start off by charging Rs 50 per month. But then, in the wonderful tradition of zero brokerage for investors buying and selling shares, they made Coin free as well. After all, the idea was to expand the market, and ultimately get some of these investors to start trading, wasn't it?

And did the strategy work? You bet it did. As of March 2022, Coin was the largest online platform for buying and selling mutual funds in India, with AUM (assets under management) of Rs 17,900 crore. A staggering 37 per cent of the total AUM across all online distributors.[*] And they haven't been sitting idle since then. At the

---

[*] Nishant Patnaik, cafemutual, 20 September 2022, https://cafemutual.com/news/industry/27581-five-major-direct-plan-platforms-manage-aum-of-rs48600-crore-in-mutual-funds.

time of writing this book (2023), the figure has gone up to over Rs 60,000 crore. And who knows where it will reach by the time you read this book?

So, Zerodha had started by letting customers trade in stocks, and from there went on to mutual funds as well.

But that wasn't the end. No sir, there was a lot more that Zerodha did, to enhance customer experience.

Wouldn't you want to know what?

Just read on, my friend . . .

16

Growing the Business

So Zerodha created Kite for trading. And then they created Coin for buying and selling mutual funds. Both great products, and both completely in sync with Nithin's philosophy of looking after the customer. But that was just the beginning. Because there were competitors lurking around, desperate to copy his model. Give them a few months, and they would probably catch up. In other words, Zerodha had to keep enhancing their entry barrier over time. And for that, they needed to keep enhancing their products, along with adding new ones.

Right? So let's take a look at what they did.

The New Products

The next product to be launched was called **Console**, which, as its name suggests, was essentially carrying out the function of reporting. So it would give the trader all kinds of reports, such as what had gone right and what had gone wrong with his trades in the past. After all, it was important to learn from past mistakes, wasn't it? It would also give him his capital gains statements, because the income tax department would want its own pound of flesh 😊.

Then, there was one more product that was really close to Nithin's heart. A product called **Varsity**. You see, he has always been keen to share his know-how with others and get them to benefit from it. Let's hear it from him directly:

> I have always had this *keeda* (literally meaning insect, but what Nithin means is 'obsession'). A keeda of wanting to share knowledge with others. Even before we started Zerodha, I used to run the largest Yahoo messenger group in India on the subject of the stock market. I've always enjoyed it, particularly when someone else benefited from my sharing. In fact, I would often spend hours answering people's queries.
>
> I also believe in the concept of 'good karma'. Where you do good to others and good comes back to you. This know-how sharing was a part of my good karma.
>
> That has been the philosophy behind Zerodha. Help people without any expectations in mind and they will come back and help you. And that's how we launched Varsity. To help our clients really understand the innards of the stock market, without charging them anything. And to help them make money. These happy clients, in turn, spoke about us to other clients, and that's how we have grown through referrals.

Varsity was developed almost single-handedly by Karthik, an old friend of Nithin. And no, it doesn't have any ads. Zerodha doesn't ask you to register and then follow up with loads and loads of emails asking you to join. No, it's pure and simple learning: completely free. I've personally tried it. I didn't need to register and I didn't see any ads. And it explains everything very, very clearly. Varsity is just one more initiative from Nithin that helps people. As you can imagine, this builds trust. And in the long run, these people come back and help Zerodha!

Nithin also launched an initiative called **TradingQnA**. Which is exactly that: a forum where people can ask questions about trading and get answers from Zerodha. Nithin believes that this gets them close to the customer, and helps them listen to what the customer is saying. By the way, Nithin personally answers some questions—just to understand his customers. And he does all this without expecting anything from the customer. There is no selling, no push to join Zerodha. They simply help people without expecting anything in return!

Nudge

Finally, let me tell you about a really fascinating product that Zerodha added to their stable. Something that I found hard to believe. And to understand this, I must ask you a question: Have you ever heard of a broker who discourages his clients from trading? I've been in the stock market for over forty years and I certainly haven't. It's just not done. As a broker, you are earning your brokerage, so why the hell would you tell your client not to trade? But now I've heard of it. Because that's what Zerodha does. Not for all trades—come on, they would be out of business if they did that. But for highly risky trades.

Let's look at some examples of such risky trades:

'Ghotala Industries is trading at just Rs 5 per share. Can you imagine such a great opportunity? Even if the share price goes up to Rs 15, that's a tripling of value!' Unfortunately, that doesn't happen. The share was trading at a very low price because the founder was fighting a criminal case. As expected, he loses the case and goes to jail. And the share price plummets from Rs 5 to just 50 paise.

Or, 'I've just discovered the most wonderful company— Phenku Services. Only Rs 4 per share. It cannot possibly go lower.' Unfortunately, it does go lower.

Phenku Services is unable to withstand the latest high-tech competitors that have entered the market. And the stock price crashes from Rs 4 to a miserable Rs 1.20.* Obviously, all the traders

---

* These examples are taken from my earlier book, *Welcome to Aaraampur: A Sleepy Little Hill Town* (India: Penguin Ebury Publishing, 2023), which you are welcome to read.

and investors who bet on these two companies would lose their money—and perhaps their shirts as well.

And that, my friend, is what we call 'penny stocks'. Stocks of companies that are trading at very low prices—typically a few rupees. The important thing is that these prices are low for a reason. In many cases, the companies are loss-making. Or the managements are dubious with the money being siphoned off. Or the future outlook is bleak. Whatever the reason, putting money into these companies is a highly risky business.

And Nithin has always been clear—he was not in the business purely to make money. He genuinely wanted to look after his customers, and ensure that they didn't lose money while trading. Remember his belief in good karma? He wanted to educate his customers about the risks associated with such trades. And that's why he started **Nudge**. Essentially, Nudge moves the trader towards good practices, such as not trading in penny stocks and other risky trades. In a way, Nudge tries to change the behaviour of both investors and traders.

And what do you think the reaction to Nudge was? Phenomenal, as you can imagine. Traders and investors alike realized that this was a platform which was not in the business purely to make money. It was there to educate them and move them towards good behaviour in the stock market. So that *they could also make money*. They trusted the platform. From the moment Nudge was introduced, there was a torrent of clients jumping onto the Zerodha bandwagon. So, while the company might have lost out on a bit of revenues by getting their clients to avoid certain trades, they more than made up for it with the positive word of mouth that was generated.

Can you see Nithin's good karma thinking in action once again?

Kite Connect: Opening the Floodgates

While growing the business, Nithin had yet another brainwave. Yes, like me, you must be wondering how this young man gets so many brainwaves. I don't have the answer to that question, but I can help you understand what this particular brainwave was. And for this, I need to take an analogy from the well-known car manufacturer, Ghata Motors. (Sorry, Tata Motors, this has nothing to do with you guys. This is an entirely fictitious company; I just liked the name.) Now, Ghata Motors was in the business of manufacturing electric cars. However, battery charging was a major issue. The company had a strong R&D team, but they realized that there were several innovative people outside the company, who might be able to come up with interesting solutions to the problem. So they threw the problem open to anyone who was interested.

And that worked brilliantly. Sunny Engineering Works, a Ludhiana-based company, named after its founder, was into providing solar energy solutions. They took up the challenge and created a rooftop solar solution for Ghata Motors' car. (When I say rooftop, I mean the rooftop of the car, not the house of the owner.) So when the car was out in the sun, solar energy was generated and stored in its battery. Then you had Windy Pvt Ltd, which placed small windmills on the roof of the car and used wind energy to charge the battery. And how can I leave out Waterfall & Sons, which used rainwater to generate electricity and charge the battery, with the entire machinery mounted on the car? (I must clarify that some of these are highly unpractical solutions. After all, how much electricity can you get from rainwater? However, please remember, this is just an analogy to explain what Zerodha did.)

So Ghata Motors' strategy worked brilliantly. Their own R&D engineers would perhaps have come up with one or two such solutions, but when they threw it open to the world, there were several solutions coming up, each more brilliant than the others.

Now the next bit is vital, so please read it carefully: For this strategy to work, Ghata Motors *had to allow all these players to access the electrical circuitry of the car*, so they could charge the car battery. *Without impacting the rest of the car in any way.* In other words, the company made the interface to the electrical system publicly available to anyone who wanted to use it and build their own product.

And now we can move away from this silly analogy and return to Zerodha. Nithin and Kailash realized that to grow, they needed to keep enhancing their product. One option, of course, was to get their own programmers to do it, which they were doing anyway. But they also followed the Ghata Motors strategy. Just as Ghata Motors made their electrical interface available to anyone who wanted to build something on top of it, Zerodha made the Kite interface available to anyone who wanted to build software on top of it. In the world of computers, we call this interface an API, or 'Application Program Interface'. Essentially, Zerodha made the APIs of Kite accessible to the outside world. And anyone who wanted, could build software on top of it and make it available to users. By the way, this software interface was called **Kite Connect**.

In fact, Nithin's team actually reached out to start-ups. The message was simple: 'We already have a trading platform, Kite, where we charge zero brokerage for investors and a flat fee for traders. There is no point in building another platform. Instead, you can build your application on top of Kite using the APIs in Kite Connect.'

As you can imagine, the strategy worked. Various software vendors came up with completely different options. One of Nithin's favourites was a product called **smallcase**. You see, unlike seasoned, battle-scarred investors, new investors tend to invest based on excitement. 'Wow, this share is at Rs 14. Can't go lower. Let me buy it in bulk.' So, the investor buys the share in bulk. Of course, that's a high-risk investment. If that one share were to tank, the investor would lose a large chunk of money. A far safer policy would be to diversify the portfolio across multiple shares. For instance, if you wanted to invest in the banking sector, rather than buying shares in one single bank, you could buy a smaller number of shares in multiple banks. That's exactly what smallcase was building—software that would allow the investor to buy a basket of shares, and therefore spread his risk. And of course, it was built on the Kite platform using Kite Connect!

So were many other start-ups such as **Sensibull**, which helped in options trading. And **Streak**, which helped traders to cut down their manual involvement and automate their trading strategies.

So Nithin's strategy worked. But there was something missing. Remember, I had told you in Chapter 13 that in this business, credibility was critical. 'Who is this upstart called smallcase? Why should I trust him with my money? I know Zerodha very well—they are market leaders—but I don't know smallcase at all!' Consequently, even though many start-ups had launched their offerings using Kite Connect, there weren't too many takers.

But by now, you probably know Nithin well. He is not the kind of guy who sits back and waits for things to happen. No sir, he makes them happen. And in this case, he had another bright idea. *He positioned the products from these start-ups as Zerodha's products.* Products that had the backing of Zerodha. And then he went to his own customers and asked them to try them out.

With this backing from Zerodha, the word spread: 'Oh, Zerodha is backing this product, is it? Then we don't have a credibility issue. We trust them. Let's try it out!' And after that, there was no stopping these smaller products. In fact, smallcase raced to 10,000 customers in just two or three months. Just compare that with the two years it took Zerodha itself to reach 10,000 customers!

Let me pause for a minute to let that sink in. If it hasn't, please pick up a cup of strong coffee. Preferably black. You see, Zerodha already had a small tech team, which was developing and improving upon their products. But now, they had brought in partners who would help them. So they kept improving their offerings without incurring any significant costs.

Can you see one more reason why Zerodha became the highly profitable giant that it did?

Rainmatter

But even that was not all. While the above strategy worked and Zerodha was able to grow its customer base, there was yet another problem that raised its head. Yes, start-ups such as smallcase and Streak did benefit from the core platform that Zerodha provided. And they also benefited hugely from the fact that they were positioned as Zerodha's products. But to scale up rapidly, many of them needed funding.

So guess what Zerodha did? They were profitable and had surplus funds. So they identified promising start-ups that were using the Kite Connect platform and actually invested in them. As a strategic investor. (Remember, we had discussed this term in the Info Edge story?) That's how Zerodha kept improving their offerings to their customers, thereby continuously building their entry barrier.

And that, dear reader, was the concept of **Rainmatter**. Throwing open the Kite platform to products developed by other companies through Kite Connect, giving them credibility by positioning them as part of the Zerodha offering, mentoring them, and finally providing funding to them as well.

That is Zerodha, the strategic investor.

We Had Our Share of Luck

As you have seen, Nithin made several decisions that really helped Zerodha disrupt a business that was over a hundred years old. But he has also had his share of luck—something that he readily admits. First of all, you must remember that Zerodha has always been heavily dependent on the number of Internet users in the country. You've already seen how the small base of Internet users made it tough for Naukri.com to grow when it was launched in 1997. Fortunately for Zerodha, their business was launched in 2010, by which time the number of Internet users was significantly higher. But it still wasn't large enough. In fact, until 2016, Zerodha could only scale up to around one lakh users. In a total of six years since the launch. That's it.

However, in 2016, an event took place that really transformed the fortunes of Internet businesses. An event that all of you living in India are aware of. Yes, that's when Reliance Industries launched their Jio network. Low-cost, fast and widely available. And of course, their competitors, Airtel and Vodafone, followed suit. That's when the number of Internet users boomed, and therefore so did traders and investors on Zerodha.

But there was more. Along with the Jio network, Reliance also launched its low-cost Jio phone. As usual, other phone manufacturers followed suit. The result? The cost of phones came down, and a huge number of users were able to access the Internet through their phones. No longer were expensive laptops required. All you needed was an app on your phone—and, of course, Zerodha was happy to provide this.

So that was one event that truly boosted Zerodha's user base. Then of course, there was the government's push towards Digital India. You see, the Government of India has always insisted that companies offering financial products conduct a 'Know Your Customer' exercise, or KYC. Perfectly okay. No cribs about this at all. But KYC required you to manually fill up pages and pages of forms and attach photocopies attested by gazetted officers. And then, having created around half a kilo of documents, you would courier all of them to your broker. And what do you think the broker would say? 'Documents missing'. Or, 'Form wrongly filled up; please fill it up again.' And if you had the patience, you would start the 'fun' process again. Of course, if you didn't, you would simply say, 'To hell with it. I won't invest in shares.'

As you can imagine, because of these lengthy processes, share markets in India lost out on lots of clients. In Nithin's own words:

> In those days, you had to fill up perhaps a forty-page document to open a trading and demat account. And with the inevitable back and forth, it would take maybe fifteen days to ultimately do so. Just to take an analogy, suppose you had to book an Ola Cab, and for that you had to sign a forty-page document. Would you take the cab?

Also, please remember, Nithin was targeting young people. And young people do not have the kind of patience that older ones do. But all that changed when the RBI started allowing eKYC, or electronic KYC. That was the time when your Aadhaar card was linked to your PAN number as well as your mobile number. Which meant that you could upload your documents and do your KYC online.

What a transformation that caused! From an earlier fifteen days, it now took just fifteen minutes or so, to open an account with your broker. Suddenly, people who were earlier reluctant to go through the entire manual process, queued up to get their eKYC done, and therefore opened their accounts in a jiffy. Of course, it not only helped Zerodha but all the other Internet brokers as well. In simple terms, the market expanded and each broker had a chance to grow within this expanding market.

Then there was the dreaded Covid-19. While the pandemic had a terrible impact on humanity and on economies, it actually helped companies such as Zerodha. You see, during those days, people were sitting at home and many of them started online trading. And that has been one more reason for their user base to boom.

Did you read boom, my friend? Yes, you did. I have already mentioned that until 2016, the company had a user base of one lakh. And at the time of writing this book (2023), they have reached well over 1 crore. Staggering, isn't it? Just goes to show you that wonderful business practices need to be complemented with a slice of luck. And Nithin openly admits this. He doesn't brag about what he has done or what the team has done.

No, sir. Our utterly humble Nithin Kamath attributes a large part of the success of his company to luck.

17

The Wonderful Culture at Zerodha

Dear reader, you've seen Nithin's views on customers. Give them products they like. Keep them happy, and they won't leave you. *And* they'll bring in more customers.

'Customers first,' he always says.

But what about internal customers? What about the team members at Zerodha? Wouldn't the same apply to them?

Well, what if I told you that of the first 100 people that joined the core team at Zerodha, almost all of them are still there? Yes, over a span of more than ten years, almost no one from the core team has left. Doesn't that answer your question? And when I discovered this, I was as intrigued as you are to find out the reason.

So I started snooping around. And this is what I discovered . . .

No 'Manager Culture' Please

You are aware that Zerodha is a market leader—a giant. And giant companies are hierarchical, aren't they? So they would have analysts reporting to senior analysts who would report to managers, who would, in turn, report to assistant vice presidents, vice presidents and senior vice presidents. With perhaps a few more designations that I might have left out. And then of course, all decisions would need to go through multiple layers of management, thereby slowing down all decision-making. And the most commonly heard phrase in the corridors of power would probably be, 'You'd better listen to me, because I'm your boss.' Isn't it? Isn't that the way large companies are run?

But that's not the way Zerodha is run. You see, Nithin has always believed in close-knit teams. Rather like families. Where everyone is involved in decisions, rather than being forced to accept what the boss says. That creates ownership. That creates bonding. And since they avoid hierarchies, decision-making is quick. So there is a small core team that looks at products and works closely with Nithin. The tech team is also tiny—just thirty people. And the total size of the Zerodha team? Well, guess what? It's just over 1000 people. That's it. For a company that is a market leader. Incidentally, this number has barely grown over the past six years, during which time revenues have gone up around six-fold. You see, in addition to small, close-knit teams, Nithin believes in the power of technology. And that makes the business highly scalable. And profitable!

As you might imagine, the primary criterion for recruiting people into Zerodha is neither qualifications nor skills. It's attitude. It's culture. In fact, according to Bhuvanesh, who works closely with Nithin, there is perhaps only one MBA graduate in Zerodha. And that is enough (sorry, MBAs 😊). By the way, since they don't go out looking for fancy qualifications, they don't have astronomical salary bills, although people are paid well and looked after. And that's one more reason for them to be profitable.

Finally, according to Bhuvanesh, there is perhaps an HR policy tucked away somewhere, but no one really bothers to read it. The policy is clear: Look after people. That's it!

The Nurturing Environment

And it's not just small teams. The best word to describe the environment at Zerodha is 'nurturing'. All the senior core team members consisting of Nithin, Kailash, Venu (who looks after operations) and Hanan (who takes care of customer support) are extremely patient with people. All of them invest time in sharing their knowledge and experience—and it doesn't matter how senior or junior you are. Here's what Bhuvanesh told me:

I was one of the early employees at Zerodha. When I joined, I had absolutely no idea about the stock market, beyond the spelling of the word 'shares'. Believe me, Nithin spent hours and hours teaching us. He literally invested in us. It was like a 'Finance for Kindergarten' course. And by the way, Zerodha was already the largest broker in India at that time, and Nithin was a busy, busy person. That's the kind of person he is.

Bhuvanesh goes on to say:

At Zerodha, we have a culture of experimentation. People are allowed to experiment and make mistakes. If things work out, great. If not, well, we just move on. And team members get a chance to grow. Good people get noticed, and they get opportunities. And Nithin never takes credit for any success. 'It's the success of the team,' he says, in all modesty. He's always in the background. More like a friend who is always there.

Of course, I don't need to mention the obvious—unlike most companies in the Internet world, there are no mass lay-offs. Not at all. In fact, Zerodha doesn't ask people to leave and people don't want to leave. Because at Zerodha, it's not just 'Customers first.' It's 'People first'.

ESOPs at Zerodha

Now, let's get to the issue of money. You see, a nurturing environment and close-knit teams are fine, but ultimately, team members also need money, don't they? Well, here's what I learnt: *Every team member at Zerodha gets ESOPs* after a year. That's right: every team member, irrespective of how junior or senior he is. Now, do you now realize why employees simply refuse to leave Zerodha? And can you see Nithin's good karma in action once again?

In this context, let's listen to him again:

> Most people do not exercise their rights to sell their ESOPs—something I'm really happy about. Because that means they are keen to stay with us and help the company grow. Essentially, ESOPs become a kind of retirement fund for them.

The Ultimate Good Karma: Rainmatter Foundation

So you've seen good karma for customers. And for team members. But what about good karma for the rest of the world? The ultimate good karma? Yes, my friend, Nithin believes in that as well. This is what he says:

> What's the point in building a business and making money, if our planet Earth is getting deeper and deeper into a hole? With global warming, and people chopping trees left, right and centre? And completely unsustainable methods of farming? I am a nature lover, and I hate it when I see all this around me. Therefore, I was keen to do something to help the planet.

And since you know Nithin quite well by now, you would also know that he doesn't just talk. (Unlike many of us who simply discuss all this over the inevitable whisky in our drawing rooms, while cursing all and sundry.) He translates his talk into action. And that is how, in 2021, **Rainmatter Foundation** was born. Unlike Rainmatter, this is a *pure non-profit organization*. It supports businesses that are into sustainable practices, aimed at saving the earth. And rather than taking equity in these businesses, the foundation gives them grants. No returns expected. In the process, Nithin and his team have been helping save planet Earth for our children and grandchildren. That's the ultimate good karma, isn't it?

By the way, I must tell you that when I heard about the Rainmatter Foundation, I was quite sceptical. 'Oh, these must be CSR funds. Corporate Social Responsibility, you know? Where the government insists that a certain percentage of the company's profit must go into social activities, such as rural education, building toilets, health care, etc. But no. *This is not CSR money. This is over and above CSR.* It's not something Zerodha is doing because the government has asked them to do it. It's something Nithin wants to do to help the planet!

One last point. Remember, I had told you that Nithin never raised any funding? Because he didn't want to run to VCs each time he had to make a decision? Now look at the Rainmatter Foundation. *It's a non-profit organization.* It is designed to *not* make money. Tell me, which VC in his right mind would allow Zerodha to start such an organization? But Nithin did start it, and he never had to get permission from any VC!

And with that, I need to stop talking about the wonderful culture at Zerodha.

We'll now take a look at where they've reached and where they are likely to go from here.

In the next chapter, of course.

18

Zerodha: Today and Tomorrow

Dear reader, you've read so much about Nithin and his baby, Zerodha. About how he always puts the customer first. 'If it's good for the customer, we'll do it: even if we don't make any money from it.' About his almost maniacal focus on the product. About not spending on marketing and instead letting his happy customers bring in others. About not taking external money and bootstrapping his business. And above all, his strong belief in good karma.

So you've seen all this. But where has it taken the company? Well, in terms of number of transactions, Zerodha is perhaps the largest online brokerage firm in the world, with about 5–7 million trades per day.* Just imagine—*the largest broker in the whole world!* The company recorded an operational revenue of Rs 6875 crore in the financial year 2022–23 (nearly a billion dollars for those obsessed with the USA). A growth of 38.8 per cent over the previous financial year. And a profit after tax of Rs 2907 crore—once again, a growth of 39 per cent over the previous financial year. Staggering, isn't it? That too, for a market leader. In fact, they've been profitable for years.

By the way, they still charge a flat Rs 20 per transaction from traders and nothing from investors, and I don't see that changing. That's the kind of company Zerodha is.

---

* In value terms, the US stock market is larger because they trade in dollars, whereas our markets trade in rupees.

What about competition? Sure, it's there, and it's growing all the time. You see, all the innovative decisions made by Nithin helped not only Zerodha but the entire trading community in India to grow. In the past few years, several online brokerages have sprouted across the country. Many of them use Zerodha's model of a flat brokerage for traders and zero fees for investors. For instance, you have Groww and Upstox. Groww is now neck and neck with Zerodha in terms of the number of active users. In fact, in September 2023, its active user base was marginally higher than that of Zerodha.[*] However, Zerodha has a much larger number of transactions. And there's a fundamental difference between the two: Groww has a huge marketing budget—I'm sure you've seen their ads on the business channels on television. On the other hand, Zerodha does not spend on marketing because Nithin believes in letting the product speak for itself. Therefore, Zerodha is likely to be far more profitable!

And now, for the icing on the cake. In February 2023, I was pleasantly surprised to see my young friend, Nithin, receiving the highly prestigious Entrepreneur of the Year Award at The Economic Times Awards for Corporate Excellence, instituted by the leading business newspaper, the *Economic Times*.

Thoroughly deserved recognition, isn't it?

Is Zerodha a Unicorn?

Actually, I don't think Nithin cares. His objective has always been to chase the business, and not valuation. In any case, valuation is really arrived at when the company gets an investor. Otherwise, it's just a notional figure, isn't it? Now, Zerodha never got investors, so how would they arrive at the valuation?

---

[*] Harsh Upadhyay, 'Groww surpasses Zerodha in terms of active users', Entracker, 12 October 2023, https://entrackr.com/2023/10/groww-surpasses-zerodha-in-active-users/.

However, they did need to figure out the valuation because they had to give exits to those few team members who wanted to encash their ESOPs. Therefore they put on their thinking caps and got into a huddle with their accountants. Based on commonly used models, they pegged the valuation of Zerodha at around $3.6 billion, when they announced their annual results in the financial year 2022–23. So the company is definitely a unicorn.

Sorry, I almost forgot—it's an earnicorn 😊!

And What Does the Future Hold?

And now for a peek into the future.

First of all, what is Zerodha working on at the moment? Well, one thing is clear: They will keep improving their existing product line. Because they are in a competitive space, with several brokers snapping at their heels. (I just told you about Groww.) Nithin has said that they are working on improving their Nudge offering, where they try to inculcate good habits in traders. They are also working on bringing machine learning into Nudge. If you are familiar with this concept, it means that the Nudge algorithm learns from the mistakes made by traders and accordingly shapes its advice. You can imagine how powerful Nudge will become if all the past data is used to figure out the advice it needs to give.

Secondly, they are also keen on bringing good practices into the area of personal wealth management. For instance, the fact that you need life insurance as well as health insurance, and the amount you need depending on your family and other circumstances. Or the fact that you should park some of your savings in safe, fixed investments, rather than putting all of it into risky trades. There is so much more to wealth management, and this is what Zerodha would like to offer its clients.

In fact, Nithin is keen on extending this service. For instance, what should an investor or trader do when the market tanks? Or, conversely, booms? He realizes that a lot of the advisory services out there are not really worth the name. Worse, they have a vested interest in recommending specific stocks. As always, Nithin is very clear that they will not recommend any specific stocks or mutual funds. Because that would lead to vested interests, which goes completely against the transparency that he so firmly believes in. This facility would simply be to help their clients. As he is never tired of repeating, 'You help clients and they, in turn, help you'.

Now, I must share something interesting with you here. Late in 2023, as I was putting the finishing touches to this story, Zerodha dropped a bombshell. They announced that they were launching two mutual funds.

Nothing wrong with that, is it? After all, anyone can launch mutual funds, as long as they get permission from SEBI. But this was different. Remember, all along, Nithin has said that Zerodha would never recommend specific stocks. Because that would be biased. And here they were getting customers to invest in their funds, which obviously had specific stocks. That would go completely against the grain of Nithin's thinking, wouldn't it? And against everything I've said in this story.

Now, you can imagine what an earthquake that caused in my life. Would I need to write the Zerodha story all over again? Or worse, should I drop the story and pick up another company? I almost tore out my hair in frustration (whatever little hair I still have, I mean 😊).

But one day, when I was reading the newspaper over my morning cup of tea (yes guys, I'm from the generation that loves to open the newspaper and sip my tea along with it; no silly Internet, please), I got my answer. There was absolutely no conflict with Nithin's thinking. No vested interest. Because they were launching pure Index Mutual Funds.

What is this new animal? Let me explain. You must have heard of the Nifty and Sensex. Each of these is an index. For instance, the Nifty is an index of the top fifty stocks traded on the NSE, where the stocks are assigned weights according to their respective market caps. Importantly, the selection of these stocks and their weightage, is decided by the stock exchange. Similarly, the NSE has an index called the Nifty Large Midcap 250, which is an index of the top 250 stocks traded on the NSE.

Now, in an Index Mutual Fund, the fund manager buys all the stocks that are part of the corresponding index *in exactly the same proportion*. So if the index goes up by, say, 1 per cent on any one day, the fund will go up by exactly the same amount.

And this is the key: The fund manager of an Index Mutual Fund does not make any decisions. He does not have to figure out which stocks to invest in and which ones to get out of. All he needs to do is follow the index. No decision-making, and therefore no bias and no vested interest. Agreed? And now, you can understand why I was at peace when I read about these funds that Zerodha was launching.

One last point before I end the Zerodha story. Nithin realizes that brokerage is a cyclical business. India has had a prolonged bull market for several years now, with a brief dip during the Covid-19 pandemic. But that will not always be the case. There will be times when the market crashes and traders step back to lick their wounds. At these times, business will fall. There will also be boom times when traders are in a frenzy. So these ups and downs will take place. But Zerodha's basic philosophy will continue. They will always be a transparent business. They will continue to focus on offering their clients better and better products. Above all, they will follow good karma. And profits will follow.

And of course, in his spare time (yes, I believe he *does* have some spare time), Nithin will keep playing the guitar and singing along with his son, Kiaan. And being the fitness freak that he is, he will keep on gymming, running, cycling and swimming with his wife, Seema. And spending time with his brother Nikhil, along with his friends and family.

While the fabulous journey of our **earnicorn** Zerodha will go on . . .

19

Let's Analyse the Earnicorn: Zerodha

So that was the fascinating story of the **earnicorn** Zerodha and its equally fascinating founder and CEO, Nithin Kamath. Now at this stage, as we had done in the case of Info Edge, let's step back for a moment and analyse the Zerodha business. And as before, I'll start with my favourite PERSISTENT model.

Zerodha: The PERSISTENT Business

First of all, is Zerodha solving a PROBLEM? Of course it is. When Zerodha was launched in 2010, most Internet-based trading platforms were somewhat cumbersome and slow. Definitely not what the young and restless needed. In addition, they charged a percentage of the traded value as their fee. Which, for an active trader with a large number of trades, could turn out to be huge. Once again, too expensive for the young trader. In other words, the young trader wanted a simple, fast and low-cost option to trade. And bingo, that's exactly what Zerodha provided them with—and still does.

Next, we come to the EARNINGS MODEL. Once again, no issues, because they take a flat Rs 20 commission for each trade. Not from investors, but traders. So they do make money.

And now for the interesting bit: SIZE of the MARKET. When Zerodha was launched in 2010, there was a decent number of traders around, so it was a large market. But it was hugely overcrowded, with banks, brokers and sub-brokers all jostling for the same customer. It was a huge RISK to enter a market with so many large and entrenched players. Players with deep pockets who could easily squeeze this upstart called Zerodha out of the business. Conventional wisdom would indicate that Zerodha should *not* have got into this market. Or, at best, identified a NICHE which was not crowded.

However, I've come to know Nithin over these past few months, and I can tell you something: He doesn't believe in conventional wisdom. My guess is that he doesn't even know the meaning of the term (sorry, Nithin, that was a joke ☺). Instead, he decided to disrupt the market. And then expand it dramatically. In this context, you've already seen how INNOVATIVE he has been. First of all, he charged a flat brokerage of Rs 20 for each trade, as opposed to the highly opaque percentage that existing brokers charged. Suddenly, the country sat up and took notice. And Internet-savvy people who wanted to trade, flocked to Zerodha. So not only did Zerodha grab market share, but they also grew the market at the same time.

Later, along with his friend and CTO, Kailash, Nithin developed a FOSS-based platform that was fast and easy to use. At the same Rs 20 per trade. With this, he was able to grow the market even further. And then of course, the blockbuster decision: zero brokerage for investors. What followed was nothing short of an explosion, as investors fought with each other to join the bandwagon. Over time, some of them started trading, which was Zerodha's core business anyway. And then there was the launch of Kite Connect, which allowed other software companies to build their products on it. And of course, the launch of Coin to get in mutual fund investors, some of whom became traders over time. All terrific examples of innovation, aren't they?

Of course, there were external events as well, which expanded the market. Such as the proliferation of the Internet, thanks to Jio, and the resultant flurry of activity amongst its competitors. And then the RBI's decision to allow eKYC, which reduced the time required to open an account from days to minutes. Yes, these events did help dramatically. But Zerodha was ready for them. And in any case, as Nithin readily admits, luck *does* play a part in any business, doesn't it?

Now, for the biggie: the ENTRY BARRIER. And since this is so, so important, I must repeat a statement I've made earlier. I hope you realize that *the flat Rs 20 brokerage was not an entry barrier*. Neither was the zero brokerage. In general, a discount can never be an entry barrier, simply because it is so easy to copy.

Why?

Well, let's assume your costs are similar to those of your large competitors. Now, if you offer a lower price than them, you are either making a loss, or at best, you are knocking out most of your profitability. And neither of these can be sustained for too long. In the meantime, what does the bigger guy do? Please remember, he will not sit back and happily watch you eat into his market share and take away his customers. He can always reduce his price for some time, so as to match or even beat your price. And since he is a bigger guy, he can sustain losses for a longer period than you. Therefore, he lowers his prices and then quietly waits for you to die. Once you are killed, he raises his prices again. And lives happily ever after!

Simple, isn't it? So lower pricing by itself is not an entry barrier. But what *can* be an effective entry barrier is your cost structure. If your costs are significantly lower than those of your competitors, you can easily charge lower prices than them and *still be profitable. That* cannot be copied in a hurry. And that's a true entry barrier.

That's exactly what Zerodha has done. You've seen it all, haven't you? First of all, they have used FOSS, which means that their software costs are lower than those of their competitors. Plus, they do not need to go to a software vendor to make enhancements to the platform, since they do it in-house. Secondly, they do not run a large, bureaucratic organization, and instead maintain small, highly focused teams, keeping their HR costs manageable. And even within these teams, the fact that they look after their employees means that people do not leave them. They stay on, hopefully until retirement.

As Nithin has always said, it is far better to hang on to people, rather than losing them and having to replace them. In other words, low recruitment as well as training costs.

Finally, please remember, these guys spend nothing on marketing. They believe in word-of-mouth. They keep their customers happy, and these customers stay on and bring in more customers through word of mouth. And of course, the earthquake caused by their flat brokerage fee and later on their zero brokerage did no harm to their brand. Along with the associated press coverage, with various media channels falling over each other to talk about them.

All in all, they have always maintained a low-cost operation, and have therefore remained profitable, in spite of the flat Rs 20 brokerage. And this lower cost structure is one of their major entry barriers.

However, that's not the only one. Remember, Nithin had mentioned that price was only a temporary reason for customers to come to them? Ultimately, it was the product. And here, they have ensured that their platform is easy to use and fast—helped by the fact that they develop their own software using FOSS. And of course, they have always been completely transparent.

Now, I've already told you that entry barriers are never permanent. They might give you a head start over competition, but sooner or later, competition can copy what you have thought of. And in fact, build something that you have *not* thought of. That's why businesses need to keep enhancing their entry barrier all the time to ensure that they stay ahead of competitors. In this connection, one of the things that has worked very well for Zerodha is the Kite Connect interface. Because they have been able to get other businesses, such as smallcase and Streak, to build their offerings on top of their Kite platform using Kite Connect. In other words, the expansion of the Zerodha product line has not been limited to what their own team can do. They have partners who have brought in additional products.

What about SCALABILITY, or the ability to grow rapidly within their chosen market? That should be obvious, isn't it? This is a pure Internet business. No manual involvement, and no physical infrastructure such as buildings, plant and machinery. And therefore, it is highly scalable!

I've already said enough about the TEAM. About the wonderful founder Nithin, the equally wonderful CTO, Kailash, and the close-knit, nimble, high-performance team they have built. More like a family than an office. And of course, the icing on the cake: no mass lay-offs. Ever. People join, they get responsibilities and they grow. And all of them get wonderful ESOPs. That's the culture Nithin has built. And that's why people *join* Zerodha; they *don't leave*.

Finally, the TRACTION. Operating revenues of Rs 6875 in the financial year 2022–23: a growth of 38 per cent over the previous financial year, with 5–7 million online trades per day. The highest in the whole world!

Can you imagine a more perfect PERSISTENT business?

And of course, I'm delighted, because both the businesses I've discussed so far follow my PERSISTENT model!

The PERFECT Attitude

Aha! My favourite section.

Like all successful founders, Nithin has always been strongly CUSTOMER ORIENTED. 'Customer First. Give customers products they like. And they will return, bringing more customers with them.' That has always been his philosophy. Now since both the brothers had been traders for several years, they were aware of the pain points faced by their potential customers: namely high brokerage fees, speed, complexity and lack of transparency. And those were the pain points they focused on when they built Zerodha. Not only that, even before starting off, Nithin was part of several trading communities, which is where he kept getting inputs from traders on the problems they were facing.

You've already seen that he still communicates with his customers—through Zerodha's TradingQnA. And that tells you something more about his attitude. His willingness to do

EVERYTHING. Where most founders would delegate this customer interaction to people down the line, or perhaps conduct customer surveys, Nithin is very clear. He connects directly with his customers. No delegation, please.

So Nithin has always listened to the voice of the customer. Equally important, he has responded to this voice, which is how the Zerodha platform is low-cost (remember the flat fee of Rs 20?), transparent and easy to use. And scalable. Even with the massive volumes they have reached today, the response time on their platform remains the fastest. And this is not just something I got from Nithin. It's something I confirmed with trader friends who are using Zerodha—and are happy to continue using it.

But perhaps the best example of Nithin's customer orientation is 'Nudge'. 'We don't want you to lose money, so if you are following bad practices such as trading in penny stocks, we'll quietly nudge you. Even though it means we lose brokerage in the process.' Outstanding consumer focus and strongly ETHICAL thinking, isn't it? And with this one step, you can imagine the level of TRUST Nithin has built with his customers.

Then, of course, there is complete transparency. And the fact that Zerodha does not recommend specific stocks, in order to avoid vested interests. Once again, extremely ETHICAL. I could go on and on, but I'm sure you get the message. This is how Nithin has been building TRUST in the minds of his customers.

And what about TRUST in the minds of his team? Obvious, isn't it? A close-knit team; no mass lay-offs ever; everyone gets responsibility and grows and everyone gets ESOPs. How can the team *not* have trust in Nithin?

Then there is RESPONSIBILITY—giving credit for success to others. I just need to repeat some facts that I've already shared earlier: Nithin credits the launch of Zerodha to his brother Nikhil, who he believes is a far better trader. And then he credits the entire tech to Kailash. And of course, Varsity to Karthik. And a lot of successes to luck. In fact, according to Bhuvanesh, the entire core team is very open about their own capabilities. If something goes right, they attribute it to luck. If it doesn't, they move on. 'Luck', according to Bhuvanesh, is one of the most common terms heard in the corridors of Zerodha. And isn't that terrific humility?

What does he credit himself with? Nothing really. As Bhuvanesh keeps repeating, Nithin is always in the background, like an elder brother. 'All successes are successes of the team.' That, my friend, is the humility of this phenomenally successful founder!

And finally, PERSEVERING. Again, I don't really need to talk about this. Ever since they launched the business, Nithin has been saying that in the world of finance, the credibility of the service provider is super, super important. After all, why would anyone give up stable platforms such as HDFC Securities or ICICI Direct or Motilal Oswal Financial Services, and switch to an upstart like Zerodha? And he was dead right. It took almost ten years for this credibility to build up. But he did not give up. He focused on the product and on keeping the customer happy. Initially, the customers came in drips and dribbles. Gradually, ever so gradually, the trickle turned into a flood. And ultimately, Zerodha became the biggest broker in the world in terms of volume of transactions. PERSEVERANCE at its best.

And that, my friend, is Nithin's PERFECT Attitude!

The Profitable Business

Finally, I must talk about the one thing that has made Zerodha an earnicorn. And I simply must repeat Nithin's statement—my favourite: *'We didn't 'take' money so we had to 'make' money'*. What an outstanding approach, in an era when all founders and their aunts were simply falling over each other to maximize their valuation, and take in more and more investor money! And that was the starting point: the strong belief of the founder, Nithin Kamath, that the business had to be profitable.

By the way, please don't get me wrong. I don't mean 'profits at any cost'. No sir, Nithin has always believed in his 'customers first' policy. 'Keep them happy and they'll keep coming back. And in the process, we'll make profits.'

Now, ultimately, profitability boils down to one simple equation: Revenues need to be higher than costs. And if you've been following this story, you might have noticed something really fascinating:

Zerodha has taken several decisions, where cost reduction was not the primary purpose. But even these have led to lower costs!

For instance, their unwavering focus on the customer ensured that they saved on marketing costs. Their policy of recruiting people with the right culture and attitude, irrespective of their degrees, led to lower manpower costs (in addition to a more productive and stable team). And then of course, Nithin's firm belief in looking after his people—giving everyone ESOPs, giving them responsibility and letting them make mistakes—meant that people stayed on. Which, in turn, meant lower recruitment and training costs.

Of course, let's not forget the whole focus on the use of FOSS. FOSS was used because it reduced the company's dependence on external software vendors and therefore made it possible to quickly respond to new requirements. But the other benefit was lower development costs.

Dear reader, when I dived into the Zerodha story, this was perhaps my biggest learning: You do not need to chase profits. If you look after the customer and your people, profits will follow.

That's the principle of good karma. That's what Nithin has always believed in and practised.

And that is how he has built such a phenomenally successful and respected organization.

A wonderful, wonderful **earnicorn**.

Agreed?

Section IV

Dream11

20

Dream11: The Early Years

This is the story of a young man named Harsh Jain. Born into a highly successful Mumbai-based business family, Harsh moved to England in 2001 to finish his schooling. Well, he did finish his schooling as planned. But he also did something else. You see, Harsh was an avid sportsman right through his school days, both in Mumbai as well as in England. His favourite sport was football and his favourite team was Manchester United. While in England, he was introduced to the fascinating world of fantasy sports or more specifically, fantasy football. I don't quite know how much time he spent on his studies and how much on fantasy football, but by the time he finished his schooling and returned to India, he was utterly and completely hooked. Not to studies—come on—but to fantasy sports.

What Is Fantasy Sports?

Now before I proceed further, I need to explain the concept of fantasy sports. Of course, if you are a normal young man or woman, you would know a lot more about it than I do. Therefore you can comfortably skip this section. But just in case you've been living with your nose in your books, removing it occasionally only to breathe and eat, I need to explain the concept to you. In any case, if you are from an older generation, well, I need to explain it to you anyway.

And I'll take the example of football, because that's what Harsh was infatuated with. So here goes . . .

Let's assume there is a football match scheduled between Manchester United and Liverpool, two top-notch football teams in England. Now, you are interested in the match, but all you can do is sit in your living room and watch it on TV. With the mandatory beer in one hand (or Coke, if you're not old enough and are also law-abiding) and a bag of popcorn in the other. That's it. You are not involved in any way. Sad, isn't it?

But that's where fantasy football comes in. You *can* be involved. How?

Well, as you know, each team would have, say, twenty players. From these players, eleven would ultimately be selected. These eleven would include one goalkeeper, a few defenders, a few half-backs and a few forwards. Making it a total of eleven players stepping onto the field. And the rest are potentially substitutes. In other words, you have forty players in all, across both teams.

This is where fantasy football comes in. Before the match starts, you—yes, you—can select a team of eleven players from these forty. *So you become a selector.* Once again, you'll have a goalkeeper, a few defenders and so on. And then of course, you need to choose a captain and a vice captain. And here's the key. This team, my friend, is neither Manchester United nor Liverpool. *This is your team.*

Now, the actual match starts. Let's say one of the forwards in your team scores a goal. Well, you get points for the goal. And if he's the captain of your team, that's wonderful, because you then get even more points. Or your goalkeeper saves a goal, in which case you get points once again.

Ah, I almost forgot: You're not the only one playing. Just as you've made your team, there are thousands of other fans out there who have made theirs. And all these teams are competing with each other for points. So in the end, whether it's Manchester United that wins or Liverpool, it doesn't really matter. Because you—yes, you—can win. And of course, there's prize money as well.

My friend, can you see how the game has suddenly come alive for you? It's no longer just two distant teams playing in a stadium far, far away. It's your team playing against the teams selected by lakhs of other fans worldwide. Suddenly, there is extra fizz in your beer, and your popcorn becomes so much crunchier. As you cheer yourself hoarse and your heart pumps furiously, you are cheering for *your team*. And when your centre forward, David Beckham, scores a goal, he's not just scoring it for Manchester United. He's scoring it for your team—and, of course, you go over the moon in delight.

That, dear reader, is fantasy football. Which is just one example of fantasy sports. And now, I'm sure you can imagine how young Harsh got hooked.

We'll Launch Fantasy Sports in India

Now to get back to our story. After finishing school, Harsh studied electrical engineering at the University of Pennsylvania, one of the topmost universities in the world. But the fantasy sports bug never left him, and he continued playing fantasy football with his friends while attending university. He returned to India in 2007, and that's when our country was hit by a tsunami. In the form of the IPL, or the Indian Premier League. Young Harsh was fascinated. He realized that in India, it wasn't fantasy football but fantasy cricket, which could be the rage. That's when the young man decided that he wanted to play fantasy cricket. So he looked around for possible options where he could play with his friends. After all, given the fan following the sport of cricket enjoyed in India, there simply *had to be* an option for fantasy cricket.

And how many did he find?

None.

That's right. There were none. Yes, there used to be an online fantasy cricket platform some time ago. But when Harsh looked for it on the Internet, he couldn't find it. It had closed down, you see.

As you can imagine, young Harsh was astounded. A cricket-crazy country of well over a hundred crore people? Where Sachin Tendulkar, Dhoni, Virat Kohli and the like were demigods? Where Mahendra Singh Dhoni was raining sixes into the stands, and you could build up points simply because you had selected him in your team? How could the country *not* have its share of fantasy cricket?

Let's hear it from Harsh himself:

India is a cricket-crazy country—that's beyond all doubt. And for years, people have been following cricket passively, starting with the radio in the 1960s, TV in the 1980s, and ultimately the Internet in the 1990s. Everyone has an opinion on cricket, and you can see that in animated discussions at paan-beedi shops, or haircutting saloons, or even bars over the inevitable single malts. Where people are willing to wage war with their friends over whether Virat Kohli should come in at number 3 or 4. That's how involved everyone is.

And fantasy cricket allows all these people to put their opinions into action. They can select their team. They can decide the batting order. Rather than simply watching matches on TV, they can actually get involved. It's active involvement, rather than passive involvement. Because each person now becomes a selector!

And this is perhaps his most interesting statement:

Fantasy sports is like popcorn in a movie—it enhances the experience.

Harsh could not believe that there was no fantasy cricket in India. Which is when he started thinking. And then he thought some more. And more. And gradually, the businessman's son took over from the avid sports fan. Playing fantasy cricket was not enough. Yes, he did want to play. But he wanted to do more. He wanted to grab the phenomenal opportunity that was simply staring him in the face. Yes sir, he wanted to launch his own brand of fantasy cricket. He spoke to his friends and they were kicked with the idea. One of them, Bhavit Sheth, actually joined him. And at the ripe old age of twenty-two, our two friends decided to launch their own online fantasy sports platform called **Dream11**.

And the rest, as they say, is history.

But It Wasn't Easy

Now, I've given you a peek into Harsh's family background. I've said that he came from a highly successful Marwari business family. And as you are undoubtedly aware, as a group, Marwaris are perhaps the most successful businessmen in India. Look at the Birlas, the Bajajs, the Dalmias, the Goenkas, the Singhanias . . . I could go on and on, but I'm sure you get the message. I've already told you that Harsh's father was a highly successful businessman. So when Harsh decided to start his own venture, he had just the right background. Unlike the other founders we've met in this book so far, namely Sanjeev Bikhchandani, Hitesh Oberoi and Nithin Kamath, all of whom came from a service-class background. Therefore, I'm sure you thought life for Harsh, the founder, was all hunky-dory. A bed of roses, if you get what I mean.

Right?

Absolutely wrong, my friend. It doesn't matter what your background is. Life for an entrepreneur is never a bed of roses. You see, first of all, coming from a highly successful business family, Harsh faced the weight of expectations. His father was successful, so he was expected to be successful as well. There was simply no option. Whether it was his family, neighbours or friends, everyone was clear. Harsh simply had to be a success at business. Fast.

Now you are aware that Internet businesses don't operate that way. There is a lot of experimentation, lots of pivoting and lots of failure. And hopefully, someday, things work out (remember the experimentation and failures Sanjeev and Hitesh went through before Naukri actually worked out?). But for Harsh, this was simply not an option. He had to succeed. Period. His relatives were expecting it. Family friends were expecting it. The neighbours were expecting it. And that led to one word: pressure!

But that wasn't all. In such families, it's almost a given that sons would join their father's business. There is simply no debate; it's almost preordained. 'You want to do something around the Internet? Well, play around if you wish, but ultimately, we know what you'll do. You'll join Papa's business.' And that's the message that came through loud and clear to young Harsh. 'When are you joining your father's business?' 'You mean you haven't joined it yet?' And snide remarks, such as, 'Ah, so you are having fun with Internet-based sports. But ultimately, we know you'll join Papa.' And so on . . .

So there was the pressure of expectations, as well as the pressure of no one taking Harsh seriously. His dream of starting an Internet-based fantasy sports company was fine, as long as it was a hobby. 'But *beta* (son), do join your father's business fast.'

However, Harsh was a determined young man (he still is). And one fine day, he went to his father. To ask for a miserable Rs 2 crore to fund his 'hobby'. Fortunately, his father was broad-minded and realized that his son had a strong desire to do something on his own. So he gave him the Rs 2 crore. Armed with this money, Harsh and Bhavit went on a spending spree. They spent on development, marketing and prize money. And before I forget, they spent on people—a total of forty of them.

But that wasn't all. At this stage, I must tell you something about the thinking of these two young founders. You see, they wanted to launch fantasy cricket in the form of Dream11. That much you already know. But that was not the only thing. Their vision was far, far bigger than just Dream11. They wanted to impact sport in India in general through technology, whether it was cricket, football, hockey or just about anything else. They wanted to create a sports tech company, of which Dream11 was a part.

And that's why the founders decided to launch several things at the same time. They had cricket news, cricket blogs, polls related to cricket and even physical cricket games. Everything under the larger umbrella of the **Dream Sports** company, of which Dream11 would be a part. Along with significant marketing and PR spends. After all, they needed to get lots of users on board, didn't they? And all this was supported by the Rs 2 crore that Harsh had taken from his father. They were so excited, you see?

And what do you think the result was?

Ha ha! Within two weeks of getting the Rs 2 crore, they were down to just a lakh and a half. Yes, believe it or not, they had only one and a half lakh rupees in the bank! And that's when the harsh truth hit the two founders: They did not really understand how to start and run a business. And this in spite of the fact that Harsh came from a successful business family. The two friends realized that they needed more money. In fact, they needed Rs 10 crore and not just Rs 2 crore. So Harsh went back to his father and asked for an additional Rs 8 crore.

As you can imagine, his father threw a fit. 'Rs 8 crore more? Of course I won't give you that kind of money.' And you should hear out Harsh on what happened next:

> My father told me that I had no respect for money, and he was dead right. He told me that I didn't value money, which was equally right. I was a spoilt brat, you see?
>
> Fortunately, that's when the Marwari business family swung into action. Or rather, the Marwari mother—my mother. *'De do na. Ek hi toh beta hai.'* (Why don't you give him the money? After all, we have only one son.) And then there was this family drama, at the end of which my father relented and gave me the money.
>
> I think my father saw this as an opportunity. In the best case, I would make something out of the money he had given me. And in the worst case, even if I were to lose all that money, at least I would learn how hard it was to make money.

Dear reader, there's something I want you to notice over here. Yes, the money was blown up. But Harsh did not blame the environment or the Internet or the fact that companies refused to pay to advertise on his wonderful platform. No, he accepted responsibility for this failure. He realized that he didn't know enough and that he definitely did not know how to manage money. And if you want to be successful, that is one of the first things you need to realize. Accept your mistakes, realize your shortcomings and work on them!

Anyhow, Harsh got the money. Or rather, Dream Sports got the money. But there was a lot more that they got. As I've mentioned, his father was a highly successful businessman and investor. And he asked all the right questions. 'What's your business plan?' 'Show me your projections.' 'What are your likely cash flows?' Questions that any investor would ask.

And what do you think the answers were?

Poor.

That's right. In Harsh's own words, their projections were poor. He admits that they didn't really understand business. They didn't understand finance. They didn't even understand simple things like debit and credit (dear reader, I assume you understand those terms). That's when his father took the young founders to the gaming gurus of those days. To get their opinion on the concept. And their opinion was unanimous. 'It's a terrible idea. The concept of fantasy sports is non-existent in India. No one is aware of it. All attempts to create a business around this have flopped. Why do you want to go the same way?'

Based on this unequivocally negative advice, you would imagine that Harsh would have given up. But then you don't know Harsh. As you have guessed by now, he was extremely passionate about the idea. It was a roaring success in the western world, and he was determined to make it a success in India. 'Terrible idea? No issues. I'll make it work.'

And that was that. Within a year—2008, to be precise—Harsh and Bhavit launched their fantasy cricket platform, Dream11. This was a version where each contest would continue for the entire cricket season in India (which, as you are aware, lasts right through the year except the hot summer months). And it was free to use: users paid nothing to play. The assumption was that advertisers would drool over the huge number of users and flood the platform with paid ads. After all, with cricket almost being a religion in the country, surely companies would pay to put up their ads on such a platform. This is the way it had worked in the West, so there was no reason why it wouldn't work in India.

And of course, you thought it would be a grand success, didn't you?

No, it wasn't. It flopped.

Why?

Well, perhaps a full season was too long. As you are aware, youngsters are impatient people. They need instant gratification. 'We need to wait for a full season? No way.'

So the founders modified their offering and launched it again.

It flopped again.

And again.

And again . . .

And while companies were happy to advertise on Dream11, they refused to pay. Yes, they were willing to test out the platform as long as it was free. 'Show us the numbers first,' they would say. So users were not asked to pay, and advertisers were not willing to pay. Where would the money come from?

By the way, you can now begin to understand the weight of expectations on young Harsh's shoulders. A scion of a highly successful business family, who kept launching new versions of his business and kept failing. No, that was simply not acceptable. And the clamour grew louder and louder, 'When are you joining Papa's business?'

The two young men kept pivoting and kept failing. But they didn't give up. They were highly passionate about what they were doing, and they were clear that one day the business would work out. It was just a question of finding the right model.

And there was another issue. Two years after raising the Rs 10 crore, they had blown up nearly all of it. And what did they have to show for it? A total revenue of just about Rs 4–5 lakh. That's it! Rs 4–5 lakh in the entire two years, on an investment of Rs 10 crore.

That's when the two young men went into a huddle. They needed more money—that was clear. They couldn't possibly continue without more funding. At the same time, there was no way they could go back to Harsh's father. Even the Marwari mother would not have been able to bail out her son this time. But they needed the money, otherwise they would be forced to shut down their baby.

So what did they do? Well, they did two important things. First of all, they decided to focus entirely on fantasy cricket. Everything else that they had initiated—the cricket news, the blogs, the forum— was shut down. Because these were gobbling up money, which they didn't have. By the way, doesn't this sound uncannily like the decision Sanjeev and Hitesh took at Info Edge in 2000, where they shut down Bachao.com, sold off Jeevansathi and focused on just the Naukri business? Doesn't it? Successful founders do similar things right, don't they?

The other thing they did was to launch Red Digital Solutions.

Red Digital Solutions: The Social Media Marketing Company

It was in 2010, more than two years after our young founders had got money from Harsh's father, that they launched Red Digital Solutions. A digital marketing agency focused on social media marketing. Why was it named 'Red'? I really don't know. Perhaps because it was the colour of the Manchester United jersey. In any case, you are welcome to ask Harsh when you meet him. However, to get back to our story, was the launch of this agency a long-term strategy? Of course not. They simply needed to generate money from somewhere. Not to blow up on discos or fancy cars. No, sir, this money would be pumped into their passion—Dream11. Which stubbornly refused to generate money on its own.

Now, I must tell you something truly endearing about these founders. You see, in today's world, when a start-up runs out of money, what's the first thing they do? Lay off people, isn't it? Isn't that the norm?

But that wasn't the norm for Harsh and Bhavit. Their norm was to look after their people. So guess what they did? When they started Red Digital Solutions, they had a team of forty people in Dream11. But Dream11 wasn't making money. So they retained just six people in Dream11 and transferred everyone else to Red Digital. No one was laid off.

And that's super important, so let me repeat it:

No one was laid off.

Great gesture, wasn't it? What a wonderful way to build a close-knit team. And to get everyone to feel they belonged.

Now, at this stage, Bhavit went to the USA to pursue his MBA. Of course, Harsh stayed back; after all, they needed at least one founder to be around. Interestingly, they *did* make money from Red Digital. In fact, within a couple of years, they became one of the largest social media marketing agencies in India, with marquee clients such as Mumbai Indians, Lufthansa, Monginis, Pepsi and Godrej, among others. And the money they earned from Red Digital was promptly ploughed back into Dream11. So they were able to fund their dream.

But there's something more. Harsh personally made a lot of sales calls to potential clients. In the process, he learnt how to sell. From his beginnings as a spoilt brat (his own words, definitely not mine), he was beginning to understand the complexities of doing business.

Anyhow, given that Red Digital was doing well and making money, and Dream11 was definitely not, what would any sane person have done? Focus on the successful business, of course. But that's not what Harsh and Bhavit did. No sir, they had no real interest in the digital marketing business. That was simply a way to generate money, which would then be used to fund their passion, which was clearly Dream11. So, even though the digital marketing agency was making money, they sold it. As you can imagine, whatever money they got from the sale was pumped back into Dream11.

And yes, since you asked, Harsh did not have to go back to his father for money again!

Dear reader, I want you to notice two very important things. First of all, our young founders were extremely passionate about what they were doing and they pursued it with single-minded focus. They were persistent. Even when it wasn't making money. Secondly, when they needed money to fund it, they started something in parallel, which would get them welcome cash. And that's what many founders do. When their core business is not making cash, they take up something else in parallel to fund the core business. Temporarily, of course.

Now, for some good news. After all those pivots and many years of trying out multiple options, finally in 2012, our young founders hit upon the right model. This was not based on paid ads. It was a freemium model, where you could play for free or you could play for money. And they had moved from the full season to 'per match' contests. This was instant gratification, because now participants did not need to wait for a full season to figure out whether or not they had won. Our founders realized that Indian consumers wanted small-size tickets. In Harsh's own words:

> *The Indian consumer doesn't want a shampoo bottle, he or she wants a sachet.*

And what do you think users did? Well, they lapped it up. And of course, word of mouth did the rest, with friends bringing in more friends to play on the platform. By the way, this version has continued until the present day.

Dear reader, please notice that it took more than four years of planning, experimentation, tinkering, pivoting—whatever you want to call it—before they hit upon the right model! Great businesses are not built in a day, you see? You need to persevere, persevere and then persevere some more. Remember the seven years of struggle before Sanjeev Bikhchandani hit upon the right model?

Interestingly, now that they had figured out the right model for Dream11, our young founders decided to bring back all their other offerings: the cricket news, the forum, the blogs etc., etc. Yes, my friend, the Dream Sports group, starting with its flagship Dream11, was well and truly on its way.

Finally, I must share something interesting that Harsh said:

> We are trying to promote sports engagement. Take, for instance, the IPL. Now if Chennai Super Kings are playing against Mumbai Indians and they need 100 runs to win with one wicket in hand and there is only one over left, what will the result be? Obviously, Mumbai Indians will win. And therefore, most cricket fans would simply switch off the TV. Match over. But the fantasy sports fan will continue till the end—*because the bowler who gets the last wicket will decide whether this fan wins or loses.* And that's how we push up sports engagement dramatically.

Dear reader, I hope you can now understand what these two young men were doing?

And on that exciting note, let's end this chapter.

21

The Funding

So after nearly five long years, Harsh and Bhavit had finally cracked the problem. They had figured out the right model for Dream11. And now, of course, they needed to grow rapidly.

Which meant?

Funding, of course. This was one business where bootstrapping would perhaps not have worked. And we need to understand why. First of all, remember, fantasy sports was unheard of in India. The founders would need to market not only the brand but the concept as well. Let me explain this with an analogy: Suppose you were manufacturing jam. Now, in a country where people were already aware of what jam was, you would only need to promote your brand of jam. But if you were in a country where jam was unheard of, well, you would need to promote the concept as well—educate people, tell them how it was to be spread on toast at breakfast time, etc. And that would take time—lots of time and lots of marketing money.

Now, if you were to replace jam with fantasy sports, you can understand the problem. Our young founders *needed to promote the concept of fantasy sports in addition to their own brand*—which would take lot of time as well as money. But there was more. Since this was gaming with real money, the founders would need to give out prize money. And obviously, to build up interest and grow, the prize money pool would need to be large, with several prizes and perhaps some big ones as well. Otherwise, players would not be interested. Can you imagine the following ad: 'Play Fantasy Cricket, put in Rs 20 and you can win a massive first prize of Rs 5?' Doesn't make sense, does it? No one would be interested. The company would need high-value prizes.

But this was a chicken-and-egg situation. Initially, they had very few paying customers, so they couldn't really take out much prize money from this source. And therefore, they needed money from somewhere else. In a nutshell, they needed funding.

But It Wasn't Easy to Get Funding

So our young friends started approaching Indian investors in 2012. And given the size and attractiveness of the opportunity, they were sure investors would bite. They simply had to.

But did they?

No.

Why? Well, this is what they said: 'No one is aware of fantasy sports in India. So you won't get investors from here. It's popular in the West; that's where you'll get investors.'

Now, by sheer coincidence, Harsh had got admission to the highly reputed Columbia Business School to do his MBA. And while he was there, he realized that he could pitch to VCs in the USA. And yes, the VCs liked the concept. But guess what they said? Their response was, 'Great idea. But if this is a fantasy sports platform for India, you should pitch to Indian VCs. That's where you'll get your funding.'

You can imagine how frustrated Harsh was at this stage. He simply couldn't figure out this game of ping pong, where Indian investors were asking him to pitch to US investors and US investors were asking him to go back and pitch to Indian investors. He recalls those days, when he must have met more than fifty investors over perhaps a hundred and fifty meetings. And this frustrating period lasted for over two years. Harsh recalls those tough days:

The investors didn't even say no. They said, 'We'll get back to you.'
And then they maintained a stony silence. Which was worse than
an outright no. Because we had no idea why they were not willing
to invest. We must have got over a hundred such rejections, and
believe me, it was extremely depressing. And of course, the snide
remarks about 'joining your Papa's business' continued. Which
only made things worse.

However, one thing that kept me going during those days,
was the support I got from my family—my wife, Rachna and
my parents. When you come home with rejection after rejection,
believe me, you need that support.

And that's where Harsh learnt one of his key lessons as an
entrepreneur: When an investor says anything other than 'yes', it is
actually a 'no'. 'We'll think about it.' Or, 'Good idea, but let's wait
for a bit.' These are all polite (and frustrating) ways of saying 'no'.

However, in this era of doom and gloom, there were two investors
who finally mustered up the courage to invest in the business. Vani
Kola of Kalaari Capital and Shashin Shah of Think Investments.
This was in 2014, by which time Dream11 had grown to three lakh
registered users. It's interesting to hear Vani Kola on why she put up
the money:[*]

What I saw in Harsh was a founder who was very mature for his
age. Unlike most entrepreneurs who paint a rosy picture, he was
very comfortable openly talking about the risks involved in his
business. Most entrepreneurs don't talk about the risks, let alone a
game plan to deal with them.

[*] Naini Thaker, 'Dream11 turned fantasy (gaming) into reality. Now it's eyeing a
diversified sports tech future', *Forbes India*, 8 June 2022, https://www.forbesindia.
com/article/sports-tech-special/dream11-turned-fantasy-(gaming)-into-reality-
now-its-eyeing-a-diversified-sports-tech-future/77065/1.

So the company got its first investment from these two investors. And then, of course, there was no looking back.

Today, when Harsh looks back on those days, he is able to laugh about them. Let's hear him out—and please notice the sense of humour:

> I fell in love with my future wife, Rachna, in school. In Class 8, believe it or not. And I kept chasing her, but she kept saying no. Finally she relented, and we got married. In a way, Rachna prepared me for all the rejections I got from VCs. I learnt that as long as you keep on at it long enough, the other person will finally say 'yes'.

By the way, Harsh made this profound statement when he was addressing an audience of a thousand people at the well-known TechSparks conference in Mumbai. Therefore, it's public knowledge. I am not sharing family secrets 😊.

And here's another gem from him:

> When you hear a 'no' a hundred times, you also learn more about your business each time. I remember, in one of our early meetings, an investor asked us, 'What's your TAM (total addressable market)?' We had no idea what this meant, and our response was, 'Who's she?'

Funding Gives You More than Just Money

Dear reader, I'm sure you thought that the predominant benefit of getting funding was the money itself. And the fact that these young men finally had a runway where they did not have to think about money all the time. But when I met Harsh, I realized that it was a lot, lot more. Harsh believes that a company that is only funded by the family of the founder has very low credibility. Because no outsider has vouched for it so far. But once an outsider invests, and that too, a highly respected outsider such as Vani Kola, the world sits up and takes notice. 'Aha. If a VC thought it was worthwhile investing in the company, there must be something in it.'

And this changes the attitude of anyone who deals with the company. For instance, potential job applicants suddenly start evaluating you seriously.

And there is still more. External investors ask a lot of tough questions before parting with their hard-earned money. But once they make the decision to invest in you, they help you. This is what Harsh had to say on the subject:

> As young founders, we really didn't understand business. We wanted help. Help in the area of the product, strategy, design, marketing, everything. We wanted someone to advise us and mentor us. And I must say that our investors were truly hands-on. They didn't just put in the money and walk out. No, they spent time with us and guided us—particularly Vani. And for this, we will always be grateful.

Of course, once the young men got their funding, there was no looking back. Over time, more and more investors got interested and put in their hard-earned money into the company. At the time of writing this book, they have raised over eight rounds in all, the latest round being in 2021. And from reputed VCs such as Tiger Global, DST Capital and Tencent. And yes, in a further confidence booster, Kalaari Capital and Think Investments invested in the company once again!

And the valuation?

Well, it was $8 billion at last count. A unicorn, if ever there was one.

But here's the interesting part: Harsh was not really interested in becoming a unicorn. He wasn't chasing valuations. He was focusing on building a lifelong business. One that would ultimately be profitable.

Makes sense, doesn't it?

The Focus Was Always on Profitability

So the Dream Sports group got several rounds of funding. And now I can guess what you are thinking: Like so many other Internet-based start-ups, the founders focused on growth at any cost. 'Let's keep growing and making hefty losses. We'll make it up through more and more funding.'

Ha ha, my friend, think again. Remember, Harsh came from a highly successful Marwari business family. And in such families, the key is 'profit'. Not exotic figures such as GMV, or LTV or CAC. Not growth at any cost. The key figure remains 'profit'. Or, as Harsh himself puts it, *dhandha*. A Marwari businessman cannot dream of growing revenues while at the same time growing losses as well. It's just not done, you see? What would the family say?

As you can imagine, Harsh had imbibed these ideas, perhaps from the time he was a toddler. And that's why he has always been strongly focused on profitability. He has never believed in chasing valuation for the sake of valuation. Yes, as I've already mentioned, in the initial years there was a problem, because he was trying to introduce a concept that was totally alien to India. Which meant a lot of time, a lot of patience, and a lot of marketing spend. And of course, he needed external funds to generate prize money for his users. But even during those years, he was extremely cost-conscious. And so was his co-founder, Bhavit. From day one, they ran a frugal business.

According to Harsh:

It's very easy to get carried away by the valuation game. Your aim cannot be to get higher valuations and exit. In any case, if the founder wants to exit, what happens to the investors? No, you should *definitely not* focus on building a unicorn. You must build a lifelong business. A profitable business. What we call *dhandha* in our Marwari business families. That was our aim. And that's exactly what we did.

Incidentally, there is one thing I learnt from Harsh (among many others, of course): his fanatical belief in 'retention' as against 'acquisition' of customers—or users, as the company prefers to call them. Obviously, getting new users is important for any business to grow, but retaining existing users is even more important. After all, getting a new user requires a lot of marketing spend. But retaining existing users requires no marketing spend. Just keeping existing users happy, which you would need to do anyway, even for new users.

And there is more. What do happy users do? They talk to their friends. They spread positive word-of-mouth. And bring in more users. It's a cycle, you see. Keep your existing users happy, and you'll keep getting newer and newer users. By the way, doesn't this sound very much like Nithin Kamath of Zerodha?

And it's not just users. The retention vs acquisition strategy applies to team members as well. New people need a lot of time, effort and money to recruit. They need to be trained. And of course, they might leave—for whatever reason. But existing people simply need to be kept happy and motivated and given an opportunity to grow. And they'll keep contributing to the company. Makes sense, doesn't it? Therefore, Harsh focused on retaining team members as well as customers.

And now, my friend, you can figure out one major reason why Dream Sports has moved towards profitability. Because they focused on retaining existing users and team members. A strategy that cost them far, far less than going all out to grab new users and new team members.

Yes, it took time—ten years, in fact—but since then, they have been a solidly profitable business.

22

Game of Skill or Game of Chance?

Dear reader, in the previous chapter, I told you that Dream11 found it tough to raise funds. Until of course, Vani Kola and Shashin Shah took the plunge. But just consider this: Here was a business that had huge potential in our cricket-crazy country. They had effectively no competition. And it was an Internet-based business, which made it highly scalable. So why weren't investors interested?

Actually, while the business was undoubtedly attractive for multiple reasons, investors stayed away because they were not sure what the government's attitude towards the business would be. You see, investors don't like uncertainty. They consider it too 'uncertain'. Too much of a risk. And in this case, they were reluctant to invest in a company that could face legal or regulatory challenges.

What challenges? Well, let's start with a basic question which has plagued Dream11 for years: Is it offering users a game of skill or a game of pure chance? You see, betting and gambling have always been a no-no in India. Online gambling is an even bigger no-no. And Dream11 was dealing in money. Real money, not stupid 'Monopoly' money. Where the user could win, but he could also lose. So wasn't it an avatar of online gambling? And therefore had to be banned by the government? Or at best, wasn't it operating in a grey area?

All over the world, fantasy sports have been accepted as games of skill and not chance, but not so in India.

Fortunately, this grey area has been resolved several times over, and the Dream11 model has been accepted as a game of skill. Let's understand why.

You see, when you play fantasy cricket on Dream11, you are not betting on one event, such as Virat Kohli scoring a century, or Bumrah taking a wicket in his third over. That, my friend, would be betting. On Dream11, you are a selector. And if your team beats the other guy's team, you win.

And this is the key: When you select your team, it's not just a random group of cricketers. You first need to look at the pitch where the match will be played. For instance, the Mohali stadium, near Chandigarh, is notorious for helping fast bowlers. Whereas the M.A. Chidambaram stadium in Chennai helps spinners and not fast bowlers. If you didn't know this, and picked only fast bowlers for a Chennai match or spinners for a match at Mohali, the chances of your team winning would go down, wouldn't they? And there's more: As the cricket season goes on, pitches tend to get slower and slower, and therefore help spinners more and more. In other words, the bowlers you choose should also depend on whether you are at the beginning of the season or at the fag end of it. To take another example, most pitches in England help fast bowlers swing the ball, whereas those in Australia are hard and bouncy, but with very low swing. And this is the key: One fast bowler might be great at swinging the ball, but poor at bowling on hard, bouncy pitches. So would you pick such a bowler for a match that is being played in Australia?

And this is the skill that you, as a Dream11 selector, need to have: the skill where you understand the nature of the pitch, and therefore pick the appropriate bowlers.

But there's a lot more. You would also need to look at current form. You may have a wonderful batsman that you can select in your team, but what if he's badly out of form? Or what if it's a spinning pitch and he's currently low on confidence in tackling spin? You see, not only do you need to understand the strengths and weaknesses of individual players, you also need to look at form. (By the way, I am definitely not an expert at cricket, but I do know a bit about the sport. And my comments here are based on my limited knowledge. If there are any errors in what I've just said, I apologize. But I hope you get the point: Winning at fantasy sports requires a solid amount of knowledge.)

I could go on and on. You would need to look at the weather, the opposition, the past record of each player, etc., etc. before choosing your team. Yes, my friend, playing fantasy sports needs knowledge and skill. If you do not have these, sorry, you are very unlikely to win.

Harsh puts it very well:

> Fantasy sports are like stock markets. You don't bet on one particular stock crossing, say, Rs 1000. You create a portfolio of stocks and expect the portfolio to perform. And you would do this based on past performance, the outlook for the industry, the current state of the economy, the competitive intensity, etc.
>
> In a similar way, on the Dream11 platform, you pick a portfolio of players. Once again, based on past performance, nature of the pitch, competition, etc. In other words, based on your knowledge of the game and the players. And you expect this portfolio of players (your team) to perform better than teams selected by others playing on Dream11.

By the way, I must highlight one important issue. Yes, there will always be an element of luck. But isn't that true of any sport? What if Dhoni were setting himself up for a huge flat-batted six and at that precise moment an insect decided to get into his eye? Isn't that pure bad luck? Or what if Rohit Sharma were to get a stomach upset on the morning of a World Cup match? Bad luck again, isn't it? Any sport has its share of good and bad luck—that's part of the game. But no sport is based purely on luck, and that goes for Dream11 as well.

Winning the Legal Battle

Dear reader, by now I hope you can see that playing fantasy sports, Dream11 style, requires knowledge and skill. It is definitely not a game of pure chance. It's not betting and it's not gambling.

However, when you live in a country of 140 crore people (this number could be significantly higher by the time you read this book, but that's irrelevant), you can bet that there would be enough people who disagree. And if they were sitting in a bar, consuming the inevitable Black Label scotch whisky, they would disagree more and more violently, depending on the number of pegs that had gone down their respective throats. Ever since Dream11 was launched, several people have indicated that fantasy sports are games of chance. And no, they did not simply finish off their glasses of scotch and go off to sleep. They actually took the issue to court. In fact, people in several states filed cases in their respective high courts, claiming that what Dream11 was doing was pure betting: a game of chance.

Now, what do you think our young founders did? Well, they were very clear—this was a game of skill and knowledge. And they would prove it in court. They would fight. In fact, I heard Harsh speak at the well-known TechSparks conference in March 2023 (more about this later), and according to him, the issue actually went up to the Supreme Court of India. Not once, not twice, but SEVEN times.

And what do you think the Supreme Court said?

Each time, they quashed the case. They said it was a game of skill and not a game of chance. It was definitely not betting. In fact, the seventh time was the best. This was in 2022, when the court actually said that the issue had been examined enough times and should not be raised again. So that was the final judgement: Dream11 was a game of skill and had been approved by none other than the highest court of India. 'Don't waste the time of this court again and again', they said. (I'm not sure if that's exactly what the court said, but I'm sure you get the idea.)

Incidentally, in case you have a legal bent of mind, you are welcome to read these judgements. I don't, so I read a simplified version* on *BW Legalworld* (a division of *BW Businessworld*).

As you can imagine, this was a major relief for the company. Because they were now at par with any fantasy sport worldwide and were accepted as a game of skill rather than chance. This also opened up the doors to investors, who had seen the numbers rise and were keen to invest, but were holding back because of the legal hangover. But as clarity began to emerge—and the business grew—investors came in droves.

The Regulatory Hurdles

So legally, Dream11 was in the clear. However, there were still some hurdles left (running a business is never easy, is it?). Yes, the Supreme Court had conclusively said that Dream11 was a game of skill. But in spite of this, some states decided to ban it.

Why? Well, it might have been for political reasons. You are aware that some states, such as Gujarat, have banned the sale and consumption of alcohol. Well, this was probably similar, and some states such as Assam, Andhra Pradesh and Odisha have banned real-money online gaming. However, in most other states, Dream11 is permitted to operate freely—and that's a huge market. If you wish to read more details, check out this article.†

But even this is changing. And you need to understand why. As you are aware, India has always been the software factory of the world, with world-class companies such as TCS, Infosys, Wipro and

---

* 'Supreme Court Affirms Fantasy Sports Offered by Dream11 As A Game Of Skill', *BW Legalworld*, 12 November, 2022, https://bwlegalworld.businessworld.in/article/Supreme-Court-Affirms-Fantasy-Sports-Offered-by-Dream11-As-A-Game-Of-Skill/12-11-2022-453779/.

† Aviral@Legal Shack, 'The Regulation of Fantasy Sports in India', *Times of India*, 7 May 2023, https://timesofindia.indiatimes.com/readersblog/legal-shack/the-regulation-of-fantasy-sports-in-india-53547/.

Zoho providing software solutions across the world. The government of India is now looking at building on this opportunity and finding the next big growth area. And after the phenomenal success of UPI (Unified Payments Interface), Aadhaar and Digilocker, among other applications, the obvious candidate is 'Digital India'.

And now for the punch line. Within Digital India, the next big thing could just be online gaming. Which could potentially bring in invaluable foreign exchange for the country. Further, investors, including foreign investors, are happy to invest large amounts in such online gaming platforms. Not only that, according to Harsh, gaming as an industry earns the country over a billion dollars in taxes. Now, which government would not be tempted to encourage this?

So much so, that in his post-budget speech of 2022, our prime minister stressed on the gaming sector, which he said had a huge international market, and that India was exploring increasing its footprint in this area.[*] I As I write this book (2023), the central government is attempting to put together legislation that would regulate—rather than ban—the gaming industry. Which would hopefully also remove the bans imposed by some states.

And that might just be the catalyst our country needs to become a superpower in this space.

Of course, Dream11 is already doing its bit in this endeavour. It is contributing to India's digital economy, creating jobs in the process, and helping to make India a gaming super power!

Meanwhile, We Will Follow Good Practices

So regulations will hopefully come, and that's a good thing. But in the meantime, what do great businesses do?

---

[*] 'Gaming sector has huge int'l market, India trying to increase its footprint in it: Modi', *Indian Express*, Updated 3 March 2022, https://indianexpress.com/article/cities/delhi/gaming-sector-huge-intl-market-india-trying-increase-footprint-modi-7797747/.

Simple. They don't wait for the regulations. They follow good practices. So when the regulations *do* come in, they are ready, or have perhaps been following those regulations anyway.

For example, what if children were to get on the site and play with money. Completely unacceptable, isn't it? And the founders agree. So every user who plays with money needs to certify that he or she is over eighteen years of age. And back it up with an ID issued by the government, such as Aadhaar. And yes, if a user wins a game and money needs to be transferred to him, he needs to share his PAN card details, which he would only have if he is an adult.

Further, some states do not permit online fantasy sports, so what does Dream11 do? Well, they ask the user which state he resides in and do not let him play if he lives in a state that has banned the activity.

But it doesn't stop there. As the market leader in the sports tech industry, Dream Sports took the lead in getting online gaming companies together, and forming what is called the Federation of Indian Fantasy Sports (FIFS). This was in 2017. According to Bhavit, 'The FIFS was formed to protect the interest of users and promote best practices for online fantasy sports.' In other words, not only is Dream11 following good practices, they have also taken the lead in ensuring that everyone in the industry follows good practices as well.

However, I must end this chapter on a somewhat cautious note. Sectors that are small tend to remain under the radar of regulators. But large sectors are always under the scanner. It happens to all businesses, so it was only natural that it would happen to fantasy sports as well. Yes, my friend, while the Supreme Court has clearly ruled that this is a game of skill, in late 2023, the GST council, which includes the Union finance minister as well as all the state finance ministers, bowled a googly. A googly which none of the players was able to pick. But more about that in Chapter 26 . . .

And that brings us to the end of the whole debate of 'game of skill' vs 'game of chance'. But before you move on to the next chapter,

I have a suggestion: I realize that legal issues can be tiring. And you must be exhausted by now.

Take a break and go for a nice, lo-o-o-o-o-o-o-ng walk.

Let's meet again tomorrow.

23

From Dream11 to Dream Sports

So everything started falling into place for Dream11. They had a great product. The Supreme Court had backed them. They were able to get funding several times, which helped in developing the product as well as in marketing. And of course, the number of users on the platform grew and grew. Cricket had always been a religion in India, and this was a way by which fans could not only watch the game but actually be involved. And then our founders decided to go beyond men's cricket. Because women's cricket was hotting up, and you now had the Women's Premier League, or WPL. Naturally, therefore, Dream11 jumped into it.

But fantasy sports does not need to be limited to cricket alone, does it? No way. So there were all the other sports, such as football, hockey, kabaddi, basketball, volleyball, etc. You name it, and Dream11 launched it. Of course, in India, these other sports have not been as popular as cricket, but the founders believe it's just a matter of time. For instance, the bronze medal that the Indian men's hockey team won at the 2022 Olympics, could just be the catalyst that the game needs to catapult itself into people's minds.

Dream Sports: Making Sports Better

So that was the fascinating story of Dream11.

But hang on. As they say in America, 'You ain't seen nuthin' yet!' (Apologies for the terrible spelling and grammar.) Remember, the vision of our young founders was far, far bigger than just fantasy cricket—or even fantasy sports in general. It was to create a full-fledged sports ecosystem. And that's where Dream Sports came in. This is what Harsh says:

> We are proud to continually serve our growing community of avid sports fans with the latest innovative offerings and contribute to the overall expansion of the Indian sports ecosystem.

In fact, Harsh and Bhavit have a simple but extremely powerful vision for their company:

Make Sports Better.

Sounds wonderful, doesn't it? But I can see that you are itching to ask a question. And yes, it's a great question. How could the company do so many different things at the same time? You see, some things were an obvious extension of the core business, Dream11. Extending that to women's cricket and also to other sports was the job of the core team. But to impact the entire sports ecosystem, there was lots more to be done . . .

And that's where the founders decided to scout around for other, well-run companies. Wherever they saw that someone else was building a great business in the area of sports, well, the company was happy to invest in them. In some cases, they incubated these businesses from an early stage. In others, they invested at a later stage. Occasionally, they simply bought out the entire company. As you are aware, such investments are called strategic investments: something that you've already seen in the case of Info Edge, as well as Zerodha. And now, you've seen it in the case of Dream Sports as well.

Along the way, in 2021, they also created a fund called Dream Capital, where they put in $250 million, or around Rs 2 crore. And from this fund, they began investing in interesting businesses that could potentially add value to their core business.

One of their first strategic investments was in a company called **FanCode**, in 2019. What does FanCode do? Well, it has an app which gives you live streaming of matches, news, statistics and content related to sports. Remember I had told you that when they launched Dream11, they tried to do everything but couldn't manage? And that they had shut down things like sports news, blogs and other kinds of content? Well, once they became profitable, they re-started the content business by buying out FanCode. And that's an interesting message: When you are burning money, you need to focus on your core business. But when you are making money, well, you can diversify!

By the way, FanCode also has an eCommerce site called FC Shop. Which is exactly that: an online shop. Where you can buy sports apparel. For instance, if you wanted to buy the jersey of the Indian cricket team, where would you buy it? I never knew the answer. But now I do. FC Shop is the place to go!

In the same year, they also invested in a business called **DreamSetGo**, which caters to sports travel and experiences. What does that mean? Well, what if you wanted to watch Wimbledon? No, no, not on TV. What if you wanted to watch it live at the Wimbledon stadium in London? You would then need to book tickets (and they would need to be real tickets, not fake ones). You would need to locate a hotel, organize your flight tickets and do all the other nitty-gritty things that go into a foreign trip. Quite a hassle, isn't it? But guess what? It's not a hassle any more. Because DreamSetGo does all this for you!

One of their most fascinating investments was in a Pune-based company called **Rolocule Games** in 2021, which they rebranded as **DreamGameStudios**. In fact, this was their first complete buyout.

What does the company do? Well, it's a studio that develops mobile-based sports games—starting with cricket, as you might expect.

According to Harsh:

> There is no awe-inspiring mobile-based game for cricket, like FIFA
> for football or NBA 2K for basketball. With DreamGameStudios,
> we're hoping to create a game like that.

There have been many more such investments, and these will continue. By the way, the founders are clear that these are strategic investments and not financial investments. They are all in the area of sports and are intended to 'make sports better'. The company doesn't want an exit from these investments. Over time, the idea is to enhance their stake and perhaps even buy out the entire investee company.

Yes, the fantasy sports platform, Dream11, is very much there. That's their core business. But now there is a much larger 'Dream Sports' umbrella, of which Dream11 is a part.

It Isn't Just about Profits: Dream Sports Foundation

But there is still more. Remember, I had told you that the vision of the founders is to 'make sports better'? In this context, they have also created a non-profit arm called the Dream Sports Foundation, where the idea is to give back to sports by financially supporting athletes, whether it is for training, sports gear or anything else that might be required to get them to improve. And the results are great: The athletes supported by them have won over 220 medals so far. Major medals. For instance, there is Jyothi Surekha, who brought home three gold medals in archery at the 2019 Asian Games.[*] And then

---

[*] Aditya Chaturvedi, "'I like to remain in my zone off the field as well': Jyothi Surekha Vennam', *Hindustan Times*, 21 October 2023, https://www.hindustantimes.com/sports/others/i-like-to-remain-in-my-zone-off-the-field-as-well-jyothi-surekha-vennam-101697595651296.html.

there is Sreeja Akula, who claimed a gold medal in the mixed doubles event at the Commonwealth Games in 2022, and was awarded the Khel Ratna.*

As you can see, the vision of the founders extends far beyond business. They support sports in whatever way they can.

And it's not just cricket.

Yes, sir, they are truly 'making sports better'.

---

* 'Sreeja Akula congratulated on her victory and felicitated by PM Narendra Modi', *Hindustan Times*, 19 August 2022, https://www.hindustantimes.com/sports/commonwealth-games/sreeja-akula-congratulated-on-her-victory-and-felicitated-by-pm-narendra-modi-101660898699509.html.

24

Culture and People

Dear reader, I've already told you that the founders of Dream Sports have always believed in retaining customers and team members.

Right?

So let's examine what they did . . .

First of all, here's something that really hit me when I started researching the company. I'm sure you've come across the term CEO. And obviously, you know that it stands for Chief Executive Officer.

But guess what? At Dream11, that's not what it stands for. It stands for *Culture Enforcement Officer.* That's Harsh Jain's designation. And those three words tell you more about the organization than I can possibly tell you in this entire chapter.

Anyway, since I've written this book—and you've bought it—I must say *something*. So let me start by quoting Harsh:

We are very clear that our organization needs to be culture-driven. When we recruit people, we check their culture fit. Skills can be learnt, but not culture. And we certainly do not want someone coming in and messing up the culture that we've built over the years. Similarly, the annual performance appraisals include culture as a key element.

In fact, the core of the organization has to be like-minded people *who don't need to be the most skilled.* Some of our people have been around for nearly fifteen years. And they are the cultural custodians of the company.

Culture Flows from the Top

That's obvious, isn't it? In this context, let me share a personal experience. I first met Harsh at the TechSparks conference organized by YourStory in Mumbai, in March 2023. He was the keynote speaker and was sharing his personal story as well as the story of his baby, Dream11. Believe me, the audience was simply enthralled listening to him. So was I. And that's when I decided that I *had to* meet him and include the Dream11 story in this book.

I quickly followed him as he was about to walk out of the conference and said, 'Hi Harsh, my name is Dhruv Nath. I'm writing a book on profitable giants in the Indian Internet world. And I'd like to include your story in the book.' Now remember, the young man was extremely busy, and this was also just before the start of the IPL season. Naturally, I expected him to hem and haw and say stuff like, 'Well, you know, I'm very busy for the next couple of months (which he was, given the IPL). Please contact my office and check with them.'

That's what I expected, and I was prepared for it.

Instead, Harsh said, 'Of course!' And he promptly gave me his email address. No secretary, no executive assistant. No, sir, he gave me his personal email address.

'Wow,' I thought. 'This is great!' And my respect for the young man went up a few notches. Here was a busy, busy founder running a huge company—a market leader—and I was trying to get time from him during the busiest part of the year. And he not only agreed, but also shared his email address.

But then I started thinking. You see, I am a senior citizen, and I look the part. No hair on my head and a sparkling white beard. Plus, my visiting card carries the word 'Professor'. Perhaps what Harsh did was out of respect for my age. Yes, that must be it, I thought. But just to confirm my thinking, I stayed on and watched him speak to some of the other people in the audience.

After me, there was a young college student who had a question about eSports. Not only did Harsh hear him out patiently, but he also answered his question. Then there was another college student who wanted Harsh to visit her college for placement. Once again, he answered her question patiently. In fact, I must have spent over fifteen minutes watching Harsh interact with several young people, and I noticed the same level of patience, as he responded to each one of them. By the way, it wasn't that he had a lot of time on his hands. He was busy and had to leave for another meeting. But he was willing to listen to people around him patiently—people whom he might never meet again—and talk to them.

And that's when my theory about Harsh responding to me the way he did because I was a senior citizen, went out of the window. It wasn't my lack of hair or my snowy white beard. It wasn't the 'Professor' against my name on my visiting card. This was the way Harsh spoke to everyone he met—young or old. Here was a man who would listen patiently to people and answer their questions. Here was a man who had no airs about the fact that he was heading the biggest sports tech company in the country. Here was a man who truly respected his fellow human beings. In a stroke, I understood the culture of the organization. I understood why people wanted to work with him and why they wouldn't leave him. Yes, my friend, I understood the true meaning of the phrase: 'Culture flows from the top. It cannot be pushed down your throat.'

Of course, in those few minutes, my mind was made up. Harsh and Dream11 simply had to be part of my book.

Now, for the next step: Obviously, the best way to understand the culture of an organization is to visit their office. Which is what I did. And I must tell you that I saw people looking happy over there. Now, they didn't know that I was there to write a story about the company, so they hadn't pasted smiles on their faces for my benefit. No, they looked genuinely happy.

Next, I was keen to see the founders' cabins. Because that would tell me how accessible they really were. So I looked around for these cabins . . .

But there were none.

I thought I had missed seeing them. After all, the CEO and COO simply had to have cabins of their own. It was the done thing, you see? So I asked one of the young team members working there (incidentally, team members there are called Dreamsters). And what do you think the response was? 'There are no cabins for anyone. We don't believe in hierarchy.'

'But where do Harsh and Bhavit sit?' was my next question.

'Come, I'll show you,' was the response, as she took me to a couple of workstations near the window. 'Here!'

I looked around. What this Dreamster showed me were two ordinary workstations—*identical to the hundreds of other workstations in the office.* And when I took a closer look, I read the names on them: 'Harsh Jain' and 'Bhavit Shah'.

'Wow,' I said to myself. I had spent over forty years visiting and working in corporate offices, but I had never seen anything like this. Bosses usually had cabins, or at least half cabins with partitions. Or at the very least, much larger desks. But no, Harsh and Bhavit had exactly the same kind of desks as everyone else. And this is when I realized that they really did not believe in hierarchy. My mind went back to the TechSparks conference, where I had seen Harsh listening patiently to each of the college students he met. And I realized that this wasn't an act that had been putting on for the press. No, this is how Harsh was: approachable, willing to listen, willing to respond and showing respect for the individual. Bhavit was exactly the same. And that set the tone for the culture of the organization.

By the way, I must clarify something. Their head office is not called an office. No, sir, in keeping with the sports culture at Dream Sports, it is called a 'stadium'. That's right—a stadium.

And now, I'm sure you'd want to know more about this stadium, wouldn't you? So, guess what? I've devoted a full chapter to it.

The next one.

Ownership

So, that's the first and perhaps the most important step in building organizational culture: The top management needs to lead by example. And now, for an equally important step. In my many years of experience as a consultant, I have learnt that the starting point for building culture is 'ownership'. The moment people start saying, 'This is *my* company', everything falls into place. And for this to happen, the company must look after them. So let's take a look at how Dream Sports looks after its people.

First of all, Dream Sports has always given their people enough opportunities to grow. The founders believe in keeping their head count low, and giving their people challenging work. 'Give challenging work to the team, and they will perform.' That's their motto. By the way, there is no micro-management, so there is no 'boss' breathing down their respective necks, checking their work. In other words, people take 'ownership' of their own work. If they prove themselves, they are given a bigger role, irrespective of their qualifications. And yes, good performers are not stuck to one role. Those who do well get an opportunity to move to another role. That's what keeps them fresh and motivated. And that's how they grow!

Okay, sounds good. People get challenging work, they get a chance to shift roles and of course, they grow. But I can see what you are thinking. 'What's the big deal? Isn't this what most companies do anyway? What's unique about Dream Sports?'

Yes, my friend, you are right. These practices are common across many good companies. But let me tell you a few things about Dream Sports which are *not* common. Starting with financial incentives, such as ESOPs. According to Harsh, *each team member in Dream Sports gets ESOPs*. Yes, you read that right. I said *each team member*. You could be a manager, a regular team member, or even an office boy. It doesn't matter. You still get ESOPs. As you can imagine, that builds a strong sense of ownership amongst the team. So you are not just an employee earning a salary. You are a part-owner of the company. If you do well, the company does well, the valuation of the company goes up, and the value of your ESOPs goes up.

But there's more. Here's something you'll really love (I certainly did). You are aware that the city of Mumbai is famous, or perhaps infamous, for its traffic. And therefore, for the time it takes to commute from home to office and back. But guess what? Our founders have always wanted people to stay close to the office. So if you were to rent out a flat that was close to the office, where the commute time was less than half an hour, the company would actually re-imburse up to 40 per cent of your rent.

Don't believe it? Well, it's absolutely true. And Bhavit tells us the reason why:

> We strongly believe that our people should be fit. They should not spend two hours travelling each way from home to office. Fit people are able to give their best. That's why we have created this benefit. It's called 'Proximity to the stadium benefit'. And it's a HUGE draw for anyone in our team who comes from outside Mumbai, and whose parents don't have a home here.

And finally, the icing on the cake. Let me refresh your memory about something I've already spoken about. During their early years, when Dream11 was not making money and these guys had to reduce manpower, what did they do? Did they resort to mass lay-offs? No way. They started the social media advertising company, Red Digital Systems. And they transferred most of their team members to this new company. No lay-offs.

Incidentally, exactly the same thing happened during the Covid-19 pandemic. As you can imagine, there were no matches during that time, whether cricket, football, hockey, or any sport for that matter. So what did that do to Dream11? Remember, this was fantasy sports, which was built as a layer on top of real sporting events. And when there were no events, well, there was no fantasy sports. Which meant—that's right—revenues were down to rock bottom.

But even during those tough times, *there were no mass lay-offs.* In fact—hold your breath—they even continued to hire people for specific roles. The founders made it clear, 'You guys have supported the company all along. Now the company will support you. There will be no job losses.'

Dear reader, if you wanted to build ownership in your team, can you think of a better way? No revenues and no idea when revenues would start, but no one lost his job.

Can you think of a better way to create ownership in the team?

DO PUT

So Dream Sports has always taken the two most important steps to build their culture: top management showing the way, and creating ownership amongst the team.

Anything else?

Yes, there is more. And to understand this, let's hear out the culture enforcement officer, Harsh, once again:

> Culture flows from the top. That much is clear. Now when the organization is small, say, twenty or thirty people, the top management is in touch with everyone in the team. Therefore, culture is simply absorbed from the top. People see you doing the right thing, and they follow it. But when the organization grows bigger, this becomes harder. Therefore, you need to write it down; and that too, in a form that people can remember and easily implement.
>
> So we tried to list down the parameters that would define our culture—and we came up with a list of eleven. Of course we were excited, but no one remembered eleven parameters. Not even me. Therefore, we had to make another attempt, and we scaled down the parameters to eight. Once again, no one remembered eight parameters. Which is when we realized that it had to be a small number of parameters, and that too, in a form that people would

remember. And that's when we finally whittled it down to just five parameters. That worked, and that's what we have been following for years now.

What are these parameters?

Simple—they have been written down in the form of an acronym: **DO PUT.** Which reads as follows:

D: Data
O: Ownership

P: Persevering
U: User First
T: Transparency

Interestingly, they believe so strongly in this approach that they have put it up at their reception—so anyone who walks into their office cannot help reading it.

Let's take a look at each of these parameters, one by one. I've already said enough about *Ownership*, so I don't think I need to say anything more. The team members at Dream Sports love the fact that their company looks after them, so they take full ownership of any role or task they get. And they are happy to follow the example set by their top management—in other words, the founders.

And now for the second aspect of culture, namely, *User First*.

User First

One of the things that sets great businesses apart from the also-rans, is their fanatical focus on their customers, or users, as Dream11 prefers to call them. Give the user products or services that he likes, keep him happy, and he'll keep coming back to you. Not only that, he'll also bring other users along. Each company that I've spoken about in this book, has had the same unwavering focus on the customer. And Dream Sports is no different.

I think the best example of this attitude is a feature called 'Dream responsibly'. And let me give you one example of this: Dream11 does not want users to lose too much money. So they let each user set his own limit. When he reaches this limit, he gets a notification asking him to stop.[*]

Can you imagine that? A business asking a customer to stop? And therefore impacting its own revenues? I certainly can't. But Dream11 does this. And that's why their customers love them! Incidentally, doesn't that sound very much like the 'Nudge' feature in Zerodha, where Nithin tried to move his customers away from investing or trading in penny stocks?

And there's a lot more. Eighty per cent of their users are still free. The platform simply wants them to go ahead and enjoy themselves. Over time, if they want to convert to paid gaming, they are welcome, of course. But no one will force them to. Once again, doesn't that sound uncannily like the zero brokerage on Zerodha?

Even for those 20 per cent users on Dream11 who do pay, the average ticket size is only Rs 45. It has been kept low, because the founders strongly believe that the Indian customer doesn't want a bottle of shampoo. He wants a sachet. (I've already mentioned this in Chapter 20, where I introduced Dream11, but it is so apt that I decided to bring it up again. And I hope you'll understand why.) The focus of the company is to keep customers happy, get lots of them on board, and thereby build scale. And believe me, they are doing it brilliantly.

Oh, I almost forgot. For paid customers, the company tries to ensure that at least half of them get their money back. And 99 per cent of their users have never won or lost more than Rs 10,000 in their entire lives. Customer orientation at its best once again, isn't it?

---

[*] https://www.dreamsports.group/dream-responsibly/trust-safety

And there is something else. Remember, these guys are dealing with young people, and that too on the Internet. Where no one—I repeat, no one—has patience. No waiting for those silly ten seconds, please. We are in a hurry. And therefore, response time becomes critical. But how do you ensure quick response times when the users are growing exponentially, often with millions of them using the system concurrently?

Aha! That's where investment in technology comes in. Along with a fanatical belief in keeping customers happy, the company has an equally fanatical belief in investing in technology. Cutting-edge technology that enables them to scale and keep pace with the rapidly growing base of active users. And of course, the user interface design—because today's young people want quick, intuitive apps. Just to drive the point home further, nearly 80 per cent of the Dream Sports team focuses on the product, on design and on technology. That's what keeps them ahead of their competitors. And that, my friend, is what separates leaders from the rest.

Finally, here's a brilliant example of their customer-oriented thinking. Now, I'm sure you have watched IPL matches. In 2019, Dream11 came out with a brilliant add-on to the fantasy cricket their fans were playing. In every IPL match, all fans who were sitting in the stadium and watching the match (the real stadium, not the Dream11 stadium) could take part in an in-match quiz. And guess what? The winner of this quiz got to be a part of the presentation ceremony and a chance to hand over a trophy and a cheque to the 'Dream11 Game Changer of the Match.' And of course, shake hands with this game changer.

Just imagine. Fans got a chance to shake hands with superstars such as M.S. Dhoni, Virat Kohli, Rohit Sharma, A.B. De Villers and the like. And then present them with a trophy. No amount of prize money could have topped this, and as you can imagine, fans fell over each other to take part in this quiz.

And that, my friend, is customer orientation. Or in the company's own words, 'User first'.

Perseverance

Once again, I don't think I need to say anything here. During the initial years, when things were just not picking up, the entire team tried all kinds of models until they hit upon the right one. Even later, during the Covid-19 pandemic, when no matches were being played and therefore fantasy sports was non-existent, the founders persisted. They used the time to plan for a post-pandemic future—whenever that happened. And since all team members took full ownership, they were happy to play along.

And of course, the long, long, LONG battle: 'Game of skill vs game of chance', the repeated court cases, the unending chase for investor money, and the regulatory hurdles put up by state governments. No one in the Dream Sports team ever gave up; they were happy to keep on at it. It took several years, but finally they won their court cases and got their funding. And knowing the founders and their charged-up team, I have no doubt they will win all future battles as well.

Data

This one is interesting (well, they are all interesting, but so is this one). Dream11—and the larger Dream Sports group—is a data-driven company. They have a tag line for this: '90 per cent data, 10 per cent gut. Experiment without bias.'

Two things emerge from this: First of all, the culture of experimentation. Team members are encouraged to experiment, and that's one of the things that keeps their ownership alive. No one is blamed if the experiment goes wrong. There is no blame game. The only issue is: 'Don't experiment in a vacuum. You believe that users are leaving for some reason and want to experiment? Sure, go ahead, but first show me data.' You see, Harsh and Bhavit believe that team members could be biased. They could have preconceived notions about why users are leaving or not playing as much as they

should. Rather than make decisions based on these biases, they insist on data.

And how do they get this data? Very simple—they talk to their users. They take feedback, so they know what the users want. And also what's troubling them. That data is then used in their decision-making process.

One last comment before I move away from user feedback. Who takes this feedback? Who takes these phone calls. My friend, get ready for another surprise. Very often, both Harsh and Bhavit have been seen picking up the phone and taking user calls. That's how grounded they are. No sitting in an ivory tower and making decisions in a vacuum. They are willing to do everything—and it shows.

Transparency

Finally, let's talk about transparency. In Dream11, the user knows exactly what is happening to his money—how much goes towards the game and how much goes to Dream11 (if you recall, that's very similar to what users experience at Zerodha). He also knows what his competing gamers are doing, so he can make an informed decision when selecting his team. That, my friend, is transparency. And that's Dream11.

Overall, the company has a happy, open culture. The founders are always willing to take feedback from their team members. Even negative feedback, which is taboo in many organizations. In fact, they keep walking around the office, meeting people and encouraging them to share feedback. Harsh and Bhavit hold town hall meetings on a regular basis, where anyone can ask anything. And all questions are answered honestly. After all, they believe in transparency. Even during the Covid-19 pandemic, when things were a huge question mark and everyone was concerned about the future of the company (and consequently their jobs), the founders were honest about what was happening and what they were doing. No hiding of facts. And that builds trust, doesn't it?

And you can see that in the numbers—the attrition rate of people in Dream Sports is an unbelievable 4 per cent. That's right, for a company in the Internet space, for a company that has had so many ups and downs, it's almost a world record.

But by now, I'm sure you can understand why.

But We Must Be Profitable

Aha! We now get back to one of Harsh's favourite topics: his obsession with dhandha, or profit. Something that he has imbibed as the scion of a successful Marwari business family. Remember Chapter 21, where I had said that Harsh believed that retention of users was a far better policy than acquisition? And now, just look at the 'User First' strategy of Dream Sports. Not letting the user lose too much money, letting most people play free, ensuring that the average ticket size is affordable, etc. Aren't these great ways to keep existing users happy? And thereby dramatically reduce acquisition costs?

Of course, the same applies to team members as well. Keep them happy and motivated, and ensure they stay. So much better than losing people and replacing them, isn't it? And that's exactly what their people policies do. Policies such as giving ESOPs to everyone, giving them a 'proximity to the stadium' benefit and above all, never laying off people, even during tough times. Once again, by keeping team members happy, motivated and stable, the company avoids repeated recruitment and training costs. And those costs go directly towards profitability.

And of course, the founders have always believed in keeping their head count low and giving their people challenging work. That motivates the team and gets them to perform. People are happy, they stick on and HR costs are low. A true win-win, isn't it?

And one more reason why Dream Sports has been profitable.

Now, do you begin to understand the meaning of dhandha?

25

A Visit to the Stadium

And now for something absolutely unique to Dream Sports. Where the concept of culture takes on a whole new meaning. To understand this, you need to visit their office in the posh business area of Bandra Kurla Complex, or BKC, in Mumbai. But till you do so, let me tell you what I saw when I went there. Of course, it's not the same thing as actually visiting it, but anyway, here goes.

I've already told you that they don't call it an office. After all, which sportsman in his right mind would ever want to enter an office? No way. They call it a 'stadium'.

Anyhow, I reached the stadium, entered the reception . . .
. . . and stopped.

And looked around.

This was not a reception. No sir, it was like no other reception I had been to—and I must have been to several hundred. This was a small football field, complete with all the markings. There was a goalpost at one end, with sofas, where visitors could wait. Just imagine: You go into a corporate office and you find yourself sitting and waiting under a goalpost. Could it get any more sporty?

From the reception—sorry, football field—I went into the main stadium, where the entire team sat. But I didn't go in through a door. I went in through a turnstile. The kind you have in actual stadiums, where they check your tickets. And once again, I stopped. And stared at the floor. You see, I expected perhaps marble flooring.

Or maybe tiles. Maybe wall-to-wall carpeting; after all, this is where the founders sat. But no. It was none of the above. No tiles, no marble, no carpeting. The entire floor was covered with *astroturf!*

Astroturf? The stuff that hockey grounds are made of?

Absolutely. The very same astroturf. Because our founders want you to feel as though you are entering a stadium and not a silly, boring office. That's why. And there is more. They had a running track going all around the office—sorry, stadium.

Now you can imagine my reaction. Here was a sports company that actually believed in what they said. Anyone could have called their office a stadium, but these guys really made it look and feel like one.

As I went around the stadium, I saw their meeting rooms. Given our country's obsession with the IPL, each IPL team had a meeting room named after it. So there was the Delhi Capitals room, which had a huge photograph of Chandni Chowk in old Delhi. There was the Chennai Super Kings room, which had an equally huge photograph of—you've guessed it—M.S. Dhoni. There was the Punjab Kings room, complete with a cut-out of a truck, with the words 'Sadda Punjab' proudly emblazoned next to it. There was the Mumbai Indians meeting room, the biggest of the lot (perhaps because Harsh is a staunch Mumbai Indians supporter), where the shelves on the wall were made of cricket bats.

And it wasn't just cricket. In keeping with the company philosophy of diversifying into multiple sports, they had the Ferrari room, the Arsenal room and the Chicago Bulls room. And how can I forget the Hockey India room with the proud slogan, 'Chak De'? All over the stadium, I was reminded of some sport or the other. So one area had hundreds of hockey sticks suspended from the ceiling. Another area had a large net with lots and lots of basketballs. There was even an interesting corner with a chandelier made up of baseball bats. With a bean bag in the shape of—that's right—a baseball. And the inevitable guitar, so when you wanted to, you could strum to yourself. In fact, all across the stadium, I saw cricket bats signed by well-known cricketers, cricket balls, wickets, bails, footballs . . .

And across the entire stadium, I saw large TV screens showing live matches. So you could work, but you could also watch your favourite cricket, or football, or tennis match at the same time. Tell me, which other company gives you this?

But it's not just about the ambience; it's the entire sports culture in Dream Sports. Let's hear out Bhavit on the subject:

> The team in our organization is like a champion sports team. So we don't have bosses. We don't have conventional CFOs, CTOs and CXOs. Harsh and I are coaches. Those you would call 'bosses' in a conventional organization are captains over here. Everyone else is a 'Dreamster'. When a team is stuck, we ask them to think like a champion sports team and solve the problem. Along with the captain, and perhaps the coach. And obviously, the environment helps.

Let me get back to the football field and goalpost at the reception. When the company gets a new batch of trainees, guess what? They meet on the football field, and each trainee gets a jersey signed by his captain (or boss, in case you still don't understand). Then, he or she kicks a football into the goal. In a way, that's how they kickstart their careers at Dream Sports.

By the way, I must mention one fact. This is the only office—sorry, stadium—that the company has. No other offices scattered across Delhi, Bengaluru, Chennai or any other cities. No sir, they have one single stadium in Mumbai, spread over two floors. And you can see the impact of the belief in dhandha. Because running multiple offices would mean more overheads, which would eat into their profitability. In any case, this is a pure B2C Internet company and they would only need to meet users online, or over phone calls. No need for any offices.

Therefore, no additional offices. And higher profits!

Finally, there is something I've said before, but it's so important that I must say it again. During my visit to the stadium, I must have seen several hundred young people. And they looked so happy. They didn't look as though they were working, doing a mundane job, with meetings, deadlines and targets. No sir, they were enjoying themselves thoroughly.

As I've already mentioned, the manpower turnover in the company is a miniscule 4 per cent per year.

And as I walked out, I understood why!

26

Dream Sports: Today and Tomorrow

So where has Dream Sports reached? Well, in the financial year 2021–22, the company had a revenue of—hold your breath—Rs 4000 crore. And yes, it was profitable. In fact, it made a net profit of Rs 147 crore. They have received multiple rounds of funding, but Harsh has made it very clear that they don't need funding any more.

Why?

Well, they are profitable, aren't they? And a large chunk of these profits are ploughed back into growth.

What about valuation? Actually, based on the last fund raise, the company has a valuation of around $8 billion, although I strongly suspect that Harsh does not really bother about these things (of course, his investors do 😊). He believes in dhandha, in real money, and not valuation. Doesn't this sound uncannily like the other founders you've met in this book?

The company has 200 million Indians as registered users. That's right: twenty crore people, or more than 10 per cent of the population of India. Of course, not all of them are active throughout the year. Typically, they become active during the cricket season, which is at the onset of winter. And then there are one lakh new users signing up every day. Yes my friend, Dream Sports is by far the biggest sports tech company in the country. And Dream 11 is the biggest fantasy sports platform, way ahead of the others, such as MPL (Mobile Premier League), Games 24x7, Fantasy Akhara and the rest.

And here's a bit more. For several years, Google did not allow real-money gaming apps to list themselves on Google Play Store. On 9 October 2022, they allowed this, and Dream11 was listed. And would you believe it? In less than a month, specifically, by 2 November, it had become the number one gaming app on Google Play Store. And that includes all the free-to-play apps, which had been around for years. Need I say anything more about the popularity of Dream11?

One More Roadblock

As you've seen so far, like all businesses, this one has also seen multiple roadblocks along the way. Right from the time when their model did not work, to the time when they were fighting legal battles over the issue of 'game of skill' vs 'game of chance'. And of course, the long and frustrating wait for funding.

But what you've also seen is that the company has persevered (remember, DO PUT?) and overcome all these hurdles over time.

However, just as I was putting the finishing touches to this story, there was one more hurdle that cropped up: that of taxation. As you are aware, the government of India charges GST, or Goods and Services Tax, on most services rendered in the country. Since online gaming companies are providing a service to consumers, quite naturally they need to pay GST. That much is fine. It's the law of the land, and Dream Sports abides by it. But how much GST do they pay? Let's take an example. Suppose a user puts up Rs 1000 to play on Dream11 (please remember, these are fictitious figures simply to explain the concept). Now, let's assume that Dream11 retains 20 per cent of this amount, or Rs 200, as their fee for letting the user play. This Rs 200 is called GGR, or Gross Gaming Revenue, and this is the revenue that goes to the company for services provided. The balance Rs 800 goes into the prize money pool, from where prizes are distributed.

Now this is important, so please stop nodding your head absently and listen carefully. Dream11 is providing a service (gaming) to the customer, for which they are charging a fee of Rs 200 and not Rs 1000. Quite naturally, they would need to pay GST on this Rs 200. Which they were happily paying, at the rate of 18 per cent. And all was hunky dory.

However, in August 2023, this situation took a dramatic change for the worse. The GST council, which consists of finance ministers from the central as well as state governments, came down hard on the business. In fact, *they clubbed online gaming with gambling*, such as betting on race horses, casinos or even online gambling. Further, they decided that *GST would be payable on the entire amount that the customer had put in*—in other words, Rs 1000. According to experts (and I'm definitely not one of them), this is not fair, because they were charging Rs 200 for the services they rendered, and this is what they should have paid GST on.

But there was more bad news. Not only was GST charged on the full amount of Rs 1000, but the rate of GST was also raised from 18 per cent to 28 per cent. And these new rules were applicable from 1 October 2023, to be reviewed after six months.

You can imagine the chaos that ensued after this decision. This decision made online gaming less attractive than earlier. Because a lot of the money that used to go to both the gaming companies as well as the prize pool, would now go into taxes. In fact, after this decision, some smaller players announced that they were shutting down their business.

However, there is hope. First of all, there is a six-month trial window, after which the decision will be reviewed (and it should have happened by the time you read this book). As I had mentioned earlier in Chapter 22, in his post-budget speech in 2022, our prime minister had stressed on the gaming sector. According to him, gaming had a huge international market and India was exploring increasing its footprint in this area. Given his interest, most companies and gaming associations have written to him, requesting him to intervene and to make this happen.

Secondly, while many smaller gaming companies will suffer losses (and some have already shut down), guess what? Dream Sports remains profitable, even after this GST shock.

Why?

Well, you already know the answer, don't you? They run a frugal business. The focus is on *dhandha*, or profitability. In fact, after this GST shock, they have become even more cost-conscious. Soon after the decision was announced, the founders got into *dhandha* mode and took certain key decisions. First of all, they cut down on advertising spend. Remember their strong belief in retention of customers over acquisition of new ones? And the fact that happy customers would get new ones through word of mouth or referrals? So guess what? As I write this chapter, the 2023 cricket world cup is on. Naturally, I expected the TV to be plastered with Dream11 ads. After all, if Dream11 ads could be seen all over the place during the IPL, surely the World Cup would see a similar advertising blitz, if not more.

But no. This was *dhandha* (sorry for repeating the term, but I find it really expressive). The company had to be profitable. And it wasn't clear what the impact of the new GST decision would be. So advertising had to be cut down. Yes, I did see some Dream11 jerseys on TV but that was it. No big-bang advertising. Period.

The founders made one more decision. Remember, they had started investing in sports-related companies through Dream Capital? Well, they have now dissolved Dream Capital and decided to focus only on large, strategic investments, where Harsh and Bhavit could be involved. So rather than investing in unrelated businesses— even if they were in the area of sports—they now focused only on investments closely related to their core business.

And yes, they still continue to recruit for certain roles. That's right, in spite of the huge GST googly. After all, they need to plan for the future, don't they? And of course, there have been no mass lay-offs. No way. That's not in their DNA, you see?

Finally, please remember, Dream Sports has survived multiple crises in its journey. They went through tough times in their initial years when business was not picking up. But they survived. They went through tough times when they couldn't get funding. But they ultimately got multiple rounds. They went through a torrid time during the Covid-19 pandemic because there were no matches, and therefore, no fantasy sports. But they not only survived but came back with a bang. And you can see the results today.

Yes, my friend, that's the resilience of this company, its founders and the entire team of Dreamsters. They persevere, they focus on the user and they figure out solutions. And there is no doubt that they will not only survive this shock but continue their market-leading growth as well. And yes, they will continue to be profitable—although the profits could be lower than earlier.

A Peep into the Future

Knowing the company and its DNA and knowing its founders, the future of Dream Sports can be described in one simple phrase: Bright, brighter, brightest. The founders realize that 'digital' is growing solidly in India. And the key is 'digital youth'. They estimate that there are seventy crore online sports fans in India. Yes, you heard that right—three quarters of a billion online sports fans. I've already told you that twenty crore of them have registered on the platform, so as you can see, that's just the tip of the iceberg. In a recent report[*] by Deloitte and the Federation of Indian Fantasy Sports (FIFS), the market size for online fantasy sports is expected to grow to Rs 1,65,000 crore by 2024–25. That's a staggering forty times the revenue that Dream Sports generates today.

So the market is very much there.

---

[*] Naini Thaker, 'Dream11 turned fantasy (gaming) into reality. Now it's eyeing a diversified sports tech future', *Forbes India*, 8 June 2022, https://www.forbesindia.com/article/sports-tech-special/dream11-turned-fantasy-(gaming)-into-reality-now-its-eyeing-a-diversified-sports-tech-future/77065/1.

And what about profitability? Well, the founders believe that profitability will only go up, because they've already spent a huge amount on marketing, and that's a fixed cost. So while usage and therefore revenues will go up in the future, marketing spend will not go up proportionately. Therefore, the margins in the business will only improve, which means higher profitability.

Finally, just to prove that Harsh is serious about future growth, here is a post he put up on LinkedIn in 2022, when mass lay-offs were the flavour of the tech industry in the USA:

> With all the 2022 tech lay-offs in the US, please spread the word to remind Indians to come back home (especially those with visa issues), to help Indian Tech realize our hyper-growth potential in the next decade.
>
>   We have 10 kickass portfolio companies in Fantasy Sports, NFTs, Sports OTT, FinTech, Sports Experiences etc., that are constantly looking for great talent, especially with leadership experience in Design, Product & Tech. If you or someone you know fits the above, feel free to reach out to us.

Harsh also shared an email address (indiareturns@dreamsports. group) for all these techies who had been laid off to reach out to Dream Sports.

And that's the confidence our young founder Harsh Jain has in the future of his wonderful **earnicorn** . . .

Finally, Some Learning for Young Entrepreneurs

Dear reader, I'm sure the entire story of Dream11 and Dream Sports has been a great learning experience for you—as it has for me. But before I end the story, here are some terrific nuggets from Harsh, especially for you:

When you look at Dream Sports, and more specifically, Dream11, you see a major success story in the Indian Internet world. You see a true market leader, well ahead of the rest of the pack. But the journey wasn't easy. And one of the things we have learnt as founders, is that to build a successful company, you must solve a problem that you care deeply about. You need to be stubborn about it. Sleep with it, wake up with it, live and breathe the problem and your solution. And keep on and on and on at it. Perseverance is the name of the game.

In our case, the problem was to introduce fantasy sports to the Indian consumer, and believe me, all our waking lives—and a lot of our sleeping lives as well—were spent thinking about this issue and working on it. That's why we succeeded.

Finally, you must remember that becoming an entrepreneur is not a part-time occupation. It's not work. It's your life. And that is why you need people around you who understand what you are going through, such as your family and friends. These are the people who will support you in tough times. But these are also the people who will slap you when you are doing something wrong and need to be slapped.

And with that, let me wish all those young entrepreneurs out there all the very best.

27

Let's Analyse the Earnicorn: Dream Sports

And now, let's analyse the business—sorry, the **earnicorn**. As before, we'll take a look at the core business, Dream11. You are welcome to analyse the others yourself!

Dream11: The PERSISTENT Business

First of all, are these guys solving a PROBLEM?

Interestingly, the answer is 'no'. There was no problem—unless you call boredom a problem 😊. But there was definitely an opportunity. An opportunity to get people to play fantasy cricket, and ultimately, fantasy sports of all kinds. By the way, this is not an uncommon situation. Facebook did something similar by providing a platform for users to post stuff that they wanted to, where their friends could see it. So did Instagram. Or even TikTok, which allows you to post videos. And that provides an interesting variation to the PERSISTENT model. Yes, in general, businesses need to solve a problem for the customer. But there are situations where you could look at an opportunity instead of a problem.

Of course, the EARNINGS MODEL is clear—although it took a lot of time for the founders to find the right one. As you've seen, initially they tried to get advertisers to pay, but ultimately it was the user who paid.

What about the SIZE OF THE MARKET? Again, this is interesting. When these guys started, fantasy sports was almost unheard of in India. Therefore, the market size at that point was nothing to write home about. But assuming they could get people hooked, the *potential size of the market* was phenomenal. In some ways, this was similar to the Naukri situation, but for different reasons. Remember, when Naukri was launched, there weren't too many users on the Internet, so the market size was small. But the potential market size was huge. On the other hand, by the time Dream11 was launched, the number of users on the Internet had grown significantly, so that was not an issue. The issue was that fantasy sports was unknown, so at that point there was no market. But if the company could popularize the concept, well, it would become a huge potential market. And as you've seen from the figures Dream11 has reached—twenty crore registered users—*they actually created a massive market*, almost from scratch.

And that's an interesting message for all of you readers (and founders) out there:

You might not have a huge market right now, but as long as the potential is large, well, you could be in business!

By the way, there was no need for the business to look for a NICHE, simply because there was no large competitor. In fact, the few that existed earlier had closed down. So it was a huge potential market, and completely non-crowded.

What about SCALABILITY? Well, it's an online business. It is not manpower-dependent. Therefore, like Naukri and Zerodha, which you've read about earlier in this book, it is highly scalable.

And now for RISKS. As always, one of the biggest risks to any business, is the possibility of competition getting in and killing you. For which you need an ENTRY BARRIER. Over time, Dream11 has been highly successful in creating such an entry barrier, because the business has grown phenomenally. And when you grow, two things happen: First of all, your brand gets noticed, and that's what attracts newer and newer customers to you. Obviously, this depends on your customers being happy, which is taken care of by the company's 'User First' policy. Remember, they have kept the ticket size small to make their users comfortable. They have also tried to ensure that at least half their users get their money back. And the icing on the cake—the feature called 'Dream responsibly', where users who lose significant amounts of money are discouraged from playing more. So that's how they are able to keep their customers happy, and that's how they have built a strong brand. And that's their entry barrier.

Secondly, when you grow, your fixed costs get amortized over a larger and larger number of users, so you are able to charge less than your competitors. That's exactly what the company has been able to do, and that only strengthened their entry barrier.

However, in the case of Dream11, there were some other risks. Initially, they faced the risk of lack of funds, which they overcame by starting the parallel business of social media marketing through Red Digital. Thanks to the persistence of the founders, they were finally able to get funding, so they were no longer dependent on the Red Digital business.

Secondly, like most organizations, Dream11 also went through a horrendous time during the Covid-19 pandemic because there were no matches and therefore, no fantasy sports. However, they used this period to develop their products further. They did not resort to mass lay-offs, and therefore kept the team motivated. So when the pandemic started receding and sports matches resumed, well, they were in a great position to restart the business with a bang.

But perhaps the biggest risks the company faced were the legal and regulatory hurdles. Initially, they were clubbed into the category of 'game of chance' as opposed to 'game of skill'. It was the persistence of the entire team, led by the founders, that helped them get a favourable judgement from the Supreme Court of India. But then there was the GST risk in October 2023, which remains unresolved at the time of writing this book. As I've mentioned in the previous chapter, the GST council has now decided to charge the highest rate of 28 per cent, and that too on the entire amount that the user puts into a game. Obviously, the gaming industry is in a tizzy. But given the perseverance of the founders as well as the entire team, and the fact that they are running a frugal, profitable business, no one doubts that they will ultimately recover from this shock as well. In fact, the company is likely to remain profitable even after this shock, and that's saying a lot!

Now for the last three letters in our PERSISTENT model. Starting with 'I' for INNOVATION. I've already mentioned the online quizzes these guys conduct during IPL matches. Where the winner gets to be a part of the presentation ceremony and a chance to hand over a trophy and a cheque to the 'Dream11 Game Changer of the Match'. Can you imagine anything more innovative?

Then of course, there are the phenomenally innovative people policies followed by the company. For example, the 'proximity to the stadium' allowance, where team members staying within half an hour of the stadium (their Mumbai office), get 40 per cent off on their rent. Just to make sure these people don't spend hours and hours commuting in the city. And the extravagant sports environment they have created in their stadium. Any team member who is crazy about sports would find it tough to leave this environment, wouldn't he?

Thanks to all these innovative policies, the company has been able to attract people, and more importantly, retain them. In other words, they have a motivated, charged-up, high-performing and above all, stable TEAM. Of course, the fact that there have been no mass layoffs, even during bad times, helps. You see, when the team believes that the company will look after them, well, they look after the company as well.

Finally, I've spoken about TRACTION several times, and I don't think I need to repeat it. Today, they have twenty crore registered users—yes, twenty crore—and they have reached revenues of nearly Rs 2000 crore. They are far ahead of their competitors and are showing no signs of stopping.

A truly PERSISTENT business, if ever there was one. And of course, I'm delighted because that makes it three in three. All three of the businesses I've spoken about so far, namely Naukri, Zerodha and Dream11, follow my favourite PERSISTENT model. And I simply cannot wait to look at the last one, Zoho!

The PERFECT Attitude

And now for the other framework: the PERFECT Attitude of the founders. Actually, I don't think I need to say much. The designation of the founder, Harsh, 'Culture Enforcement Officer', says it all, doesn't it?

Interestingly, several aspects of this PERFECT attitude are already included in the 'DO PUT' culture of the company. CUSTOMER ORIENTED is the same thing as USER FIRST: Look after the customer, keep him happy, and not only will he come back to you, but bring friends along as well. And you've seen enough examples of this when I talked about Culture in Chapter 24. Then of course, the idea of 'Dream responsibly', so that no customer loses too much money. Just look at the phenomenal ETHICS of the founders here: They were willing to lose revenues just to ensure that the customer did not lose too much. Then the fact that they let users play without any charge—and even if they *did* play with money, they kept the average ticket size low. And of course, they ensured that at least half their customers got their money back while playing. Customer orientation at its very best, isn't it?

What about RESPONSIBILITY? Very simple. Remember when Harsh took Rs 2 crore from his father and blew it up within two weeks? And then he went back to his father to ask for Rs 8 crore more? Remember what happened?

Harsh accepted full responsibility for this failure. He realized that he didn't know enough and that he definitely did not know how to manage money. And he was more than willing to learn from his father. Even later, when he got funding from investors, he was happy to learn from his investors. And of course, he gives much of the credit for the success of Dream Sports to these people.

What about the willingness to do EVERYTHING? Remember, I had told you that both Harsh and Bhavit often pick up the phone to take user calls. Just to get user feedback, first-hand. Can you imagine the CEO and COO doing this? Well, these guys have been doing it all along!

FLEXIBILITY is obvious, isn't it? The founders had started off with multiple offerings: fantasy cricket, cricket news, cricket blogs, polls related to cricket and even physical cricket games. But they soon realized that they needed to focus on one product, which is why they stuck to fantasy cricket and dropped the others, at least for the moment. And once fantasy cricket took off in the form of Dream11, well, they brought everything else back. Even within fantasy cricket, they experimented with different models for several years until finally zeroing in on something that gamers were willing to accept.

And, of course, the big GST googly. What did the founders do? Well, they realized that they would need to become even more cost-conscious, so they reduced their ad spend dramatically. Minimal advertising during the 2023 World Cup—although I did see some Dream11 jerseys. And that, my friend, is flexibility. Incidentally, the number of users on their platform has not gone down since this announcement. It's actually gone up.

PERSEVERING should not need any explanation either. The founders persevered through the initial years, where they had to experiment with multiple models. They persevered through the entire legal battle over 'game of skill' vs 'game of chance.' They persevered for years, trying to get investors to fund them. Remember the 150 odd meetings Harsh and Bhavit had with investors? And of course, they persevered through the Covid-19 pandemic, when everything was at rock bottom.

Finally, how can I forget how Harsh persevered with wooing his future wife, Rachna, and finally got a 'yes' from her 😊.

What about building TRUST? Again, obvious, isn't it? When a customer realizes that the platform does not want him to lose too much money, thanks to the feature they call 'Dream responsibly', his TRUST in the platform shoots up, doesn't it? And what about team members? *No lay-offs during bad times.* And this happened not once, but twice. First during their early years, when they started their social media marketing outfit, Red Digital, and transferred most of their team members there. And then again, when the Covid-19 pandemic hit and there were no matches, so there was no revenue either. Their philosophy has always been just great: 'You guys look after the company during good times. So during bad times, the company will look after you!'

And that, dear reader, is the PERFECT Attitude of the founders!

The Profitable Business

Now for the one thing that this book is all about. How did Dream Sports become profitable? How have they become an earnicorn? And how have they remained that way?

Clearly, the starting point was Harsh's family background. If you have any idea about business families in India, you would know that Marwari business families are right up there in the pecking order, starting with the Birlas, the Goenkas, the Bajajs, the Dalmias and so on. So the operative word for Dream 11—and by extension, Dream Sports—was dhandha. It wasn't growth while making a loss year after year. Business for Harsh meant profits, not valuation. He and his co-founder, Bhavit were creating a business for life, not something that they would sell off in a few years. That's the mindset they started off with. And that's the mindset they continue to have today. As you can imagine, this mindset percolated down to the entire team. Yes, initially they were loss-making, and had to raise several rounds of funding. But that was natural, given that they were trying to create something that didn't exist in the country, and therefore needed huge marketing spends. And of course, they needed external funds to generate prize money for their users. But once they turned the corner and became profitable, well, there was no looking back.

But how did they ensure profitability?

Very simple. The company has always run a frugal business. And I don't think there can be a better example of this than the founders' strong, almost fanatical belief in 'retention' as opposed to 'acquisition', whether it is customers or team-members. Their strong customer orientation—for instance, ensuring that at least half their customers get their money back or preventing the customer from losing more money when he reaches a certain limit. Great practices such as these have ensured that their customers stay with them.

Similarly for their team members. Where the standout decision was 'no lay-offs' ever—even during Covid-19 times, when business had plummeted to zero. Which built a strong feeling of ownership and loyalty amongst their team. And of course, the focus on maintaining small, close-knit teams, giving them challenging targets and getting them to grow. All of these wonderful practices have ensured that their manpower costs have remained low.

Overall, of course, the founders have always run a tight ship. Just imagine, for such a huge company—a market leader in its field—they have only one office, spread over two floors in Mumbai's BKC. No overheads of maintaining multiple offices. And that's one more step towards the famed dhandha.

So, that's it. That is the fascinating story of Dream11 and the larger Dream Sports group. The third **earnicorn** in this book.

Finally, let me just end this story with my favourite punchline once again: If you have a start-up, or are planning to build one, do learn from these giants. Make sure it's a PERSISTENT business. With you as the founder having just the PERFECT Attitude.

And of course, focus on PROFITABILITY—sorry, DHANDHA!

Section V

Zoho

28

Zoho: The Early Years

Let me start with a question. Think about India's largest and most respected software products company. Now, where do you think the founder and CEO of this company operates from?

Bengaluru, isn't it? Or perhaps Mumbai? Or maybe, just maybe, Gurugram?

Sounds logical, doesn't it?

But what if I told you it was Mathalamparai (I hope I've got the spelling right).

Matha . . . ?

Yes, you heard right. It's Mathalamparai.

Haven't heard of it? Well, neither had I. So let me give you a hint. It's a village in the district of Tenkasi.

Still haven't heard of it?

Okay, let me give you a bigger hint. It's in the state of Tamil Nadu, around 650 kilometres from Chennai.

Ah!

That was my reaction as well.

But wait. There's more. The founder starts his day at 4 a.m. That's right, it's a multinational company with many of its clients in the USA, so he must adjust to US timings. Then he moves out of his office into the adjoining fields, and does what his ancestors used to do—farming. Which includes cultivation of paddy, coconut, mangoes and several vegetables. And yes, there is the occasional snake to be caught.

But then, like all human beings, he also needs to take a break from time to time. So, what does he do during this break?

Well, play cricket with the children in the village, of course. What a silly question!

Now as you can imagine, the more I got to know about this gentleman and his company, the more fascinated I became. And I kept asking myself one question: Why was he operating from a village? And why was he pursuing farming—in addition to developing world-class software?

And as I probed deeper, I realized that Sridhar Vembu, the founder and CEO of Zoho Corporation, hadn't always operated from the village of Mathalamparai. He was earlier in Silicon Valley, California, living in and around San Francisco. The hub of the software world, as you are aware. But he came back to India with a vision: to personally bring Silicon Valley to the villages of Tamil Nadu.

Can there be a more fascinating story than this?

That's exactly what I thought. And the moment I learnt this, I made my decision. Zoho and its amazing founder simply had to be featured in this book.

Where It All Began

Let's start at the very beginning. Sridhar Vembu was born in a village in the Thanjavur district of Tamil Nadu. As you might expect, many people in his family were farmers, although his father worked in the High Court. Young Sridhar was a brilliant student. He went to IIT Madras, from where he got his BTech degree in electrical engineering in 1989. As if that wasn't enough, he went to Princeton, one of the top universities in the world, to do his PhD, once again in electrical engineering. And then he got a great job as a wireless systems engineer with Qualcomm, the well-known giant in the field. And you would think that he was all set for a wonderful career, working for large American corporations.

But that didn't happen. No, sir. By now, as in the case of many bright engineers who left India for the USA, the entrepreneurship bug had begun to bite. And bite hard. Sridhar realized that India had great talent, but produced virtually no software products. Yes, there were software service companies such as TCS, Infosys and Wipro—all world-class companies—but these were *service* companies, not *product* companies. And that's how our young electrical engineer decided to start his own company, which would build software products for network management.

He spoke to Tony Thomas, his senior from IIT Madras, as well as two of his brothers, Kumar and Sekar, and they all agreed with him. And that's when they launched their company in 1996. Shortly afterwards, two friends, Shailesh Kumar Davey and Sreenivas Kanumuru, also joined them. At that time, the company was called **AdventNet Inc**. As the name indicates, it was headquartered in the USA, specifically in Pleasanton, California, in the heart of Silicon Valley. But most of the development took place in Chennai. Tony became the CEO: After all, he *was* Sridhar's senior at IIT Madras. And since the USA was their biggest target market, Sridhar stayed on in California, evangelizing and marketing their products.

The first series of products AdventNet created was aimed at network service providers—in other words, companies that set up computer networks for their clients. Under the brand name **WebNMS.** You see, after having installed computer networks for their clients, these network service providers would need to manage these networks as well. What if the network went down? What if it was slow? What if a part of the network was not functioning? They couldn't have an engineer rushing to the client's site to resolve the problem every time, could they? No sir, they would diagnose the problem and try and fix it remotely, without even visiting the client location. And that's where WebNMS helped. (I must clarify that this is a highly simplified version of what the software did. Enough for you to appreciate the AdventNet story. After all, I don't expect more than perhaps 1 per cent of the readers of this book to be network engineers. Neither am I, for that matter 😊.)

By the way, AdventNet was among the first Indian companies to develop *software products*. And they did phenomenally well. In fact, among their early buyers was the world leader in the field, Cisco Systems. By 2000, the company had clocked a revenue of $10 million (remember, the market for AdventNet was global, which is why I'm giving you the revenue in dollars and not rupees). Even more, it was profitable.

Incidentally, at around this time Tony moved out, and Sridhar took over as the CEO of the company while staying on in the USA.

Thanks, But We Don't Want Your Money

Now at this stage, something fascinating happened. AdventNet had good growth, a global presence and profitability. A very rare combination, as you can imagine. And who do you think was attracted because of this combination?

Investors, of course! Venture Capitalists, who were used to loss-making companies, suddenly saw this as an opportunity to park their money. They came in droves. But Sridhar would have none of it. It's interesting to listen to him on the subject:[*]

> When you take external funding, you lose your freedom. And you would probably be forced to make some compromises, which might be good for the investor but not for the company. For instance, one VC had come to us with a term sheet. This term sheet had a clause which said that we had to provide an exit to the VC within seven or eight years. Tell me, how can I make such a

---

[*] Harichandan Arakali, 'The Bootstrapped Buddhist: How Sridhar Vembu built Zoho', *Forbes India*, 6 June 2016, https://www.forbesindia.com/article/boardroom/the-bootstrapped-buddhist-how-sridhar-vembu-built-zoho/43383/1.

commitment? How can I guarantee an exit, and that too, within a fixed time frame?

That was perhaps the only time Sridhar spoke to investors. He realized that they would lose their freedom to experiment, and be forced to make compromises if they took external funding. They would not be able to invest in long-gestation projects because the investors would expect returns within a specified time frame. And that's when he made his decision: no external funding.

To this day, he has stuck to his guns. The company has never taken money from external investors. Yes, they did take some money from a few friends and family, and obviously the co-founders put in money. But that was it. Incidentally, they could perhaps have grown faster had they taken money. But that is not the way they wanted to run their company. No sir, Sridhar wanted to build the company his way, without any pressure from investors.

And there is something more. Sridhar has always had a firm belief that getting too much easy money from outside builds bad habits. 'It's not real,' according to him. 'It builds bad habits. It distorts behaviour all around.' (Dear reader, doesn't this remind you of what Sanjeev Bikhchandani said in the Info Edge story?)

In fact, very early on in the game, Sridhar had predicted the demise of frenetic funding at higher and higher valuations, especially for loss-making companies. He has always believed that these valuations were quite ridiculous, and he was clear that the bubble would burst one day. Which, of course, it has.

Finally, this tells you something about Sridhar. One of his strengths is his uncanny ability to predict trends. You'll see more of this as you read on.

Yes, my friend, you do need to read on . . .

29

AdventNet Becomes Zoho Corporation

So the journey of AdventNet continued, with Sridhar at the helm and without any external funding. However, as you might have guessed, in 2000 they were hit by the dot-com bust. With companies around them collapsing, there was a need for AdventNet to diversify. But into what? That was the key question.

Let's look at Sridhar's thought process. You see, WebNMS was aimed at network service providers. Companies such as Cisco Systems, which would set up and manage networks for *their* clients. That much you already know (if you don't, please go back and read the previous chapter properly).

But what about the clients themselves? Let's take the example of an FMCG company such as Hindustan Unilever, or HUL, where such a network had been set up. The IT department of HUL would now need to manage each desktop or laptop that was connected to the network. They would need to ensure that the right people got the right access to resources. For instance, while the top management would need access to all the data in the organization, the more junior people would be given access on a 'need to know' basis. The IT department would also need to manage data security. They would need to get reports on the usage of their IT resources. And so on . . .

Now, the next bit is extremely important, so please listen carefully: These tasks would be managed by the IT department of

HUL, and not their network service provider. Obvious, isn't it? Can you imagine the chaos if Cisco Systems had to get involved each time a new employee joined HUL? Or resigned and left? Or was transferred from one department to another? There was no way that Cisco Systems could manage these micro transactions. (By the way, I've just mentioned Cisco as an example. It could be any network service provider.) It was the IT department of HUL that would need to do it. And for this, they would need software to help them manage all of this.

That's when Sridhar smelt another huge opportunity. It was also a great way to diversify and de-risk the business in the aftermath of the tough, tough dot-com bust. That's when he and his team swung into action, and began developing another series of software products. These products would help the IT departments of user organizations manage their network and all the devices on it. The products were aimed at mid-sized organizations, but obviously they could be used by larger ones as well. The products were rolled out in 2003 under the brand name **Manage Engine.** As you can imagine, they were an instant success and the company now had two sets of world-class products in its stable!

The World Moves towards Cloud Computing

So AdventNet had diversified their user base. They had started with network service providers, and had then moved on to user organizations as well. But there was more. You see, around 2004, the concept of SaaS and cloud computing was beginning to take shape. Obviously, you know what these two terms mean. But just in case you have forgotten, here's a mini tutorial—which you can safely skip if you're an expert:

I'll start with an analogy. In today's world, everyone has electricity at home. Now, there are two ways to get this electricity. You could, of course, buy and install a diesel generator, for which you'll spend a lot of money. Then there is the hassle of buying diesel for it on a regular basis. Plus of course, when it goes down, you would rush to the market to buy spares. And then you would need to pay your technician a huge amount to repair it. And so on . . .

But of course, you don't follow this approach (at least I hope you don't). Instead, you would get a connection from your local electricity provider. No buying an expensive genset. Instead, you pay per month for the electricity you have consumed. No hassles of ensuring that diesel is available. And of course, maintenance is not your headache; it's the supplier's headache. To summarize, you do not install your own mechanism for generating electricity. Instead, you *buy* and *use* electricity as a *service*.

Of course, you know all this. But what you perhaps do not know is that these two diverse approaches apply to software as well. The first one has been the traditional approach, where you buy the software from the vendor (actually, you buy a licence to use it—you never really buy software). And then you would need to buy a server as well, on which the software would be installed. Both expensive propositions. Maintaining both the server as well as the software is once again your headache.

However, as in the case of electricity for your home, you have another solution for software as well. Because *some vendors have made their software available on their own servers.* All you need is your desktop or laptop and an Internet connection. And you can log into their software and use it. You don't need to buy the software, and you don't need to buy a server. Taking care of maintenance, bugs, etc. is the responsibility of the vendor. All you have to do is pay him on a monthly basis, based on the usage. Exactly as you would for your electricity connection.

This concept is called 'Software as a Service' (SaaS for short), just as you had electricity as a service. Further, since the software is not running in your premises but somewhere out there, we say that it's running on the cloud. And that, my friend, is the origin of the term 'cloud computing'. (By the way, please do thank me for the new terms you have learnt today—SaaS and cloud computing. Let me tell you, these are great terms to throw around nonchalantly at a party. Even more so, if you know what they mean 😊.)

As you can imagine—and I hope you can—when this concept started catching on, the world sat up and took notice. SaaS was a far more convenient way to use software than buying and installing it. And Sridhar sat up and took notice of it as well. What a great opportunity! So far, AdventNet had been providing software that their customers would buy and install on their own servers. This was true of both WebNMS and Manage Engine. But now, Sridhar decided to jump onto the cloud bandwagon and provide SaaS-based software to his customers.

That's when, in the year 2005, the company launched its first SaaS-based product, **Zoho Writer**, an online word processor. And then in 2006, they launched one of their star products, **Zoho CRM** (Customer Relationship Management). Once again, running on the cloud in SaaS mode. Perhaps the most well-known product to come out of the Zoho stable. And an instant success!

Dear reader, I want you to notice something interesting. The company had started off by offering network management software, aimed at network service providers. Software that was installed on the server of the client organization. From there, they graduated to software that the IT departments of user organizations could use, to help them manage day-to-day operations of their networks as well as the devices on it. Once again, to be installed on the server of the organization that was using it. And finally, they moved on to software that users themselves could use—in SaaS mode, of course.

Very soon, the company realized that offering SaaS products to users was a huge opportunity. And that's when they started developing software to help users across all the functions they needed to perform. Software such as email, collaboration and other office productivity tools such as chats, as well as software for managing customers, partners and vendors. All running on the cloud, of course. Remember, I had told you that Sridhar was great at catching trends early? And this was a major trend that he foresaw. A trend where companies would not buy software, but would simply access it over the Internet and pay as they went along. Yes my friend, Sridhar was clear that his company would be at the forefront of this trend.

And that's when something interesting happened, so please stop doodling and read the following carefully (if you must doodle, please don't do it on the pages of this book—I dislike having my books damaged). While the company had started with network management software, it had now gone far beyond it. Their major growth area was now SaaS-based software for users. And in this context, Sridhar realized that AdventNet was perhaps not the best name for his company. There was a lot of soul-searching and debate, and finally, they hit upon the interesting name, **Zoho Corporation**. In any case, some of their products, such as the word processing software, were already being sold under the brand name Zoho.

Why was the name Zoho chosen? Well, Sridhar liked the sound of it. Wasn't that enough reason for the founder to pick the name?

So that was it. AdventNet became Zoho Corporation in the year 2009. Or Zoho Corp., in case you wanted to save precious time and not pronounce those three extra syllables. By the way, at this stage, Zoho Corp. shifted its headquarters to India. Specifically to Chennai, even though Pleasanton in California continued to be their base for global sales.

And now, for something really fascinating. Perhaps the biggest reason why I included the Zoho story in my book (apart from the fact that they are a rare product company to come out of India).

Yes, I'm referring to their journey into the heart of rural Tamil Nadu.

Want to read about it?

Sure. Just pick up a glass of filter coffee (no one drinks filter coffee in a cup, you see?).

And I'll take you to rural Tamil Nadu . . .

30

Zoho Goes Rural

Guys, this is the most fascinating part of the Zoho story. Don't miss it.

You see, for the first few years of his career, Sridhar's life followed a familiar pattern: brilliant engineer from one of the IITs, does his doctorate from a premier US university, works with a major multinational, launches his own software company, and of course, lives in Silicon Valley—where else?

But that's where there was a major break from the pattern. That's where he broke off from the path that so many Indians before him had followed. Because somewhere along the line, Sridhar Vembu decided to go rural.

No my friend, not rural California.

Rural Tamil Nadu!

How and why did this happen? Well, it's a long story but a truly fascinating one, so just read on . . .

I've already mentioned that when the company was launched as AdventNet, it was headquartered in Pleasanton, California, with its development centre in Chennai. Later, when it was transformed into Zoho Corp., the headquarters shifted to Chennai, with global sales being run by Sridhar from Pleasanton. But there was always something at the back of the young man's mind. Something that made him restless. Something that made him realize that he was destined for bigger things. And to understand this, you must hear him out:[*]

> An old lady in my father's village—this was probably when I was 12 or 13—told me, 'You are a smart kid. You're going to do well in life. But however well you do, don't ever forget that you come from this village, as the village can't afford to lose you.'

Those words stayed with Sridhar. They haunted him. He had always wondered why there was so much poverty and unemployment in India—especially when you moved away from the major metros to smaller towns and even villages. Having travelled in the USA, the difference between India and the West became even more stark. In fact, it's interesting to hear what he once told his brother, Kumar:

> We have so many problems in India. Why doesn't someone do anything about them? In fact, we guys are perhaps in the top 0.1 percentile of educated people in India. If we don't do something, who will?

That was Sridhar's thinking. And gradually, an idea began to take place in his mind. He wouldn't just talk. He had to do something about the problem. He had to make a difference. He had to create employment. And the old lady's words kept coming back to him. Which meant that he had to make this difference in rural India.

In any case, Sridhar had never been keen on the idea of people migrating from villages to cities in search of employment. After all, migrating to a city to take up a job is tough, isn't it? With the traffic, pollution, soaring rents and all the other goodies that cities are so well known for? It's far more comfortable to stay at home,

---

[*] Harichandan Arakali, 'The Bootstrapped Buddhist: How Sridhar Vembu built Zoho', *Forbes India*, 6 June 2016, https://www.forbesindia.com/article/boardroom/the-bootstrapped-buddhist-how-sridhar-vembu-built-zoho/43383/1.

in an environment where you've been brought up. And if people are comfortable, that would have a huge positive impact on their productivity as well. Yes, Sridhar was hooked on the idea of giving young people good employment in or near their village. Perhaps by setting up small offices in different villages and connecting all of them through the Internet.

In fact, his thinking went even further. He wanted his city-based employees to spend some time in villages. That would bring in cross-fertilization of ideas—from cities to villages and vice versa. In addition, senior people from the city could mentor and coach people from the village, making them more employable.

That's when he decided to build a software development centre for Zoho in one of the villages in Tamil Nadu. As you can imagine, this was a completely unique experiment. No one had tried it out before. Software being built in villages? No way! But Sridhar has always had strong beliefs. He was determined to make this experiment work. And that is how the company bought four acres of land in Mathalamparai, in the district of Tenkasi, Tamil Nadu. And set up an office there in the year 2011. So employees could live in the village (or in a nearby village) and come to work within the village itself. No migrating to cities and living in tiny, rented apartments. They could comfortably stay at home with their parents, in an environment where they had been brought up, and yet develop world-class software.

That's right, I said world-class software. Because one of their best-selling products, **Zoho Desk**, which enables customers to interact with their vendor for their queries and complaints, was built in Mathalamparai.

Zoho Schools: The Unique Experiment

But there's a lot more. By now, you must have realized that Sridhar Vembu doesn't like doing things the conventional way. He does things differently. Not because he wants to be different, but because he genuinely believes that there are better ways to do things, and he is willing to experiment. The fact that he does not have investors breathing down his neck helps, because it allows him to experiment.

And one of the most dramatic experiments that he and his company carried out was in the area of people.

You see, when you set up a software company, what do you need? Programmers, isn't it? And which country do you get your programmers from? India, of course. Silly question. So while Zoho (at that time AdventNet) had clients all over the world and Sridhar was based in Silicon Valley, their development centre was in Chennai. Which is exactly what you would expect.

But I can guarantee you would not have expected the next step. Sridhar had always believed in taking on people with potential and the will to succeed. Too bad if they didn't have an appropriate degree, such as a BTech or an MCA. He believed that many such people—without degrees—could actually perform better than those with a degree, provided they received the appropriate practical training and mentorship. Fortunately, his co-founders as well as his senior management agreed with him. And that's when the company did something unthinkable. Something no other software company had done. They decided to take on bright youngsters with potential, *straight out of Class 12*.

That's right. No degree. And that's when, early on in their journey, in 2004, they launched Zoho University (now called **Zoho Schools**), where these youngsters would be trained.

Let's hear what Sridhar has to say on this subject:*

Formal education only takes you so far, but most of the contextual knowledge comes from actually doing something. The Internet is a force multiplier. Now, if one wants to learn something from

---

* Harichandan Arakali, 'The Bootstrapped Buddhist: How Sridhar Vembu built Zoho', *Forbes India*, 6 June 2016, https://www.forbesindia.com/article/boardroom/the-bootstrapped-buddhist-how-sridhar-vembu-built-zoho/43383/1.

scratch, it takes perseverance, but the tools and the lessons are available almost for free. It's very powerful. It is changing the way education works, companies and organizations work. That's why Zoho University is about this contextual knowledge. We impart that kind of thinking to the trainees so that they can themselves go on to acquire what they need.

So now that you know the thinking behind the concept of Zoho Schools, let's dive into some more details. First of all, it runs a two-year programme. They take in students from all kinds of backgrounds. And this is the key: Many of these students come from low-income families—often with a rural background.

Why?

Well, let's hear out Rajendran Dandapani, director of technology at Zoho and the president of Zoho Schools:

We wanted young people with fire in their belly. Those who had a strong desire to do something in life, but had not been able to proceed with their education because of their family backgrounds. These were the ones that were likely to perform well. And that's why we have always focused on students from low-income households.

For these young people, becoming an engineer was a distant dream. But at Zoho Schools, we have made this possible—not through a degree, but through actual hands-on learning and mentorship. By the way, by the age of twenty one, these students are earning and already have experience, while others of their age are still studying.

Zoho Schools is located within the Chennai campus of the company. To enable the youngsters to work with the experienced software professionals there, and thereby learn from them. So most of their learning is on-the-job rather than theoretical. Yes, they do have some formal classes, but most of their learning comes from actually working on the company's projects.

Finally, how much do they charge these young people?

Nothing.

That's right. They don't charge them at all. Instead, they pay them a stipend of Rs 10,000 per month, as long as they are part of the programme. After that, most of them are absorbed into Zoho. So it is a combination of formal classes along with an internship, where these students work along with experienced software professionals and pick up the required skills in the process. The other great thing is that these students are productive almost from day one.

Brilliant concept, isn't it?

Costs Down, Productivity Up

Dear reader, just take a look at the win-win situation here. Software professionals are expensive. And they are notorious for jumping ship. 'Fifteen per cent higher salary? Wonderful! I'll jump. Too bad if my project gets messed up. Not my responsibility anyway.' But here, you have young people from low-income families who are have got a wonderful opportunity in life. They are not as expensive as BTechs and MCAs. But given their background, they are earning wonderful salaries. Nowhere else would they get such a great opportunity to work, learn and grow professionally. And they are delighted to stay on. In fact, as you would imagine, manpower turnover among this category of programmers has been virtually zero.

Can you think of a better win-win?

And now for profitability. Since Zoho had never taken investor money, they had to make profits. That was the only way they would survive. Now, one of the key factors in profitability is the ability to control costs. In this context, look at Zoho Schools. Sridhar's primary idea was not to reduce the cost of manpower—it was to do his bit in developing the rural economy of Tamil Nadu and providing jobs to youngsters, which they would never have got otherwise.

But in the process, his manpower costs came down. Yes my friend, Zoho Schools is one of the factors that has led to lower costs, and thereby to the company becoming highly profitable. And of course, remaining that way.

But that's still not all. Not only did costs come down, productivity went up as well.

How? Simple. Let's say you were running a conventional software company based out of Bengaluru. (Bengaluru is just an example. I could have taken any of the other software hubs in the country, such as Gurugram, Hyderabad or Pune. The argument would remain the same.) Now you would be competing for manpower with all the other companies based out of Bengaluru. Yes, you would undoubtedly get some excellent programmers, but you would perhaps have to take on some average ones as well—simply because you needed numbers.

Next, many of these programmers would perhaps be staying in rented accommodation, and their attention would be divided between their programming assignments as well as the need to survive in a big, bad city (sorry, my friend, if you happen to live in one of them). And of course, they would always have one eye on Naukri.com for the next wonderful opportunity that might come along . . .

Get the point? Productivity suffers in the process, doesn't it?

But now look at Zoho, and specifically at Mathalamparai. The company has been able to get the best and brightest minds, perhaps across the entire district. No competition. And these young men and women live comfortably at home with their parents. No need to worry about rent, food or flat repairs. Their parents ensure that they get the best possible home-cooked food. And no one looks around for better opportunities. Because they already have a phenomenal opportunity in life with Zoho.

The result? Great young people, staying in a comfortable environment, not planning to leave, and not worrying about day-to-day problems. Can you imagine a better concoction? Yes, my friend, Zoho's programmers have always been extremely productive. In fact, Sridhar is fond of saying that the manpower productivity at Zoho is significantly higher than the productivity at most major software companies in India. And it's not difficult to understand why.

So costs came down and productivity went up. No wonder Zoho has always been an extremely profitable venture.

Let's Meet Some Alumni

And now, let's meet some of the people who have had the good fortune to attend Zoho Schools. Starting with Abdul Alim, who used to work with Zoho as a security guard. Yes, you heard it right. He was a security guard. But he was passionate about programming and used to work on the computer at the reception desk whenever he had time. The result? Someone at Zoho noticed him and realized that this young man had potential. That's when he joined Zoho Schools. And now, he is no longer a security guard. No sir, he is a proud and committed programmer at Zoho. And he's been there for ten years.

Or take the case of Paramasivam Saran Babu, who came from a typical lower-income family in Tamil Nadu. In the year 2005, Babu was studying in Class 12 at a government school. But he couldn't think of going beyond that. After all, family finances were tight. In fact, the family needed additional income. That's when an opportunity came along in the form of Zoho Schools. And then, of course, there was no looking back. Babu is now a proud product manager with Zoho. And life for him has only been up and up since then.

By the way, before joining Zoho Schools, Babu couldn't even operate a computer, and could barely speak English. Today, he doesn't have a degree, but drives a fancy car and has bought his own house. Of course, he makes frequent trips to Silicon Valley in the USA, in addition to several other countries. Incidentally, he has also convinced his brother to join Zoho Schools, and both brothers now work with Zoho.

And now for something really interesting. Guess why his in-laws agreed to get their daughter married to him?

Because of his career prospects.

That's Zoho Schools for you!

Then there is Sivakumar B., whose story really hit me. His mother was employed by Zoho as a security guard. She introduced him to Zoho Schools, and for some time they used to come to Zoho together—she as a security guard and he as a student. And now, guess what? Sivakumar is working as a security analyst at Zoho. Can you imagine how proud his mother would be today?

One last story about alumni at Zoho Schools. This one is from Prem Vishwanathan. Here is what he says:

> I opted for Zoho University (the earlier name for Zoho Schools)
> over higher studies in the US. It is interesting to learn from people
> who practice what they teach.

In fact, I would suggest that you check out their website: Zohoschools.com. And you'll see many, many more such success stories.

Today, around 1500 of Zoho's programmers have come through Zoho Schools. That's nearly 15 per cent of their total staff. They're giving highly qualified software engineers across the world a run for their money. Looking at the success of this unique experiment, this number will only increase in the future.

And here's the best part. This experiment worked so well that a couple of years after Zoho launched its office in Mathalamparai, they started a branch of Zoho Schools there as well. And Sridhar says that the next step is to go all-digital!

One final point before I end this section. I had mentioned earlier that Sridhar never took external funding. 'Why lose our freedom?' he would say. And now you can see what he meant. Can you imagine any VC in his right mind agreeing to an experiment like Zoho Schools? I certainly can't. But Zoho Schools was set up, it worked and it makes talented youngsters available to Zoho.

Finally, Sridhar Moves to Mathalamparai

So Zoho had migrated to the village. And so had Zoho Schools.
And of course, Sridhar would keep hopping between California
and Mathalamparai. After all, the rural push was a unique
experiment, and he was determined to make it succeed. This had
become a personal mission for him. In fact, he did not want to
stop at Mathalamparai. He wanted to build a whole network of
offices in rural Tamil Nadu—perhaps even in adjoining states such
as Andhra Pradesh and Kerala.

There was, however, one problem. This was a gigantic project.
Making it work was no joke. Sridhar realized that sitting comfortably
in California and coming to Mathalamparai every few months was
not enough to fulfil his mission. He had to be on the ground, in one
of these villages. He had to take on the responsibility of making the
experiment work.

So, what do you think he did?

That's right; in 2019, he moved bag and baggage to the village
of Mathalamparai. And now he runs his company from there. Yes
my friend, you have a quiet revolution taking place in the world
of software. A world-class software company is being run, not
from Bengaluru, or Hyderabad or Delhi, but from a village in
Tamil Nadu!

By the way, this shift from Silicon Valley to rural Tamil Nadu has
had a major impact on Sridhar, personally. Let's hear him out:*

> I feel more connected to my roots now, and enjoy this kind of
> life where you get rid of your comparisons. You don't have to
> worry about things like: Does my neighbour have a Ferrari; or

---

* Naandika Tripathi, Sridhar Vembu's vision from the village, *ForbesIndia.com*,
18 March 2021, https://www.forbesindia.com/article/big-bet/cover-story-sridhar-
vembus-vision-from-the-village/59833/1.

does my neighbour take a vacation? You kind of reduce it to a more elemental simplicity in life. I'm at peace and this is the way I like to live. In any case, I've always been a low consumption person. When any new phone is launched in the market, I won't be the first in line to buy it; I may buy it after a couple of years after everybody has it.

Dear reader, I hope you are getting the message. Zoho is more than just a company. It is Sridhar's life mission. And that is why he has made it clear that he will never sell the company.

After all, you don't sell your life's mission, do you?

31

Culture and People

You've just seen how Zoho has gone rural. In a big way. So you have youngsters from villages joining Zoho Schools and subsequently joining the company.

Now, I'm sure you have a question. I certainly did, so let me ask the question: On the one hand, Zoho had people from low-income families in villages who could barely speak English, at least when they joined. And with no real degree. On the other hand, you had engineers and MBAs from cities such as Chennai, Delhi and Mumbai. Didn't that create a kind of caste system within the company. A kind of divide between the 'haves' and the 'have-nots'? Where the haves would get the plum postings and the career growth, and the have-nots would be left behind?

Didn't you think this was the case? Well, I certainly did, so I simply had to delve deeper. And guess what I found?

There is no difference.

None at all.

The company values competence, not degrees. It doesn't matter whether you are a BTech, or an MTech or have gone through Zoho Schools. If you are good, you are recognized, rewarded, and above all, respected.

Here's a view from Babu, who you met in the previous chapter:

I was just seventeen years old when I started working at Zoho. But I was never treated as a trainee without a degree. I was respected. And today, while I still do not have a formal degree, I have become a product manager with global responsibilities. If you show results in this company, you are recognized, irrespective of your background and your degree.

At Zoho Corp., people who show promise are given a chance to experiment. And that includes making mistakes, as long as they learn from them. By the way, that's how people grow. Listen to the story of Girish Mathrubootham, who started his career in pre-sales at Zoho in 2001 (for those who are not aware, pre-sales is a tech function that helps the sales team in software companies). But he didn't just stick to pre-sales. He shifted gears and grew to become vice president, heading the Manage Engine division in 2010. And with the phenomenal amount he had learnt at Zoho, he founded his own software company, Freshdesk. This is what Girish has to say about his stint at Zoho:*

> The answer is very, very clear in my mind—it was the operational freedom (that helped me grow). Zoho as a company is very open to experimentation, and people like me, who had no background in product management, were given opportunities to do such work, to make mistakes and learn. There was freedom to do what you thought was right.

Now, you are aware of one of my favourite statements, which I've repeated again and again in this book: Culture begins at the top. The CEO cannot shout about the culture of the organization. He must practise it. And as he gets noticed, people below him follow. You've

---

* Harichandan Arakali, 'The Bootstrapped Buddhist: How Sridhar Vembu built Zoho', *Forbes India*, 6 June 2016, https://www.forbesindia.com/article/boardroom/the-bootstrapped-buddhist-how-sridhar-vembu-built-zoho/43383/1).

seen this in all the companies you've read about in this book. And Zoho is no different.

Let me take an example: once again, from our young friend, Babu (by the way, considering the huge contribution Babu has made to this book, I must consider sharing my royalty with him):

> Sridhar would come to Zoho Schools to meet us. And the first time he came, we didn't know him. We had informal discussions with him and found him to be extremely approachable. In fact, we added him to our chat group, and would chat regularly with him. It was only after he went back from his visit that we realized that he was the founder of the company.

And that, my friend, is Sridhar Vembu. No airs. No bragging about the fact that he is the founder and CEO. Very happy talking to young trainees as an equal—not as a boss. In fact, you should hear him out on the subject:*

> Clearly, technology is affecting how organizations are structured. The traditional hierarchy of top-down structures is giving way to more fluid networks—it doesn't matter what title you have. Competence is the key.

That's the view of the founder, Sridhar. And that's the culture that he has been able to build in the organization.

Concern for People

Now there's something else that really hit me. You see, when Covid-19 hit the world, and specifically India, our prime minister declared a nation-wide lockdown and everything was shut. Following this directive, obviously all offices and factories had to shift to 'work-from-home' mode. Of course, you know all this.

But hang on. Have you heard of any company that moved to work-from-home *before* the lockdown? In fact, well before?

Well, now you have—and you're right, it's Zoho. Remember, I had told you that Sridhar had the ability to catch trends early? Well, he saw this trend as well, where Covid-19 would spread and companies would be forced to get into work-from-home mode. And therefore, *he closed Zoho's offices two weeks before the government announced the lockdown.* That's right, a full two weeks. When other organizations were not even thinking about it.

Why?

Simple. He wanted Zoho's employees to reach their home towns before trains, buses and flights became crowded with the sudden panic that the lockdown would cause.

That, my friend, is Sridhar Vembu once again. Deeply concerned about his people. And of course, I don't need to mention that there have never been any mass lay-offs at Zoho. No way. That's not Zoho.

And that's not Sridhar.

Concern for Customers

So Sridhar is extremely concerned about his people: That much is clear. But what about his customers?

Well, first of all, I have a question for you: When you're accessing an Internet site, what's the one thing that really makes you angry?

Come on, my friend, you know what I'm referring to. It's the fact that the site picks up data about you and sells it to third parties, isn't it? So that they can optimize their ads, which they keep pushing at you.

But guess what? Zoho does not believe in sharing your data with anyone. That has never been the way they operate. Zoho is a phenomenally ethical organization. Absolutely no hanky-panky. Had they sold data, they would have lost the trust of their customers. And that's the one thing you can never do. Customers come to you because they trust you. Because they have faith in you.

And by the way, since this is so, so important, it's mentioned in big, bold letters on the Zoho website:

Your privacy is our responsibility
We believe that trust is paramount in a relationship. We do not own or sell your data, and we most certainly do not bank on advertising-based business models. The only way we make money is from the software licence fees you pay us.

Wonderful, isn't it? And by the way, I have spoken to some of their customers, and this is 100 per cent true. Your data is safe with Zoho. QED.

In fact, they take it a step further. You see, a lot of SaaS companies do their hosting on servers in third-party data centres. And that's a problem, because the SaaS provider is dependent on the data centre for protecting customer data. Now, that was simply not acceptable to our own SaaS provider, Zoho. They have always been very clear. 'We respect the customer's data. And we respect his need for security and privacy. Therefore, *we will not use a third-party data centre* to host our applications. We will set up our own data centre. Thereby, we have complete control over the security and privacy of the client's data.'

Wonderful, isn't it? How many organizations would do a thing like this? Not many. But Zoho has done it. You see, for Sridhar and for Zoho, customers are priority. That's the reason why customers love them, and don't want to leave them!

And now, we need to take a look at the products that they offer their customers.

For which you'll need to make a bit of effort.

Yes, you'll need to turn the page . . .

32

Zoho.com

Let's now take a look at the products of Zoho Corp. in a bit more detail. No, I don't want to make you an expert, but I think it's important that you understand what these products do. After all, if you were to buy one of them based on what you've read, I can demand my commission, can't I 😊?

Right? So let's start with their most well-known division. The one where they offer products to users in SaaS mode. A division that they proudly call **Zoho.com**. And we'll start with the most popular product within Zoho.com, namely **Zoho CRM**.

Zoho CRM

Of course you know what CRM is: it's short for Customer Relationship Management. But just in case you don't, here's a simple example: Let's say your company manufactures and sells office equipment to businesses. And you have taken part in an exhibition where interested people gave you their visiting cards. We call these sales leads, or simply leads. Obviously, you would need to enter them somewhere. And then your company also put out ads, based on which you got some more leads. In addition, the sales guys made some cold calls, where they knocked on doors, and hopefully didn't get thrown out too often. That created more leads as well. Now, all these leads would be entered into your CRM software.

Next, you would need to keep track of these leads: what was happening with each lead and the steps you needed to take in each case. Your friendly CRM would help you do that. Then you would need to make a proposal, and guess who helps? CRM again. So right through the sales cycle, CRM would be your best friend, helping you at each step. And then the management might want to compare the performance of salespeople across geographies. Who closes deals faster, who gets better terms, etc. Or they might want to compare the effectiveness of different forms of marketing, such as advertising vs participating in exhibitions vs cold calls. And since the data is all there in the CRM system, that's exactly what they would use.

By the way, this is just the tip of the iceberg. I don't want to make this a manual on CRM; in any case, there are enough books on the subject. But I hope you get the message: Anything and everything to do with managing and looking after customers and potential customers, can be done using CRM. And that's exactly what Zoho CRM offers.

We Have Everything You Need

Now let's build further on this example. Hopefully, the customer likes one of your products, so he buys it from you. But you now need to provide him with an online help desk, where he can ask queries and raise service requests. Or even make an angry complaint (hopefully not too many of them). And both you as well as the customer would like to follow up on each service request to figure out what's happened to it.

What would you use for this? **Zoho Desk**, of course. And then you might want to do some analysis. For example, is there a link between unresolved customer queries and missed orders? For this, you would need to pick up data from both Zoho Desk as well as Zoho CRM. Right? And what would you use for such a query? **Zoho Analytics** at your service.

As you can see, you can use Zoho CRM as a stand-alone application. Or you could use a far more powerful combination of Zoho CRM, along with Zoho Desk, Zoho Analytics and a few other applications. And Sridhar realized this. So he created what he called a business suite, called **Zoho CRM Plus**, which includes all these.

Then, of course, you might want to go well beyond CRM. Where you would use inventory management software to figure out whether or not you were in a position to meet the order that you just got. And what would you use for that? **Zoho Inventory**, of course. You might also need to integrate everything with your payroll software, because the sales guys would need to be paid their commission. So you would use **Zoho Payroll**. And before I forget, you would need to integrate everything with your accounting software, or **Zoho Books**. And so on . . .

In other words, you've now gone way beyond Zoho CRM Plus. You've gone to a full suite of products that you need for your business, which the company calls **Zoho One**. And all these products are integrated.

Incidentally, Zoho.com has a few products even beyond Zoho One. In fact, at the time of writing this book (2023), Zoho.com has over fifty five different applications, accessible both from the web as well as through an app on your mobile phone. And just as you have Zoho CRM Plus, you also have **Zoho People Plus**, **Zoho Finance Plus** and **Zoho Marketing Plus**. Can you now see why the world is sitting up and taking notice of Zoho?

Sridhar has an interesting term for Zoho One. He calls it an 'Operating System for Business'.[*] Let me explain. Obviously, you are familiar with operating systems for your laptop, such as Windows. What does Windows allow you to do? Well, it hides all the details of the underlying hardware and other nitty-gritties and allows you to interact with your laptop using simple commands. For instance,

---

[*] Harichandan Arakali, 'The Bootstrapped Buddhist: How Sridhar Vembu built Zoho', *Forbes India*, 6 June 2016, https://www.forbesindia.com/article/boardroom/the-bootstrapped-buddhist-how-sridhar-vembu-built-zoho/43383/1.

you can locate a file, save it, load additional software, connect your laptop to Wi-Fi, connect it to a printer and do all the hundreds of other things you usually do on a laptop. All using simple commands without getting into the innards of the machine.

According to Sridhar, Zoho One does something similar for your business. It lets you send emails, keep track of your customers, do your accounting, collaborate using chat across continents and most other things you would need to do. You do not need to worry about how to do any of it: how you would keep track of your customers or how you would collaborate over chat, etc. It's all part of Zoho One. And that's why Sridhar likes to call it an 'Operating System for Business.'

Neat, isn't it?

By the way, the fact that they have a product for virtually everything that a business needs, is a major benefit for their customers. For two reasons: First of all, these various apps are integrated and have a similar user interface, so it's far easier to use them. Secondly, any organization that adopts Zoho will only have to deal with one vendor. And that's a huge blessing. How often have you gone from software vendor to software vendor, tearing your hair out? Simply because you simply cannot get two products from different vendors to talk to each other? With each vendor blaming the other guy? Familiar, isn't it? But if you use Zoho, your hair will remain intact (you might lose it for other reasons, but that's beyond the scope of this book). Because it all comes from one single vendor—Zoho.

Yes, Zoho gives you virtually everything you need. But what if you don't want everything? For instance, what if you already have your favourite SaaS-based inventory management software installed and running? And you don't want to replace it, but you *do* want Zoho CRM? And yes, you want to integrate the two? Is that possible?

Yes, it is. Sridhar has realized that you might already have implemented products from other software companies, and therefore you would want only a few of Zoho.com's products. And he has always been clear: He will not force you to replace what you already have. But he also realized that you would need to integrate these multiple applications, so that data can flow smoothly between them. And that's exactly what he has done. Zoho's products are already integrated with many standard products from other vendors. And even if you have a product with which Zoho is not integrated, don't worry. Just wait for the next chapter, where I'll tell you all about another product from Zoho, called Zoho Creator. That will help you integrate the two.

Oh, I almost forgot—some products from the Zoho stable are free. They are not just priced lower than competing products. *They are free.* For instance, **Zoho Invoice**, which helps small businesses generate invoices, complete with GST. In fact, many of their products have a free version as well.

And that, my friend, is customer orientation for you.

Competing with Giants

Now, for something important. You see, I have been associated with the software industry for over forty years. (Yes, you heard right—forty years, although I'm still young at heart.) During this time, I have personally used some of the leading software products available worldwide, such as Salesforce.com, Oracle and SAP. And when I came across Zoho, I naturally had a question: 'How can this upstart from rural Tamil Nadu compete with these giants?'

Yes, we do have terrific software companies in India, such as TCS and Infosys, which compete successfully with the best in the world. But they are in the business of developing customized software for their clients. They are not software product companies. Zoho is a rare company coming out of India which offers world-class software *products*. And by the way, please remember, for Zoho, the market is not India. It's global. So, to put it bluntly, how the hell does Zoho compete?

Fascinating question. And as I delved deeper and deeper into the Zoho story, I began to get my answer.

Let me go back once again to their star product, namely Zoho CRM. A product where they have always faced competition from global giants such as Salesforce.com, which is also a SaaS product. Now, you've already seen that Sridhar is an extremely smart person. And when he launched Zoho CRM, he took a major strategic decision: *He did not try and compete head-on with Salesforce.com.*

You see, market-leading products such as Salesforce.com are undoubtedly powerful. They have lots and lots of features, which I won't get into because that would take up this entire book. The point is, how many organizations actually use these features? I have been a consultant to several organizations, and I can say with confidence that only a fraction of all these features are used. But—and this is an important but—these features took time and money to develop. A whole lot of time and a whole lot of money. Therefore, software companies such as Salesforce.com had to charge for them. So you have an interesting situation where *client organizations have to pay for features that they might not use.*

And there's more. These products are complex. So it takes time and money for client organizations to implement them—usually by calling in expensive consultants.

Now, many large companies are willing to shell out the extra amount needed to buy these products, as well as the extra effort required to implement them. But what about smaller companies? SMEs (small and medium enterprises) would certainly want something that costs less and is easier to implement. In any case, they would not need all those extra frills and features. They would much rather get simple solutions.

That, my friend, is the opportunity Sridhar spotted, way back in 2005. He realized that in the crowded market for software products, there was a major gap. Where a simpler, easier-to-implement, and above all, lower-cost product was required by SMEs. And that is exactly what Zoho offered.

And did it work? Well, it took a long time. Many years, in fact. After all, you wouldn't expect a client organization to say, 'Aha! Here's an upstart called Zoho. They are offering a simpler solution than the market leaders. Great. Let's dump the well-known giants and pick up Zoho.' No my friend, things do not work like this. It would perhaps start with one or two brave organizations taking the plunge. Others would wait and watch. Based on the feedback that they got, a few others would start using Zoho's products. Perhaps only use them for non-critical applications in the beginning, to minimize the risk. That's how usage would spread.

So, it took time. But it did work, as more and more SMEs started using Zoho CRM. Over the years, Zoho CRM has been able to compete successfully with the big guys in the segment they have targeted. By the way, this is one more reason why Sridhar did not go in for funding. Because VCs have a timeline. They have taken money from *their* investors, and they are under pressure to give their investors an exit within a fixed number of years. Sridhar was clear that he didn't want this kind of pressure from VCs. If it took ten years for Zoho.com to come good, so be it. He was willing to wait, whereas VCs would not. And over time, Zoho CRM became extremely popular within the segment of SMEs that it was targeting.

Need more proof? Okay, here's an extract from the highly respected Forbes.com advisor magazine:[*]

The choice between Salesforce and Zoho CRM will likely come down to which software can accomplish what your company needs for a better price. Salesforce is a veritable powerhouse of CRM software with a list of features and integrations numbering in the thousands, but Zoho CRM's top-tier plan is still less expensive than even Salesforce's second most affordable plan. (And) for the majority of applications, Zoho CRM remains capable.

(Also), because Zoho CRM is not as complex a software, it is significantly easier for beginners to start using it quickly. Salesforce,

---

[*] Chauncey Crail, Kelly Main and Rob Watts, 'Salesforce Vs. Zoho (2023 Comparison)', *Forbes*, 12 July 2003, https://www.forbes.com/advisor/business/software/salesforce-vs-zoho/.

on the other hand, may require a dedicated IT professional to supervise its use if your company's use is particularly heavy-duty.

And here's something really interesting from the same article:

> Zoho prioritizes some aspects that Salesforce's software requires paying more for. For example, Zoho CRM has a built-in social media feature that pulls data from Google, Facebook and Twitter to track conversations with leads, prospects and current customers, while Salesforce requires an add-on for its similar feature.

Got it? Zoho has been smart. Some features that several clients need are built into the software. Whereas in Salesforce, you need an add-on.

Finally, having read all this, can you guess the ratings that the article has assigned to these products?

Here they are:

Salesforce.com: 4.2
Zoho CRM 4.6

Yes, even I was surprised. But that's how popular Zoho CRM is!

Incidentally, I've taken Zoho CRM as an example, but the logic I've used applies to the other products from Zoho.com as well. Most of them are simpler and lower-cost than those offered by global giants.

Finally, here's something really interesting. Over time, even some large organizations realized that these products were a godsend, even for them. You see, many of them also required simpler products that were easier to implement. And of course, which organization would say no to lower costs? Therefore, while Zoho.com started off by targeting SMEs, over time, even large organizations became customers. And today, these products are aimed at any company that wants a simpler, easier-to-implement and value-for-money solution.

And of course, the icing on the cake is that the organization only needs to deal with one vendor for all their software needs!

But How Does Zoho Make Money?

So Zoho has created world-class products that successfully compete with giants. And these products are priced much lower. Now, the obvious question is, how do they make money?

Well, first of all, I've already told you that their products have left out several features that customers do not need. They created products that are simpler and easier to use. Obviously, that reduced their development time and cost.

Secondly, just take a look at where their development centres are located. Not in the super-expensive Silicon Valley in the USA. Not even in India's Silicon Valley—Bengaluru. Many of them are in villages in Tamil Nadu and now, Telengana and Kerala, too. Which means far, far lower costs.

Next, look at their manpower. A large number have come through Zoho Schools. Very bright youngsters, great programmers, but definitely lower-cost resources than BTechs and MCAs in Bengaluru and elsewhere. And they are happy to stay on for life rather than jump from job to job, which means that even manpower replacement costs are low.

But of course, you already know all this; I'm simply summarizing it once again. What you perhaps don't know is the fact that the company has always run a frugal business. There is very little marketing spend. In fact, the ratio of R&D to marketing spend is something like 3:1. Just to understand the implication of this fact, it's the other way around in many companies. And by the way, this high R&D spend is because they are constantly working on improving their products.

Of course, there is no ostentation. No showing off. No unnecessary spending on fancy hotels and business-class travel. It's plain, simple and functional. And a lot of this flows down from the founder, Sridhar. As I've already mentioned, he is a man of simple tastes and that's the way he runs his company, too. In fact, if you were to take a look at his office in Mathalamparai—and there are photographs available on the Internet—it looks like a typical large village house. Definitely not the kind of plush office that you would expect from a world-class multinational company.

So, that's it. Zoho's costs are significantly lower than those of their competitors, whether it is development costs, manpower costs, establishment costs or marketing costs. At the same time, their productivity per person is higher. That's why Zoho is able to charge so much less than their competitors and still be profitable. Yes, my friend, now you know why Zoho is a proud earnicorn.

And with that, I must end this chapter. Close the book (don't forget to put in a bookmark or at least fold the page) and get back to sleep.

Just make sure you wake up in time for the next chapter!

33

The Siblings

So that's the story of Zoho.com—the most well-known and fastest-growing business within Zoho Corp. But that's not their only product line. There are other siblings as well, so let's take a look at some of them . . .

Zoho Creator

This is a really interesting product. And to understand it, let's take the example of a teacher, who has a brilliant idea for teaching public speaking to students online through an app. But he also needs to market this business through the app. And perhaps keep accounts as well. Now, this is a unique requirement, and I'm sure no one—not even Zoho—would have any ready-made product for it. Therefore, what would this teacher need to do? Very simple. He or she would need to write a program to create this app.

But hang on. The poor guy is an expert in public speaking, not programming, or coding, as we call it. He would probably go bonkers trying to come up with an appropriate program. And even if he does manage to write the program, it would take a huge amount of time (remember, he's not an expert). Of course, it would also have bugs which would need to be removed. Once again, that would take a lot of effort and time, perhaps making him pull out his hair in frustration.

But what if he had a software tool that permitted him to develop this app with minimal coding? As long as he was clear about the processes he would follow, all he needed to do was drag and drop, the way you do with most software tools today. Wouldn't that dramatically simplify his life?

That, my friend, is a concept called Low-Code. Given the name, I obviously do not need to explain it further, do I? It's a way to create software that is completely intuitive, predominantly using drag-and-drop with minimal programming, if any. And as you might have guessed, Zoho Corp. provides this kind of low-code platform. It's called **Zoho Creator** and it lets you do exactly this.

By the way, I took the example of a teacher, but it could be any other business situation. For instance, a lady who bakes cakes at home and wants to make them available across the city. Or a restaurant serving yummy pizzas. In fact, any business where the requirements are somewhat unique and therefore existing products cannot meet them. And that's where Zoho Creator comes in!

But that's not all. Let's say you want to implement a product such as Zoho CRM in your organization. But you want an additional feature that the product does not have. What do you do?

Aha! That's when you can use Zoho Creator and build this feature. Once again, with minimal programming—if any. Or, you might want to integrate Zoho CRM with a software product for inventory management which you've picked up from another vendor (remember this example from the previous chapter?). And this vendor happens to be a small, local guy, so Zoho does not have a ready-to-use interface with this software.

So what would you do? Well, use Zoho Creator once again. In other words, Zoho Creator is a tool that can be used for multiple purposes. You could use it to develop your own unique application. Or add functionality to one of Zoho's existing products. Or even to integrate a Zoho product with just about any other product that you've picked up.

Powerful, isn't it? And by the way, that's one more reason why more and more clients are flocking to Zoho. Because of the flexibility, as well as the ability to quickly integrate Zoho's products with anything else.

Manage Engine

I've spoken about this division earlier, so please don't ask me to repeat myself again and again. But just to summarize what I had said, this division creates software products for the IT departments of user organizations, to help them manage their internal networks. Obviously, with technology changing over time, these products have been upgraded. But the idea remains the same: help IT departments manage their resources better.

What about WebNMS?

Ah! Zoho's first product line. The one the company started off with. Over time, based on market needs, Sridhar and his senior team members felt that there were better opportunities out there. Opportunities such as Zoho.com and Manage Engine. Therefore, this product line has been phased out. Completely logical, isn't it? Products do get phased out and are replaced by other, better-performing ones.

So what happened to the people in this division? Did they get laid off?

Come on. Of course they didn't. Zoho does not lay off people. They were simply absorbed into other divisions. And are now happily contributing to Zoho's business in those divisions!

And that's all I wanted to share about Zoho's products. There are others, of course, and more will keep coming out.

But now, it's time to look at where the company has reached. And where it plans to go from here.

In the next chapter . . .

34

Zoho: Today and Tomorrow

So that was the story of AdventNet—sorry, Zoho Corp.

And where have they reached today?

Well, their annual results for the financial year 2022–23 have been filed with the Registrar of Companies, so they are publicly available. According to this filing, they have achieved a revenue figure of Rs 8703 crore, a huge jump of 29.7 per cent over the previous financial year. And their profits are a staggering Rs 2836 crore. (For more details, you are welcome to read the Entrackr article on this.[*] Of course, if you prefer to make life complicated, you are welcome to go to the website of the Ministry of Corporate affairs.)

But there's a bit more I need to tell you: Zoho One forms the lion's share of this revenue. Yes, my friend, the company that started off developing networking software has well and truly moved to developing SaaS products. And customers are lapping them up.

Lapping them up, did I say? Well, just go to the Zoho.com website and take a look at their list of clients. It's a veritable who's who of industry. And I'm not talking of Indian industry, although they have lots of Indian clients as well. I'm talking about global industry. So they have Ikea, Dell, Toyota, BigBasket, Stanford University,

---

[*] Upadhyay, Harsh, and Ashrafi, Md Salman, Zoho posts Rs 2,800 Cr profit in FY23, revenue up by 30%, Entrackr.com, 1 February 2024, https://entrackr.com/2024/02/zoho-posts-rs-2800-cr-profit-in-fy23-revenue-up-by-30/.

Swiggy, Bosch, FedEx, Meesho, etc. The list goes on. And please note, their clients come from completely diverse industries: whether it is furniture and home décor, or computer hardware, or food delivery, or automobiles or universities . . .

At the time of writing this book, Zoho.com has over 700,000 clients spread across more than 150 countries, and is being used by a massive 100 million individuals. Just to give you an idea of how rapid their growth has been, this number has doubled in the past five years. And all this has been made possible because of their 15,000 plus employees worldwide.

And what about valuation? Actually, since Sridhar never raised external funding, valuation is, well, whatever the analysts figure out. Obviously, different analysts would have different views, but in general, there is agreement that it is somewhere in the vicinity of $6 billion. For instance, Traxn, the well-known site that analyses such companies, has pegged the valuation at $5.94 billion as of December 2022.[*]

There are other figures, of course, and you can take your pick. In any case, as I've already mentioned, Sridhar doesn't really care. He focuses on his customers, his products and his business. Definitely not on valuations.

Finally, what about their rural outreach? As you can guess, they've been going ahead full steam. At the time of writing this book, they have over thirty-five offices in India. Let me share some of the locations with you:

- Rampally (Telangana)
- Thuthipet (Tamil Nadu)
- Periya Seeragapadi (Tamil Nadu)
- Kadachanallur (Tamil Nadu)

---

[*] https://tracxn.com/d/companies/zoho/__nGqGUzgulP1GCqqp47DM8-6vVowKLM8i_NG31Xfiv2Q

- Palakkad (Kerala)
- Poigaikaraipatti (Tamil Nadu)
- Pathanamthitta (Kerala)

Satisfied?

The Future

With all that these guys have achieved, you might think that Zoho would rest on their laurels. But no. That's not the way Sridhar is made. And neither are any of his other co-founders. Ultimately, Sridhar wants to see Zoho as a global leader in technology, and in what he calls the operating system for business. He is constantly on a mission to make Zoho more and more attractive for more and more companies and individuals to use. And for that, the key focus is R&D.

Sridhar is very clear that if you want a long-term business, you need to focus on R&D. And this is not just an empty statement; he actually puts this into practice. I've already told you that Zoho Corp. spends three times as much on R&D as they do on marketing. They have also created a division called Zoho Labs, which they set up in 2015, and which now spearheads their R&D activities.

What does Zoho Labs do? Let me give you a couple of examples: You are aware that most software products have a database at their core. Now, there are a few standard databases out there in the market, from giants such as Oracle, Microsoft and IBM. And most software companies use one of these. Obvious, isn't it? Why would you develop your own database when there are such market-leading products available?

But hang on. I've told you repeatedly that Sridhar is different. And therefore, Zoho is different. Zoho has developed its own database. And all its products are built around this database!

Why?

Well, let's hear out Ramprakash Ramamoorthy, one of the key people leading research at Zoho:

> All the software we build uses a database at its core. It's a bit like the database is the engine, and we are building the car. But that's like building a car without knowing anything about the engine. That's when we decided to build our own engine—our own database. All our products now use our own home-grown database. And obviously, we are able to optimize and improve the database continuously.

Incidentally, this also means that their costs have come down, because they did not need to buy expensive database licences. And of course, you know what happened next. Zoho has passed on these lower costs to their customers.

But even that is not the end of the story. I've already told you that these guys use their own data centres to house their software. Now, if you wanted to improve the performance of your software, one of the things you would need to do is optimize the design of the database. But you would also need to optimize the hardware on which it runs, wouldn't you? And now you can guess what Zoho has done. That's right, they have actually moved into hardware as well, so as to optimize the performance of their data centres, and therefore, their databases.

An all-in-one solution, as you can see!

Incidentally, Zoho's R&D team is now working on projects in completely diverse areas. For instance, in agriculture (remember, Sridhar comes from a family of farmers). They are experimenting with drones to chase away wild boars that destroy crops. They are also working on automatic water purifiers for use in rural India. Yes, even I was surprised when I read this. But then that's Sridhar the visionary for you.

But before I end the Zoho story, I must share with you the tag line from a campaign they had launched in 2014. Something that I really liked. And something that showcases their DNA like nothing else:

Made in India
Made for the World

And that, my friend, brings me to the end of this fascinating story about the fourth earnicorn in this book, Zoho Corp.

And its equally fascinating founder, Sridhar Vembu.

35

Let's Analyse the Earnicorn: Zoho

And now for the analysis. As before, I'll focus on the most well-known and fastest-growing business, Zoho.com.

Zoho.com: The PERSISTENT Business

Clearly, Zoho.com is solving a PROBLEM. Or rather, lots of problems. And obviously, all clients are happy to pay for these solutions—especially because Zoho's solutions are simple and low-cost. In other words, they do have an EARNINGS MODEL.

In fact, companies such as Zoho that offer SaaS products have a very stable earnings model.

Why?

Simple. They don't charge an upfront licence fee. Instead, they typically charge a monthly or annual fee as you keep using the software. And if you like the software and are hooked on it, well, you keep paying. So the earnings model goes on and on.

What about the SIZE of the MARKET? Huge, isn't it? Potentially all organizations across the world. Yes, it has always been a crowded market, with global giants such as Salesforce.com, Microsoft, Oracle and SAP jostling for space. But Sridhar smartly focused on a NICHE within this market—the market of small and medium-sized businesses, where the giants really didn't have an offering. Actually, it's unfair to call it a NICHE because it's huge in its own right, but I'm sure you get my point.

The interesting thing here is that Zoho started by focusing on SMEs, but over time, even much larger companies started coming to them. Simply because their products were lower-cost, easier to use and easier to install. And that's an interesting message for all of you founders out there: Rather than competing head-on with giants, start by focusing on a niche. Over time, as you get known and people see the benefits of using your product, you might actually be able to compete with these giants on their own turf.

Now for SCALABILITY. Clearly, Zoho is a technology company. And it develops products. To double its revenues, it does not need to double either its manpower count or infrastructure. Therefore, it is a highly scalable business, as you can see from the figures it has clocked over the years.

What about the RISKS to the business? As I've mentioned earlier, one of the biggest risks to any business is the fact that competition can enter, take away your customers, eat into your market share, and ultimately kill you. Which is why you need an ENTRY BARRIER.

Actually, there are several entry barriers that Zoho.com has been able to build. First of all, it started off by offering a suite of products that its major competitors did not have: products that were simpler and easier to implement. Sure, competitors could also build similar products, but that would take time, wouldn't it? And that's what created an entry barrier.

The second barrier is the cost structure of the company. Here, let me repeat something that I've said earlier, when I discussed the Zerodha story in Chapter 19: *Lower pricing by itself is NOT an entry barrier, unless it is matched by an appropriate lower 'cost structure'.* Now, you've already seen that their costs are low. Some of their programmers have come through their INNOVATIVE and highly successful experiment, Zoho Schools. Obviously, their salaries are lower than those of most conventional programmers.

And then many of their offices are in villages—another phenomenally innovative concept—so you can imagine how low their establishment cost is. Plus, their marketing spend is low. They prefer to focus on their products and invest in R&D. Finally, from Sridhar downwards, there is no ostentatious expenditure. Everything is simple. Overall, they run an extremely low-cost operation. Something that is very tough to copy. And that's what we want from an entry barrier, don't we?

Over time, the company has built a solid brand for itself—a brand which stands for simple, low-cost and reliable software. And that's the icing on the cake. You see, brands take time, effort and money to build. They cannot be built in a day or a month. Anyone trying to get into the same business as Zoho would necessarily take several years to build their brand. By which time, of course, Zoho would have moved further ahead, thereby maintaining their entry barrier.

Now, for the TEAM. You've seen how Sridhar, with his revolutionary ideas, has been able to get great people through his Zoho Schools project. Most of whom had given up hope of ever getting a good education after school. These people have grabbed the opportunity that Zoho provided. They have joined Zoho and given it everything they had. Of course, the top management at Zoho has provided just the kind of nurturing culture that these young people need to develop and grow. The fact that they stay at home with their parents, rather than being forced to migrate to one of our cities, obviously helps as well.

Finally, let's come to TRACTION. The final proof of any business. I've just told you that these guys achieved revenues of over Rs 8000 crore in the financial year 2022–23. And have crossed 100 million users. Can you possibly ask for more?

And that, my friend, is Zoho Corporation for you. A truly PERSISTENT business.

By the way, that made me really, really delighted. Because all the four businesses I've discussed in this book follow my favourite PERSISTENT model.

A 100 per cent record.

The PERFECT Attitude

Now for the PERFECT attitude of the founder, Sridhar Vembu. Actually, I don't think I need to write this section—it's fairly obvious, isn't it? But just to add a couple of pages, here goes.

Sridhar is nothing if not FLEXIBLE. When the dot-com crash hit the world, he realized that they would need to diversify and therefore de-risk the business. Which is when he started Manage Engine. And when the world started waking up to the concept of SaaS, he launched his own version of SaaS. Starting with Zoho CRM. And not only is he FLEXIBLE, he is PERSEVERING as well. If you recall, Zoho.com took several years to reach any significant traction and make decent amounts of money. Beating global giants such as Salesforce.com, Oracle, Siebel and SAP was not going to be easy—and believe me, it wasn't. But he stuck to his guns. And you've seen the results—revenues of over Rs 8000 crore!

And now I'll take you back to my favourite story. When Sridhar moved bag and baggage from Silicon Valley in California to the village of Mathalamparai in Tamil Nadu, to live and work there. Why? Well, he realized that having a network of small offices in villages was a major experiment. If it succeeded, it could transform the way software was developed. And it would give a huge fillip to his view that people from villages should have employment opportunities in or near their villages, rather than migrating to the inevitable cities. But this experiment would have to be managed and monitored very closely, to ensure it succeeded. Of course, he could have handed this over to a manager—after all, he *was* the CEO. But that would not have been Sridhar. Instead, he decided to oversee this massive project personally—by being present on the spot. That is Sridhar. Willing to do EVERYTHING! And taking full RESPONSIBILITY for the success or failure of the project.

Of course, he has always been CUSTOMER ORIENTED. In fact, he has gone a step ahead. He *anticipated* what customers were likely to need in the future and built his products keeping these needs in mind. A classic example once again, was the huge bet he took on the world moving towards SaaS-based software, rather than buying and installing it on their own servers. Then of course, I've already told you that some of the products that Zoho.com offers, such as Zoho Invoice, are absolutely free. CUSTOMER ORIENTATION once again, isn't it?

And then you have ETHICS. Sridhar has always made it very clear that the customer's data belongs to the customer. That's a stated policy of the company—just go to their website and check it out. But that's not all. Zoho has set up their own data centres, and that's where their applications are hosted. To prevent the possibility of a third-party data centre misusing the customer's data. And guess what? This cut down their costs as well—and these lower costs have been passed on to the customer. Phenomenal ethics and transparency, isn't it?

And of course, when you do something like this, what happens? You build TRUST in the minds of the customer.

What about the employees? Wouldn't he need to build trust in them as well? Of course he did. Once again, the best example I can think of is the 1500 people he recruited through Zoho Schools. All those young men and women realized that Sridhar meant what he said. He would give them responsibilities based on their performance—not degrees. So the fact that you had gone through Zoho Schools and not a top-notch engineering college, would not go against you.

The result?

People joined Zoho. They TRUSTED Sridhar and they trusted Zoho. They stayed on to make a career. A career that they had never thought possible earlier. And they do that to this day.

So that's Sridhar—the founder with the PERFECT attitude.

And by the way, I hope you've noticed something. All the founders we've met in the book have just the PERFECT attitude.

The Profitable Business

Finally, how did Zoho Corp. become an earnicorn?

Well, as you've seen all along in this book, making profits is simple. Ridiculously simple, in fact. Just spend less than you earn, and you'll be profitable 😊. But seriously, this has been the mantra for Zoho, just as it has for all the other earnicorns in the book. In fact, they have a cute saying, which I heard over and over again while researching the company:

We spend what we earn.

Interestingly, in many of the strategies Zoho has followed, the primary purpose was not to reduce costs. However, they had the natural consequence of cutting costs. Take, for instance, the famous Zoho Schools experiment, where they take in bright young men and women from rural Tamil Nadu and groom them into software engineers. Clearly, this has reduced their manpower costs, while at the same time enhancing productivity. The fact that many of their development centres are in villages has reduced their establishment costs as well.

The other big thing is that they focus on the product and the customer, not on marketing. Let me ask you this question: Have you ever seen massive, expensive ads from Zoho? Have you seen film stars or cricketers endorsing the brand? No? Well, I haven't either. Because that's not Zoho. You see, if you focus on getting the right product to the customer, you do not need to spend much on marketing. Because the customer comes to you.

So that's it: a simple, uncomplicated company, led by a simple, humble man from rural Tamil Nadu. A company that has been profitable ever since it started. And from what I've seen, it will continue to be profitable in the future as well.

And will perhaps transform the way software is developed in our country.

A true **earnicorn**, if ever there was any.

Section VI

Let's Compare These Earnicorns

36

What's Common across These Earnicorns

So, those were our four stalwarts. Each of them a market leader in its chosen space. Each one a unicorn, although none of the founders really cares, because that's not what they were aiming for. (Strictly speaking, Info Edge is not a unicorn, since it reached a valuation of over a billion dollars after it got listed. However, I couldn't possibly leave out one of the pioneers of Internet businesses in India, could I?) Each of them has been running a profitable business. In other words, they are all proud **earnicorns**. And that's why I decided to include them in my book.

And now I come to the real 'fun' part of the book. Where I compare these businesses. What's common across them, and more importantly, what's different.

First, what is common: You've already seen that all four businesses follow my favourite PERSISTENT model—although there are some variations. And all the founders have an attitude that is just PERFECT. You can imagine how delighted I was when I realized this: All these highly successful businesses and their founders follow the models that I've created.

Wow! You can now figure out why I am strutting around all over the place, looking so smug 😊!

However, before I get carried away—a very common phenomenon ever since I was born—I must clarify something. These businesses are not following my PERSISTENT model. It's the other way around. *I have created the model after studying successful businesses.* Similarly, these founders have not modelled themselves based on what I suggested—the PERFECT attitude. I have figured out the PERFECT attitude based on what I saw in successful founders. But in any case, it's great to know that both my models apply to giant businesses just as well as they do to fledgling start-ups.

Here's a summary of the most important things that are common across these businesses, and of course, their founders.

Now, before you start getting angry with me, let me clarify something. I am NOT repeating all the analysis I've already done. For that, you are more than welcome to read those pages all over again. However, there are a few common features that really stand out. And these I simply *must* talk about, because they form a great set of guidelines for any business that hopes to become an earnicorn.

One clarification: Some of these companies have been running multiple businesses. For instance, Info Edge has Naukri, Jeevansathi, 99acres and Shiksha. Zoho has Zoho.com and Manage Engine. Now, I will not compare all these businesses with each other, because that would make things extremely cumbersome (mathematicians would say the number of comparisons would be nC2, but if you don't understand maths, just ignore this statement). Instead, I will focus on the major business in each case. Which means Naukri, Zerodha, Dream11 and Zoho.com.

I assume you are okay with this. If not, that's just too bad. In any case, you are welcome to write your own book!

So here goes . . .

The Starting Point: Customer, Customer, Customer

As I spent more and more time with the founders and the senior management of these companies, I realized that the starting point for all of them was an obsession. An obsession with the customer. Here are some of the comments I heard:

Keep the customer happy, and he'll come back to you. Not only that, he will bring along other customers with him.

Retaining an existing customer is better than trying to get a new one.

If you focus on the product and keep the customer happy, you will need to spend a lot less on marketing.

The customer's money is far better than the investor's money. If you get the customer's money, you'll get the investor's money as well—assuming you want it. But if you only get the investor's money and not the customer's money, even the investor's money will dry up.

Sounds familiar, doesn't it? Let's take a look at each of these businesses, starting with Naukri. When Naukri was launched, employers did not really understand how to use their portal. So guess what? Naukri did everything for them—right from formatting the ad and uploading it onto the portal, to downloading the resumes of applicants, and even printing them out and giving them to these employers. Effectively, Naukri was doing the customer's job by handholding him at every stage in the process. And all at a much lower cost than conventional advertising in newspapers and magazines.

Zerodha understood the pain points of the customer. The customer wanted a simpler and faster portal through which he could trade. And of course, he wanted to know the exact amount that he would be spending on each such trade. That's exactly what Zerodha provided: a faster, simpler and completely transparent trading platform. And then of course, they provided the free Varsity, where users could learn all about investing and trading. And how can I forget Nudge, where traders were discouraged from trading in questionable stocks—just to ensure that they didn't lose money? Even though Zerodha lost their own brokerage in the process.

Of course, you are aware that Zerodha never spent anything on marketing. Instead, they focused on the product offering. And that was enough to attract—and retain—their customers.

And then we had Dream11, which actually documented their culture, and one of the key aspects of this culture was 'User First'. Perhaps the best example of this was the feature they called 'Dream responsibly'. In other words, sending messages to customers who had reached the limit they had set for themselves. Because they did want them to lose too much, even though this would mean that Dream11 lost revenue. And of course, the company has always tried to ensure that at least half their customers get their money back.

Finally, we have Zoho, where Sridhar predicted trends. He figured out what the customer was likely to want in the future and created products around this. For instance, the launch of the SaaS-based product line, Zoho.com, when SaaS was just about coming into existence. All along, he realized that the customer wanted products that were easy to install and use, and that's exactly what he provided—at a much lower cost than competing products. And of course, I'm sure you remember his famous statement, 'Your data is safe with Zoho.'

And yes, all four businesses have let their customers use certain services without any charge. You've seen Zerodha, where the investor pays zero brokerage. And several services, such as Varsity, are free to use as well. Zoho makes some of its products, such as Zoho Invoice, free to use. Naukri doesn't charge the jobseeker at all. And of course, Dream11 is happy to let their users play for free if they don't want to pay.

One extremely important question: Where did this fanatical focus on the customer come from? Easy question, isn't it? From the founders, of course.

All of them have an obsession with keeping their customers happy. And it shows!

People and Culture

So that was the focus on the external customer. But what about the internal customer—the team member? Once again, something that is common across all four companies is their strong belief in building and nurturing their teams. All founders consider their teams to be a key strength. All of them believe that small, close-knit, informal teams are the key. All of them have built an environment where hierarchy is minimal. In fact, whether in recruitment or in rewards, qualifications and titles really don't matter. What matters is competence—and that competence could come from very junior people or senior ones.

Now, don't get me wrong. Nowhere am I saying that these organizations have not taken on IIT graduates or IIM MBAs. Sure, they have. All I'm saying is that capability and culture are far more important for them than qualifications. So, if these companies found someone good but he was not qualified, well, no problem. They would take him on and give him responsibility.

And the best part. All these organizations went through incredibly tough times, whether it was the dot-com bust, the global financial crisis of 2008 or the Covid-19 pandemic. But there were no mass lay-offs. A rarity in Internet organizations isn't it, where pink slips are the first thing to be doled out in any crisis? The message in each case was clear: You have looked after the company during good times, so the company will look after you during bad times. As you can imagine, this built a tremendous bond between team members and the organization. It created trust in the management and a strong sense of ownership. 'It's my company,' is what people would say. That's why people have joined these companies—and most of them have stayed on over the years.

Once again, all this flowed from a strong belief amongst all the founders you've met. The belief that retention of people was a far better option than letting them leave and then replacing them. Belief in creating ownership amongst their people. Because people who have strong ownership stay on and are far more productive than people who chuck up their jobs at the drop of a hat.

But the Business Had to Be Profitable

By now, you know this, don't you? All four businesses that we have discussed have been profitable for years. Yes, Dream11 went through

its first few tough years when they were trying to create a demand for
fantasy sports, but once that was done, even they have been profitable.

As before, in all four cases, this flowed from the top. All the
founders have been clear: the business simply had to make profits.
That's the only way it would be sustainable, and not dependent on
external funding. Of course, they used different terms for this. For
instance, Harsh Jain used the Marwari term *dhandha*. Nithin Kamath
famously said, 'We didn't take money, so we had to make money.'
Sanjeev Bikhchandani has always said, 'Run a frugal business; if you
have too much money sloshing around, you get into bad habits.'

And none of these was simply a 'nice to hear' statement being
thrown around. Each of these founders actually practised what
he preached. Each of them led by example. So you had Sanjeev
Bikhchandani running his office out of the servants' quarters above
his father's garage, using second-hand furniture and computers. And
moving around on his father's old scooter. Once Hitesh joined him,
they would both travel in autos to make sales calls, and stay in low-
cost hotels. Then, you had Sridhar Vembu staying in a simple village
house in his adopted village of Mathalamparai. Nithin Kamath has
been living an equally simple, unostentatious life. And of course,
you know all about Harsh Jain and Bhavit Sheth, who could easily
have had large cabins in their 'stadium'. Instead, they just have
workstations, like all the other team members at Dream Sports.

Dear reader, if you are running a start-up or are planning to start
one, I hope you are noticing this. Leadership through nice-sounding
statements does not work. It only works when you set an example!

As you've repeatedly seen, all four companies run frugal
businesses. Zoho has offices in villages and takes in employees from
Zoho Schools. Low-cost and stable manpower, isn't it? I challenge
you to find a lower-cost operation. And, as Sridhar loves to say, the
manpower productivity at Zoho is significantly higher than that of
other software companies, which has obviously had a huge impact
on profitability. Dream Sports has just one office—the stadium
across two floors in Mumbai's Bandra Kurla Complex. And you can

imagine the amount they have saved by not maintaining multiple offices across the country. Zerodha spends nothing on marketing. And of course, taking a cue from the founders, the employees at Info Edge move around in autos and avoid five-star hotels.

One more important issue: None of these founders—I repeat, none of them—has chased valuations. They have all chased their business. It wasn't growth at any cost. If that meant they had to grow slower and not at the break-neck speed that many Internet companies try to, so be it. If it meant conservative growth, that was fine. None of them have followed the age-old approach of making losses year after year and getting heftier and heftier valuations. They were not interested in becoming unicorns—although, interestingly, three of them became unicorns very early in the game, and the fourth, Info Edge, has a valuation far higher than most unicorns.

Interestingly, in all four cases, the focus on keeping customers happy has had a direct impact on their costs and, therefore, their profitability. Because their existing customers stay on and bring in new ones through word of mouth. Therefore, these businesses need to spend much less on marketing and sales to acquire new ones. And as you've guessed, that goes straight to the bottom line.

And so has the focus on their teams. Since all businesses take care of their employees, the employees don't leave, which obviously means lower recruitment and training costs as well as higher productivity. Plus, their focus on getting good people, irrespective of their qualifications and seniority, helps to cut manpower costs further. Once again, this goes straight to the bottom line.

My friend, isn't it obvious why all these businesses have always been profitable?

Ethics and Transparency

This is something else that these businesses have in common. Remember, Info Edge wrote off the entire investment in 4B Networks, the moment they realized that something was wrong.

After all, the shareholders had to be informed, and bad news had to be shared upfront. No hiding, please. And then of course, you had the famous incident of Sanjeev joining the board of MakeMyTrip. Where he was offered shares in his personal name, but insisted on taking them in the name of Info Edge. Why? Because the time he would spend in board meetings was time that belonged to Info Edge!

Sridhar has always been very clear that the customer's data belonged to the customer. And for this, Zoho set up its own data centres, so no third-party data centre could access this data and misuse it. And of course, the lower costs of running their own data centres have been passed on to the customer.

In the case of Zerodha, the customer knows exactly how much he would be spending before he made the trade—a far cry from the opaque policies followed by several brokers. And then, their famous 'Nudge'. Where traders who are taking too much risk, for instance, trading in penny stocks, are dissuaded from doing so. Just so that they don't lose money, although Zerodha would lose brokerage in the process.

Dream11 has done something similar, where they've brought in the concept of 'Dream responsibly'. So a user can set this limit, and once he reaches this limit, he gets a notification asking him to stop. And like Zerodha, even in this case, the company loses potential revenues.

Dear reader, ethics and transparency are the cornerstones of any successful organization, and you've seen exactly that in these four companies. Because that builds trust—in your customers, your team members, your partners, your investors and just about anyone else who is dealing with you.

And that's why everyone stays with you!

And There's So Much More in Common

And there's more. All four organizations started off with one major product, but kept adding more and more along the journey.

Info Edge started off with Naukri.com and later added Jeevansathi, 99acres and Shiksha, and even moved into corporate VC mode when they invested in Policybazaar and Zomato. Zerodha began with their trading platform and then added Varsity, smallcase, Streak and more. Similarly, Dream Sports started off with Dream11 and then added FanCode and DreamGameStudios. And of course, Zoho Corp's first business was WebNMS, after which they added Manage Engine and later on the blockbuster Zoho.com. Even within Zoho.com, they started off with Zoho Writer, added Zoho CRM, and now have over fifty five different applications.

Finally, all these highly successful founders have a strong belief in giving back to society in areas that are close to their heart. Both through their organizations as well as personally. Whether it is the investment in Ashoka University for Sanjeev and Hitesh, which focuses on education in humanities and science, or Rainmatter Foundation from Nithin, which focuses on areas such as climate change, or Dream Sports nurturing sportspeople, to 'make sports better', as Harsh says. And of course, how can I forget the massive impact Sridhar and his company have had on rural Tamil Nadu. Where deserving young boys and girls, whose parents cannot afford higher education after school, get a chance to work on world-class products with a world-class company. And many of whom stay in the comfort of their homes in their village, rather than migrating to cities. Because Zoho had moved closer to them.

Yes, my friend, all the founders you've met in this book have had many, many things in common. And so have their companies.

But they also had differences. Major, major differences in some cases. For instance, in their views on taking external funding. Or their approach to marketing. Or . . .

Wouldn't you like to read about these differences?

Yes?

Next chapter, please.

37

And What's Different

Dear reader, this is probably the most fascinating part of my book. Where I compare these four businesses and look at what's different. You see, these companies have sometimes followed strategies that are diametrically opposite to each other. And yet, as you've seen, they have all been ultra-successful.

That'll be fun to read, wouldn't it?

So let's go . . .

The State of the Market

One of the most interesting differences between these businesses has to do with the state of the market when they launched. Let's start with Naukri.com. Sanjeev started the business when the Internet in India was just about finding its feet and there were only around 14,000 Internet users in the country. Now, that's a miniscule market by any standards, isn't it? However, the Internet was beginning to take off in the western world, primarily the US, and Sanjeev believed that it was only a matter of time before it became widespread in India. And that's why he launched Naukri.

Interestingly, at that time, there was no one else in the same business, although their primary competitor, JobsAhead, came into the market soon after. In other words, Naukri was launched when the market was tiny and there was virtually no one else around. If you go back to my PERSISTENT model, it was a very small, non-crowded market. But the *potential market* was huge. And as you've seen, the market grew and grew, and with it, Naukri grew as well—to become the giant it is today.

The story of Zoho is similar. They started their flagship group of products, Zoho.com, in the year 2006. At that time, cloud computing was just about catching on. However, Sridhar was convinced that the benefits of SaaS and cloud computing were so compelling that the market simply had to grow. Once again, while the current market was not large, the potential market was huge. Over time of course, the SaaS market grew and grew and is still growing. Today, Zoho is used in more than 150 countries worldwide.

Dream11 is an equally interesting story. When it was launched in 2009, the Internet was well and truly entrenched, so that was not an issue. The issue was that fantasy sports was non-existent in the country. In fact, there were companies that had started out in this space but had closed down since. Now, Harsh and Bhavit were convinced that the potential market was huge. All they had to do was get people excited enough to play fantasy sports. It wasn't easy, as you've seen, but over time this is exactly what happened. And today, you can see how they've grown. There are twenty crore fans on Dream11 as I write this book.

So all three of these businesses launched their offerings in a market that was small but had the potential to grow really big— for different reasons. And of course, the fact that there wasn't much competition.

And that's where the fun really begins, because Zerodha was just the opposite. Nithin Kamath started his company when there were lots of traders around, and many of them were online. So it was definitely a large market. But—and this is the important 'but'—it was hugely crowded. Many large banks, such as ICICI Bank, HDFC Bank and Kotak Mahindra Bank were already in the business. And so were several specialized brokers, such as Motilal Oswal Financial Services,

India Infoline, Sharekhan and a host of other major players. In other words, it was a large market, but it was also extremely crowded.

What does conventional wisdom—and my PERSISTENT model—say? *Do not enter a crowded market—particularly if there are giants in the space.* But Nithin had belief. He was clear that the broking services that were offered by existing players were cumbersome and non-transparent. In addition, the response time was slow. Finally, the percentage brokerage fee charged by all brokers was misleading, because for large-value trades, the brokerage rose steeply. He was convinced that if he offered a fast, transparent, easy-to-use platform, he would be able to get users. Definitely younger users. And that's exactly what happened. His platform was different and traders began to flock towards it. The sweetener, of course, was the flat brokerage fee of Rs 20 per trade. So even though the market was crowded, Zerodha's offering was sufficiently different to attract users. And look where they are today!

Marketing Spend

Another interesting area where these four companies differ is in their approach to marketing. Yes, what is common is the fact that all of them have focused on the product and keeping the customer happy. And thereby retaining customers, rather than losing them and getting in new ones. That much is common.

But beyond this, there are significant differences. As you've seen, Zerodha is at one extreme because Nithin Kamath does not believe in spending on advertising at all. Yes, Zerodha got a lot of publicity in the media, thanks to its flat fee structure of Rs 20 and later on, the free brokerage for investors. But that was it. There has been no spending on ads. Nithin strongly believes that happy customers don't leave and they bring in more customers as well. Therefore, he has always focused on the product and on keeping his customers happy. Not on marketing spend.

On the other hand, Dream11 has been spending a significant amount on marketing, right from their early days. If you follow the

IPL, you would have seen all those ads splashed on the television, saying, '*Aap Dream11 par team banaa lo* (You can select your team on Dream11)'. And you would get what I mean—major advertising spends.

The other two are somewhere in between. Zoho focuses more on the product than on marketing (reflected in the fact that their R&D spend is three times their marketing spend). Naukri has two categories of customers: the potential employer and the jobseeker. They started off with some level of advertising to get employers interested, but soon realized that it wasn't really working out. Then they switched to a far more efficient method—face-to-face sales calls. Of course, they continue to advertise for jobseekers, but it isn't the hefty kind of advertising that Dream11 does.

So Dream11 spends heavily on advertising, Zerodha spends nothing at all, and Zoho and Naukri are somewhere in between. And they are all highly successful.

Interesting, isn't it?

Funding

Aha! The big one. Funding. Something that has become almost synonymous with Internet companies. And this is one area where our founders differ dramatically from each other. On the one hand, Nithin Kamath and Sridhar Vembu have always been clear—they wouldn't take external funding. Both of them feel that taking money would lead to investors getting involved in running their business and they would lose their freedom (the founders, not the investors). Because the founders would need to go to them before making any decisions, which would slow down the business. And in the world of the Internet, the ability to make quick decisions and run with them is vital. Further, investors would have their own interests in mind, such as increasing the valuation and looking for an exit. But that might not be great for the company.

Incidentally, you've seen some major examples of this freedom in these stories. For instance, Nithin and Kailash decided on their 'zero brokerage' strategy, while waiting for a flight at Bengaluru airport. Over beer and peanuts, if you please. And it was implemented overnight. Sridhar launched the major experiment of Zoho Schools, which did wonders for the productivity and profitability of Zoho, in addition to bringing about a phenomenal impact on the lives of young men and women from rural Tamil Nadu. Can you imagine them taking such decisions with investors in the picture?

On the other hand, Dream Sports took in investor money several times. Why? Remember, Harsh and Bhavit were trying to popularize a concept that did not exist in India, namely fantasy sports. They wanted to grow it fast before someone else jumped on the bandwagon and beat them to it. And that meant marketing spend. For which they needed money. Also remember, they needed to give out decent amounts of prize money, and what they were getting from players was not enough. They had to top it up. Which again meant external money.

But there's more. Where Nithin and Sridhar were clearly delighted with the fact that they did not take investor money, Harsh Jain was equally delighted with the fact that he had. And the reasons went beyond money. First of all, he has always said that his investors were great at guiding him and his co-founder, Bhavit, at a time when they were not really sure how to run the business. Not just that, he also believes that getting well-known investors, such as his first investor, Vani Kola of Kalaari Capital, gave a lot of credibility to the business.

What about Info Edge? Well, they were somewhere in between. Remember the early years of Naukri, when investors approached them and Sanjeev clearly told them, 'We don't want your money'? But later, when they came up against a well-funded competitor in the shape of JobsAhead, he and Hitesh realized that they needed to compete, for which they needed funding. So they *did* take money from ICICI Venture. But they put half of what they had taken into a fixed deposit, so as not to get into bad spending habits. In fact, in the twenty-plus years since then, they took money only thrice more. Once when they launched their IPO and later, when they offered shares to select investors twice, through a QIP. The first time, it was to compete with well-funded competitors in the real estate space, and the second time was when Covid-19 hit them.

By the way, I must clarify something: It's not that Sanjeev had changed his belief about the customer's money being far better than the investor's money. It's just the fact that there are times when you *do* need external funding.

So that's another major difference between these businesses. Zoho and Zerodha took no investor money at all, whereas Dream11 took funding several times. And Info Edge was somewhere in between.

And There's Still More . . .

There are several other differences between the businesses we've seen.

For instance, the founders of Naukri, Zerodha and Dream11 decided that India was their market—at least for the moment. On the other hand, Sridhar of Zoho was clear: he was building products for the world.

Dream11 has always been highly data-driven, which is evident from their statement of culture, DO PUT, where D stands for data. The founders are willing to listen to everyone and are also willing to act on these suggestions. But suggestions need to be based on hard data. On the other hand, Nithin Kamath of Zerodha has based his decisions on instinct. Remember him famously saying, 'We don't have a single data scientist in the company'? And I'm sure you remember the earth-shattering decision to charge zero brokerage to investors over beer and peanuts at the departure lounge of Bengaluru airport!

Similarity in Diversity

So there has been significant diversity in the thinking of the founders we have met in this book, and therefore, in the strategies they followed. However, even in this diversity, I learnt that there was something common across all these founders. And that something can be summed up in two words: *belief* and *perseverance*. None of the founders was entering a market that was ideal. Naukri entered the market when the Internet was in its infancy in India. But Sanjeev Bikhchandani, and later on, Hitesh Oberoi strongly believed that it would grow. Yes, it meant lots of time, and the founders had to persevere for years. But ultimately, it did happen.

Sridhar Vembu of Zoho believed that companies would increasingly opt for SaaS-based software solutions, although it was very, very nascent when he launched Zoho.com in 2006. He also realized that the market leaders in software products, such as Salesforce.com and Oracle, had complex products and were catering to large companies. He saw a potential market for simpler products based on SaaS. He backed his conviction and was willing to wait for the results. And today, Zoho.com is used by over 100 million users across the world.

Harsh Jain and Bhavit Shah launched Dream11 in an environment where the Internet was common in India, but fantasy sports was almost unheard of. Worse, a couple of fantasy sports platforms had come up earlier but could not survive. Once again, these two young founders were convinced that they could get Indian sports fans hooked on fantasy cricket and later, other sports as well. They persevered for years, and today they are clear market leaders in the field, with a registered user base of twenty crore people.

And what about Zerodha? The upstart who dared to challenge all the large, existing brokerages out there? Well, Nithin and Nikhil Kamath had been traders for several years and had faced multiple problems with existing online platforms, such as speed, cost and lack of transparency. They believed that they could create a platform which would take care of these issues. Once again, it took time and patience, but it did happen. And today, they are the biggest brokers in the world by number of transactions.

And that's it. Even though these founders followed different strategies, they all had belief. And they persevered for years. That's how they were able to build the hugely successful earnicorns that they have!

Who Was Right?

And that brings me to the last bit in this book. You've seen four highly successful market leaders, all of whom have several things in common. But there are significant differences as well. And that leads me to the big, big question: Who was right? Was it Zerodha or Zoho, who never took money? Or was it Dream Sports, who took funding repeatedly to build the business? Was it Naukri, who entered a market when there were only 14,000 Internet users in India—a tiny market by any standards? Or was it Zerodha, who entered a large, highly crowded market? Was it Dream Sports, who had major marketing budgets? Or was it Zoho, who spent three times their marketing budget on R&D?

Yes, my friend, I have been asking myself these questions ever since I started writing this book. Who was right?

And after a lot of soul-searching, I have come to one conclusion—and I hope you agree. When running a business, there is no right or wrong strategy. No formula. Each founder followed the strategy that he was convinced about (remember, I spoke about belief) and was willing to pivot, persevere and give it time. And ultimately, all four of these companies have been market leaders—that too, profitable market leaders—for years.

In other words, they are proud **earnicorns**!

However, it is still interesting to speculate about what might have happened if these founders had followed a different strategy. For instance, if Zerodha and Zoho had taken investor money, where would they be today? If Zerodha had resorted to a mass advertising campaign, would they have grown faster? If Dream11 had not advertised and banked on a great product and happy users, would that have been enough to make them the market leaders that they are today? Or would a competitor have come in and overtaken them?

As you can imagine, I didn't have answers to these questions. So I decided to ask God.

And guess what God said?

He simply smiled.

I suspect he doesn't have the answers, either.

Acknowledgements

Dear reader,

Before you start reading this book, I must share something with you. Yes, I'm the author of the book. After all, it *does* have my name on the cover. And the miserable royalty I get out of it *does* go into my bank account. But what about the contents? And all the gyan that I hope it contains?

My friend, the contents and all the gyan have been contributed by lots and lots of people. My role was simply to put it all together, add my masala (I call it value-add), bring in my inevitable humour and proudly put my name on the cover.

So here are some of the people who have contributed to the book—and fortunately, they have not demanded a share of the royalty:

Out of all these people, there is one person who stands out: Sanjeev Bikhchandani, a stalwart of the start-up world, highly respected by the entire industry and someone who built the first earnicorn in India—Info Edge. Over the years, I have learnt so, so much from him, and this learning has gone into each of my books. And I'm sure you will learn a huge amount from him, as well.

And of course, the founders of the four earnicorns I've spoken about—Hitesh Oberoi, the co-founder of Info Edge, along with Sanjeev Bikhchandani, Nithin Kamath of Zerodha, Harsh Jain and Bhavit Sheth of Dream11 and Sridhar Vembu of Zoho. All of them have been pioneers and leaders in their respective fields, and I was extremely fortunate to get their views.

My senior from IIT, Saurabh Srivastava, the co-founder and chairman of Indian Angel Network, for his valuable comments on the book.

I've had great discussions with several people in the four earnicorns I've written about, and I must thank them. These are: Sumeet Singh, Esha Arora, Kitty Agarwal and Vivek Agarwal from Info Edge; Bhuvanesh from Zerodha; Pooja Sabharwal, Ishanee Roy and Gauri Sharma from Dream11; and Praval Singh, Nanya Srivastava and Mayank Kalra from Zoho. And of course, Rajiv Kumar, Sunil Lalvani and Ashish Kila.

Ankit Khandelwal, my former colleague at Lead Angels, for patiently explaining the concept of F&O trading to a not-very-bright student (read: me).

Penguin Random House India has been a great publisher, starting with my wonderful young friend and editor, Radhika Marwah. And of course, Vijesh Kumar, Manali Das, Sameer Mahale, Harish Shenoy, Anuj Sharma, Gopal Kabta, Saleheen Mohammed, Sparsh Raj Singh, Rahaman and Ishan. Along with all the other 'Penguinites' who I've never met, but who have worked brilliantly behind the scenes to get all my books to the shape they have finally taken.

My family deserves a special mention for putting up with a peculiar father/grandfather/son, who gets into long spells of hibernation to write some silly books. In spite of which, they have supported me through and through.

Now if you've watched movies, you would know that the most important person is mentioned last of all—the director. The one who is not seen on the screen but has a key role in everything that is done. That is Rajni, the only girlfriend I've ever had, and who I married several years ago (just to clarify, we did not meet on Jeevansathi.com ☺). It is not easy to manage a job, home, kids and grandkids almost single-handedly, when your husband has got it into his head to write what he fondly imagines are great books. But she has come out of this with flying colours (by the way, I hope she reads this part)!

Finally, I hope I haven't missed anyone. But even if I have, I believe I have given you enough names.

To blame, just in case you don't like the book!

Scan QR code to access the
Penguin Random House India website